1950

1950

Crossroads of
American Religious Life

ROBERT S. ELLWOOD

Westminster John Knox Press
Louisville, Kentucky

Book design by Sharon Adams
Cover design by PAZ Design Group
Cover photograph: Willinger (FPG)

First edition
Published by Westminster John Knox Press
Louisville, Kentucky

This book is printed on acid-free paper that meets the American National Standards Institute Z39.48 standard. ♾

PRINTED IN THE UNITED STATES OF AMERICA

00 01 02 03 04 05 06 07 08 09 — 10 9 8 7 6 5 4 3 2 1

Library of Congress Cataloging-in-Publication Data

Ellwood, Robert S., 1933–
    1950, crossroads of American religious life / Robert Ellwood—
    1st ed.
        p.   cm.
    Includes index.
    ISBN 0-664-25813-1 (alk. paper)
        1. United States—Religion—20th century. 2. Christianity—
    United States—20th century. 3. Nineteen fifties. I. Title: Nineteen
    fifty, crossroads of American religious life. II. Title.
    BL2525.E425   2000
    2009.973'09045—dc21   99-056256

For Barbara and Patrick,
Great and good friends.
Both born in 1950.
Makers of the future.

CONTENTS

PREFACE

Nineteen fifty, the midtwentieth-century year, was pivotal in more ways than one. In a new century it is worthwhile to look back fifty years or more to that brief epoch with interest and reflection. Much happened then that was both auspicious and ominous for the American future. The purpose of this book is to examine religion in the United States in that year with a view to understanding its relation to the great events of the day. We shall also highlight religious events, unrecognized as significant at the time, that foreshadowed the hidden future.

Lisle A. Rose, in *The Cold War Comes to Main Street: America in 1950*,[1] has emphasized that the intensive study of a single year can illumine an era. The present study is founded on the same concept, in our case using 1950 to illustrate something of what religion and religious institutions meant in the middle years of the twentieth century, and in important respects the entire century. Rose maintains that this tortured year—the year of the conviction of Alger Hiss, the emergence of Senator Joseph McCarthy, the decision to build the hydrogen bomb, and the unexpected war in Korea—was a watershed for the nation between an essentially optimistic four and a half postwar years, from 1945 to 1949, and a mood of pessimism, reaction, and cold war anxiety characteristic of 1950 and after. We will examine and in some ways endorse this view of 1950, though noting that a reactionary intellectual mood, at least in much of the religious sphere, had been in place since the end of the war and that some important religious events, such as the Roman Catholic Holy Year and the founding of the Protestant/Eastern Orthodox National Council of Churches, had other kinds of significance. But religious indicators such as Cardinal Spellman-style Roman Catholicism, Norman Vincent Peale and Billy Graham Protestantism, and even the

ix

remarkable upsurge of churchbuilding and religious life generally, though not unique to the midcentury year, undoubtedly had a relationship to the crisis mentality of 1950.

On the other hand, this year was the heyday of what Tom Brokaw, in his best-selling book of that name, called *The Greatest Generation*.[2] This was the generation, born chiefly in the 1920s, that endured depression childhoods, fought the greatest war in history through to victory, returned to receive unprecedented education under the GI Bill—typically graduating in 1950—and went on to create an America affluent and technologically advanced beyond anything the past had imagined outside of science fiction. Theirs was the first generation of television, routine air flight, elongating freeways, rapidly increasing lifespans, mega-universities, and much else. It was the generation that parented the "baby boom," already making for overflowing church and school nurseries by 1950. Despite the supposed gloom of 1950 and its very real crises, Brokaw and others who have interviewed members of that generation in depth found that even then, at least in retrospect, they saw themselves as profoundly confident and optimistic.

Brokaw does not overlook the negatives of that generation: its lingering racism, its sometimes too-uncritical patriotism, its materialism. But its members also believed that problems could be solved, even as had been the awesome issues of the war years. They had a special opportunity to shape their own and their nation's future and were prepared to take it. Its African American constituents would no longer accept denial of the freedoms for which they had fought. All this generation's people were beginning to experience the prosperous future and to recognize that abundance can enrich as well as malnourish the spirit. Perhaps that was one reason the 1920s-born generation was exceptionally active religiously, and not only out of fear and anxiety. They constructed new churches, often as parts of their evolving suburban lifestyle, out of hope and affluent exuberance as well as spiritual unease. This side of 1950 will also be a part of this study.

As for myself, born in 1933—the deep depression year that had the lowest number of births in the United States of any year in the century—I cannot claim to be a part of the great generation. My cohort, in college in the early 1950s, was usually called the Silent Generation instead. We did not passionately argue causes like 1930s students; we fought no heroic wars like those who came of age in the 1940s; we had none of the countercultural and radical effervescence of the 1960s. Nonetheless, this book is inevitably something of an exercise in nostalgia for one who became a high school senior in the fall of the year under study, in a small college town out on the Great Plains of western Nebraska. I remember the returning GIs on campus in their jerry-built housing, inevitably nicknamed Fertile Acres, with their burgeoning young families, their war-seasoned serious interests in life and God, and their oft-rehearsed plans for the future. As a newspaper carrier, I was among the first persons in town to see some of the *Omaha World-Herald*'s screaming headlines of the year as the bundles of papers arrived at the local station: Spies! H-bombs! McCarthy! War in Korea!

Being interested in religious issues even then, I recall the traditionalist, antimodern flavor of spiritual life that seemed to characterize those years, at least in the sector of the Episcopal church with which I was familiar. This mood, taking different forms in different denominations, is reviewed in the present study along with the many other spiritual and theological strands of the year. Religiously as well as politically and economically, 1950 had its distinctive flavor, and that taste was a blend of multitudinous currents, but most of them were old favorites.

If this little book contributes to the commemoration of religious life in 1950, putting that year in the largest perspective now possible, it will have served its purpose. In closing this preface, I would like to express my deep appreciation to Auburn University for offering me the position of Goodwin-Philpott Eminent Scholar in Religion for the 1998–99 academic year. Much of the research and writing for this book was accomplished during that time, with the help of that distinguished university's excellent library. I wish to thank the editors of Westminster John Knox Press for their splendid assistance in bringing this project to completion.

Journey to the Heart of a Century

The year 1950 was a happy and a grim time in the United States. Though blessings were far from evenly distributed, it is fair to say that more happy young couples were raising children and enjoying pleasant homes, and their breadwinners working at good jobs, than ever before. In the realm of religion, new churches and synagogues were rising and expanding into vast parish halls alive with classes, parties, concerts, and innumerable meetings planning even greater works in the name of God. Not a few of these were in the blossoming new suburbs.

Great fear also stalked the land. No one put it better than the anticommunist founder of the Christian Crusade, Billy James Hargis, who by 1950 was devoting full-time to this cause. According to Mark Sherwin, Hargis once boasted that he had "the feel of the people" and went on to comment, "They wanted to join something. They wanted to belong to some united group. They loved Jesus, but they also had a great fear. When I told them that this fear was Communism, it was like a revelation. They knew I was right, but they had never known before what that fear was."[1] So it was that despite all the outward signs pointing toward prosperity, anxiety, anger, and mistrust haunted the hearts of many in America, and some of them joined churches in part because churches were seen as a bulwark against communism.

Religion in the United States, in that era of near-record

Atomic bomb test (Frenchman's Flat, Nevada).

church attendance and church building, was a mirror of both the fear and the dreams. Young families, their husbands and fathers back from the War, wanted the solace and, in a word of the times, the "togetherness" of churches and synagogues. Their fast-growing families—the cradles of the "baby boom" generation—were populating the nursery rooms and kindergarten classes of countless religious institutions. During 1950 alone, Roman Catholics reported an inclusive membership increase of 2.71 percent, and Protestants, relying more on burgeoning church membership figures, an increase of 4.15 percent, compared to an overall population increase of 1.68 percent—itself a "baby boom" figure that marked the beginning of a decade in which the U.S. population increased more than in any other decade in its history. But all this had historical reason behind it: the Second World War and the present war against communism were increasingly understood in America as wars of faith against faith, of the "American Way of Life" against other ways, finally of the cross against diabolical evil. In 1950, perhaps more than in any other American year before or after, the present war was of the spirit as well as on the ground, and it was total.

Religion helped fight those wars, and it was also a way out of the unbearable world created by total war, whether of the flesh or of the spirit. Religion has the power to mythologize wars into crusades, the messy battles of nations into cosmic conflicts of the children of light against the demons of darkness. It also has the ability to give people respite from the war, for religion can offer rest and refreshment from battle and the experience of other realms untouched by shadow. It can connect people with their roots, and with a past from which treasures old and new can be excavated to serve needs of the moment or to be enjoyed for their own sake. Religion in 1950 was, for all its attention to present need, also half-consciously preoccupied with the past, for it assumed that only by recovering what religion meant when it was stronger and better could it redress what had gone wrong with the modern world.

But in America spirituality is never just one thing, and

Americans attending church in 1950 heard a diversity of messages. Norman Vincent Peale, the eminent New York pastor whose books were on best-seller lists all through the early 1950s, declared that in the expansive postwar era the levels of "success" one could attain through positive thinking and belief in oneself and God were virtually unlimited. Mainstream Protestant ministers, imbued with the neoorthodoxy now streaming out from Switzerland, Germany, and Union Theological Seminary in New York, emphasized the sinfulness of human nature and the brokenness of the world, so well taught by the dreadful recent events of history, and the need for utter dependence on God's grace alone. Billy Graham, the suddenly rising star of evangelical Protestantism and a cultural pessimist in his own evangelical way, proclaimed then that the United States had only three or four years in which to repent, and characteristically put both sin and the war of faiths in highly personal terms: "If you would be a true patriot, then become a Christian. If you would be a loyal American, then become a loyal Christian. . . . The world is divided into two camps! On the one side we see Communism . . . [which] has declared war against God, against Christ, against the Bible, and against all religion! . . . Unless the Western world has an old fashioned revival, we cannot last!"[2]

Roman Catholics, then followers of the austere, saintly, and militantly anticommunist Pope Pius XII, last of the pre-Vatican II breed, embraced a view of the world no less dualistic. Millions of their coreligionists were part of the "Church of Silence" in the "Captive Nations" behind the Iron Curtain, and those fortunate enough to be elsewhere were never allowed by the popular Catholic media to forget the suffering of those captives, or the name of the diabolical power that held them in thrall. Millions of American Catholics had ethnic roots in those distant lands and doubtless were deeply moved by their pleas. Shaped by highly traditional Catholicism, with its Latin mass, fish on Friday, and strictly run parochial schools and colleges, they held firmly to the church as the last and greatest redoubt against the evil that seemed to be sweeping over the planet. Theirs was a virtually dualistic world, divided clearly and sharply, like their individual lives, between the lights and shadows of godliness and sin, betwixt objective Catholic grace and satanic dark. In 1950 little conscious desire could be found among devout Roman Catholics to partially abandon this clear-cut world and to change the church in the dramatic and radical ways that were to obtain little more than a decade later, in the aftermath of Vatican II. In the anxious and, in some ways, deeply "spiritual" year 1950, it would have seemed far better to leave such a highly disciplined and outwardly self-assured bulwark against the evil abroad in the world as it was, without even subjective acknowledgment that the church militant on earth could be other than the "perfect institution" its advocates claimed it to be.

The evil was no less to be found at home, for it was the Catholic Senator Joseph McCarthy who in 1950 told the nation, in the manner that would be forever associated with his name, of communist infiltrators at high levels of the State Department, as well as in American education and the entertainment industry. Many Catholics, edgy about their place in Protestant-dominated America, at first gave him considerable support, as did others. Some Catholics noted with a certain satisfaction the number of names from the old Protestant establishment among the Senator's targets. The year 1950 was moreover proclaimed by the pope to be a Holy Year, a year for renewing one's loyalty to the church and of special pilgrimage to Rome. It would culminate with the infallible papal definition of the dogma of the Assumption of the Blessed Virgin Mary bodily into heaven, and the exact significance of this definition at this anxious moment in the world's history, in this year of spiritual warfare, was much discussed in Catholic intellectual circles.

Other bands also colored the religious spectrum of America in 1950. A few Americans, reading such writers as Aldous Huxley and Alan Watts, or GIs on occupation duty in Japan finding the great peace of the Buddha in Zen gardens, were beginning to explore Eastern traditions like Vedanta and Zen.

Eastern Orthodox Christians whose homelands were, for the most part, either under communism or threatened by it, were eager for a larger share in American religious life. A very small number of churchmen, holdovers from the "red decade," the 1930s, or the wartime era of Soviet-American friendship, still looked with sympathy on the Russian "experiment." Theological liberals, also by and large relics of a more sanguine age, continued to preach in many churches and wondered what had gone wrong with their vision of the future and their expansive concept of American values. American Jews, on the other hand, as they moved increasingly out of inner-city neighborhoods and into the new suburbs and a better future, tended also to migrate from orthodoxy to the more liberal Reform interpretation of Judaism. However, counterindicators to Reform rationalism could be noted in the popularity of the great Jewish philosopher Martin Buber's I-thou existentialism and his wonderful Hasidic tales, and in the still-fresh memories, or rather nightmares, of the unspeakable Holocaust of Jews under Nazism.

What almost all of these voices of 1950 had in common was belief that the right way to do religion in that pivotal and threatened year was to do it in a traditional way, and do it well. Nineteen fifty was not a time for religious innovation, whether in theology or worship or institutional structure, but rather for maintaining traditions in their authentic forms and rediscovering their forgotten power. What was wanted then was for the church to be a rock, not Peter's bark setting out for new shores. In that profoundly conservative slough after the smashing of so many modern idols and icons, the assumption was that somewhere within age-old traditions, not in anything newly minted today, was to be found a power and vision equal to the desperate times. Betrayal was not too strong a word for what many in 1950 felt they had been handed by modernity; it had promised so much, and had ended in Auschwitz, the gulags, Hiroshima, and at home in mindless materialism and spiritless industry, the fuel gauge pointing to empty but the engines of "progress" still running on momentum. Unfair, perhaps, in an age also giving far more Americans better education, better jobs, better health, better homes, and better incomes than ever before. But that was how some felt at the time, amidst the great fear and the anxieties of the age. Religion was an appropriate repository for a generous portion of that anxious antimodernism.

Indeed, a significant strand of thought in 1950 was, despite the appearance of some progress, profoundly pessimistic, anticipating the imminent end of the world as we knew it, if not by nuclear holocaust, then by moral and cultural collapse. Influenced by books like Oswald Spengler's *Decline of the West*, many pundits—ranging from "Beat" writers to mystics like the postwar Aldous Huxley, to sophisticated traditionalists such as T. S. Eliot and the new American political/cultural conservatives like William Buckley and Russell Kirk—saw signs everywhere of epidemic materialism, self-centered individualism, no less self-centered conformism, and the eclipse of real spirituality behind false liberalisms. Even the rise in churchgoing failed to appease many of these critics; to them it was no more than sentimental culture-religion.

Religion in 1950 was by and large a religion of nostalgia, or to put it more positively, of old wine in old bottles newly brought up from the cellars, wiped clean of dust, sometimes given new labels, and placed on the dining table. Pealeism harked back to a supposed traditional America of small town warmth and virtue. Neoórthodoxy strove to recover the dynamic of the Reformation in a way suitable to our time, and Graham yearned for the power of the old-time religion of the frontier revivals. Roman Catholicism in 1950 saw itself as nothing if not the perpetuation of the intellectual subtlety of the Thomistic Middle Ages, and the hard surety of the Counter-Reformation, in an age all but devastated by the Enlightenment and its progeny. Its confidence was aided on deep spiritual levels by the monastic revival sparked by the writings of Thomas Merton. Even nonconformists to the mainstream of 1950 religion seemed to have their own nostalgias: for the golden ages of Asian spirituality; for those bygone days when it seemed that communism just might be the future that worked; for the 1920s of the Scopes "monkey trial" and of mighty battles in several Protestant denominations between liberals and fundamentalists, battles that in those days the liberals usually won; and for the Judaism of the Enlightenment or of the wise old Hasidic rebbes.

Popular religion, which focused more on personal needs than the "high brow" versions of faith, had its own nostalgias: for an imagined time somewhere in the past when faith could be simple and pure, when families were loving and together, and when emotions better than those evoked by war could be freely felt and expressed. *Publisher's Weekly* for February 18, 1950, offered an editorial on "The Phenomenal Interest in Religious Books." The interest, it said, had been mounting since the end of the war and was now at an all-time peak: "People have been dreaming of something permanent in a world shaken to its core, and many of them have sought to learn through books." Characteristically for the times, the titles were neatly segregated into Protestant and Catholic lists; Protestants were reading works like Linus Poling's *Faith Is Power—For You*, Norman Vincent Peale's *The Art of Real Happiness*, and Emmett Fox's *Alter Your Life*. Catholics, enjoying a wider field of vision, at least geographically, as members of a great, worldwide institution, traveled with Alexis Carrel on *The Voyage to Lourdes*. With Oscar Halecki they visited *Eugenio Pacelli, Pope of Peace*, returned with Fulton Oursler to the days of *The Greatest Story Ever Told*, and finally recognized with Father Keller that *You Can Change the World*.

Like popular religion generally, faith in the bookstores and at the feet of the popular preachers in 1950 was faith more of images than of ideas. Above all, it was personal, seeking to appropriate the power and faith of the past in a way accessible today for oneself, one's family, one's career, one's world. The mavens of popular faith were well aware of this. Note the frequency of the words "you" and "your" in the previously mentioned book titles. In the same vein, advertisements for Norman Vincent Peale's books asked, "Are *you* missing the life of success?" Fulton Sheen, the dynamic Catholic spokesman whose radio programs and, after 1952, TV lectures were followed by millions, would open by saying, "Thank you for inviting me into your home." Billy Graham would end his fervent appeals for conversion with lines like "You come forward and give your heart to Jesus Christ. You come." The intellectual theologians talked about "man"; the populists about "you."

"You" religion was also a talisman, for another great fear of 1950, a year of many fears, was dread of "mass man." That expression evoked dark fantasies of a modern assembly-line, conformity-ridden society in which all individuality was reduced to urban anonymity and all personality to acceptable sameness. Many Americans in 1950, while enjoying the amenities of the comfortable new life in the suburbs, were only a few years removed from farms or small towns—and the foxholes. They wanted to be against conformity, a bad thing, while at the same time conforming to "The American Way of Life," definitely a good; they wanted to live like everybody else they knew while nourishing something that was themselves. Again, religion could come to the rescue, saying one could have it both ways, as it offered highly personal religious experience in the context of safe, well-ordered religious communities. Only the packaging was new; the experiences and communities were really of ancient vintage. One was called by Billy Graham—in a modern amphitheater or even over television—to a kind of conversion as old as the book of Acts; one prayed the same rosary and heard the same Latin mass as an old-country peasant—now in a suburban Catholic church with a big parking lot; one rediscovered what the Protestant Reformers meant by sin at Union Theological Seminary in New York, not too far from Wall Street and Madison Avenue.

The fact is that America in 1950 was not only troubled in soul at the same time that it was building countless new suburban churches to bring in the young families looking to be fed; it was also profoundly weary on a level having to do with spiritual creativity. It had few truly new ideas, nor did it want them; it wanted only to recover the religion of times past, changing the trappings enough to suit a world of cars, TVs, and consumer culture. It was weary because it had not yet wholly arisen from the trauma of the great war, though that war had changed the world so much that only a serious reorientation of mind and soul could have really fit the new realities. That was not yet psychologically possible, so 1950 hung suspended between old and new, looking both ways without decision, unable to cope, anxious and frantically busy because it did not want to decide, or even to acknowledge that decisions must be made.

The immense reality lying behind American experience in the year 1950 was the greatest war in history, World War II. It had ended only five years before. Directly or indirectly all that was good and all that was bad in the midcentury year had been shaped by that terrible and glorious conflict, which in the end was the work of one person. It was not for nothing that a recent poll of historians declared Adolf Hitler the most influential person of the twentieth century. Even the way people thought to themselves about love and the meaning of life, about friends and enemies and the meaning of America, about God and religion, was not what it would have been without that man and that overwhelming event.

Those had been days of horror and moral splendor, of bloodied beaches from the South Pacific to Normandy, of war bonds and USO canteens, of Ernie Pyle's and Bill Maulden's GIs, and of an entire nation mobilized to one end—Victory. The experience of war had culminated in the virtually apocalyptic year 1945, the year that brought the death of two of the great antagonists, Franklin D. Roosevelt and Hitler, only a few weeks apart; then giddy victory in Europe sobered by the discovery of the unspeakable abomination of Hitler's death camps and darkened by the beginnings of tension among the victors, especially between the Soviet Union and its western Allies; then the bombs that released the power within the sun and stars to bring victory over Japan in August and usher in peace, and the ominous new atomic age. For in those days good never came without a shadow.

Nineteen fifty, until Korea in the middle of the year, was peacetime in America. For most Americans the rewards of peace were obvious. In its editorial for July 31, 1950, *Life* magazine exulted in its proclamation that 1945–1950, the postwar years, had been "the most bountiful five year period in U.S. history." Americans had built four million new homes. Flocking to the suburbs in the greatest internal migration since ox-drawn covered wagons had made their plodding way westward a hundred years before, people had built thousands of sprawling ranch houses where once had been open country. And in these new settlements "the two-car family was becoming a commonplace," and Americans were beginning to "think of air-conditioning and sound-proofing as necessities, not luxuries."

More statistics told the same story. Between 1945 and 1950 high school graduates (as percentage of all persons over sixteen years old) rose from 47.9 to 59 percent, automobile registrations rose from 31 million to over 49 million, the gross national product ascended from 212 billion dollars to 285 billion—and the number of military personnel on active duty fell from over 12 million to 2,357,000. On another level, new drugs, the antibiotics first developed during the war, had "made human life far less hazardous than before." *Life* could also have mentioned television; 1950 was the first year in which the new medium truly began to be a part of popular culture and a major shaper of opinions and values. The flickering screen was now starting to tell Americans what they ought to know and how they ought to live.

Life also claimed gains in race and labor relations; progress in the arts; the vast expansion of education, especially at the higher levels; substantial growth in real income and in what was called the "standard of living"; and growth even in "political maturity." Rightly or wrongly, the editors of that great national magazine claimed, "[I]n world affairs, which involved spiritual values as well as power politics, the U.S. had definitely grown up since 1940. In 1950 the U.S. people were ready to accept a world role, whether they were to do it well or badly."[3]

In 1950 the churches and the print media, such as Henry Luce's immensely influential *Time* as well as *Life*, both identified as a major postwar phenomenon the American "return to religion." Which religion it was perhaps did not matter much from the national perspective, at least so long as it was part of the Protestant-Catholic-Jew troika proclaimed a little later in the decade by Will Herberg's book of that title. Around 1950 American Judaism was definitely moving from outsider status to official Third Faith.

Media piety further hinted to uneasy Americans that the unprecedented postwar affluence was good insofar as it suggested divine blessing and the superiority of American democracy and capitalism over the ways of the cold war opponent; the "American way of life" was the antithesis of godless communism and was to be preserved at all cost. This was the "American exceptionalism" espoused by Henry Luce as early as 1941 in his book *The American Century:* the belief that the United States, with a history apart from the evils of the Old World, had a special mission to preserve its own virtue, and moreover to present it to the rest of the world as the more excellent way, while defending earth from evil forces bent on destroying such righteousness. The theologian Reinhold Niebuhr, a "cold war liberal" and a favorite of Luce and his camp, was at the height of his power as a purveyor of similar sentiments, which would be encapsulated in his 1952 book *The Irony of American History*.

Never would the notion that the United States somehow led a charmed life apart from the rest of the world, whatever its mission to that world, seem more self-evident than in 1950. Half the wealth of the largely devastated postwar world was either in or on its way to America. Despite McCarthyism and the virulent racism still widely prevalent and still enforced by law in the American South, the United States was, by 1950 world standards, a land of astonishing freedom and opportunity. Most of the rest of the world was, if not under totalitarianism or colonialism, wracked by poverty and struggle; even western Europe, though "free," was ridden by an oppressive social class system and only beginning to overcome the destruction of the war. As the *Life* editorial indicated, keeping less fortunate lands from starvation with American surplus was another virtue on which America could pride itself in 1950. Even in religion the United States in 1950 was "exceptional"; few other places enjoyed its religious diversity, freedom, and equality, even if American faith was still dominated by an old Protestant "establishment." Few had the United States's remarkable immigration-based religious pluralism, or even its wealth of "new" religions.

But despite ringing declarations about the American Way of Life, the American Dream, or the American Mission, and the prosperity that might have been thought to confirm them, all was not well in 1950 with America's public and spiritual life. The U.S. monopoly on atomic weapons, which had given the nation and its allies a measure of security during four years of disarmament despite rising tension with the Soviet Union, was over. On September 23, 1949, President Truman had announced that the Russians had tested an "atomic device." In January 1950, in his first major decision of the new half-century, the President declared that the United States, in order to maintain its edge, would proceed to develop the next level of nuclear deterrence, the hydrogen bomb. By midsummer, the growing hostility between the two competing political systems of the world, the Western and the Communist, would break into open warfare in distant Korea. American GIs would once again, only five years after the end of the greatest war in history, be facing enemy bullets.

Strife in 1950 also deepened at home. J. Edgar Hoover, Director of the FBI, declared that the U.S. Communist Party had 55,000 members and 500,000 sympathizers, and anti-communist feeling spread rapidly. Most communists were assumed to be working secretly. Where were they? Next door? Teaching in the schools one's children attended, and making the movies they watched? Pulling the levers of power in the State Department?

This great fear was abetted by news from abroad of the expansion and intransigence of the Communist world. Much of eastern Europe was brought under its sway at war's end, then Czechoslovakia in 1948, and vast China in 1949. By the summer of 1950 Red armies were pouring into South Korea. Whatever Communism took in those days, it held by whatever means necessary, which not seldom were extremely brutal. Newspapers, radio commentators, political figures, and often enough the religious media registered those portentous events in the most graphic manner, spreading alarm. Above all it was the 1949 "loss" of China and the need to attach blame for that tremendous disaster that provoked the powerful upsurge of anticommunism in 1950 going under the name of McCarthyism. For Senator Joseph M. McCarthy's first and most inflammatory charge was that the State Department was "riddled" with communists, who were responsible for the China failure.

The idea that the United States was being betrayed from within even as it was challenged from without was not a new notion by 1950. For the previous two or three years the American people had been treated to a fascinating, disturbing, and sensational series of hearings and trials involving communist espionage, "infiltration," and "subversion" in public institutions. In 1948, historic hearings before the House Un-American Activities Committee aired the charges of Whittaker Chambers, a *Time* editor, that Alger Hiss, a sometime official at State and later respected president of the Carnegie Endowment for International Peace, had been a communist and a spy known to Chambers in the 1930s. These were the sensational hearings that did so much to advance the career of Richard Nixon and led to Hiss's trial for perjury. Hiss was finally found guilty and sentenced to five years' imprisonment on January 21, 1950.

In early February 1950, about the same time as McCarthy's first public charges, Klaus Fuchs, a German-born atomic scientist who had worked for the British nuclear energy establishment and at Los Alamos as the atomic bomb was being developed, was convicted in Britain of passing nuclear secrets to the Russians. This case led to the arrest of five Americans alleged to have been his accomplices—Harry Gold, Julius and Ethel Rosenberg, Morton Sobell, and David Greenglass. The subsequent trial and execution of the Rosenbergs (the only Americans actually to receive capital punishment for treason in the days of the great fear) were to be another sensational case.

Then on March 7, 1950, Judith Coplon and Valentin Gubitchev were convicted of espionage. Theirs was a story that might have come straight out of Hollywood: an attractive young woman with leftist leanings who worked for the Justice Department, an alleged lover who was a Russian employed at the UN, her heedless agreement to pass to him copies of certain documents and their arrest after a dramatic FBI pursuit through New York City. (Although Coplon was twice found guilty, her convictions were overturned on appeal on the ground of improperly gathered evidence, including illegal wiretaps by the FBI; Gubitchev was sent back home to whatever fate Stalin had in mind for him.)

All of this, together with the anxieties generated by the see-saw Korean war and the McCarthy charges, prepared the way for the McCarren Internal Security Act of September 1950, passed over President Truman's veto and the vehement protests of religious progressives and other liberals. It required communists and communist-front organizations to register with the Attorney General, forbade communists to work in defense plants or use U.S. passports, provided for their detention in time of national emergency, and made it illegal to conspire to establish a totalitarian government in the United States. Almost lost amid the news from Korea was the June 23, 1950 firing of 137 members of the University of California staff for failing to sign an anticommunist pledge, and the June 29 conviction of eight Hollywood directors, producers, and writers on contempt charges for refusing to tell the House Un-American Activities Committee whether they were communists.

But there was another side to 1950, a youthful and hopeful side, and it also culminated in that momentous month of June 1950. Young veterans of the greatest war in history, their eyes still haunted by sights of which many would never speak, were by now finishing college or trade school on the GI Bill and settling down to careers and families. That June the education boom climaxed; twice as many young Americans graduated in 1950 than in any prewar year. The alumni of 1950, who had for the most part entered academic life in the fall of 1946, right after demobilization, represented a new and confident cohort. They knew, first of all, that they represented a generation whose numbers and level of education had never before been equaled. Some fifteen million veterans had been eligible for the first GI Bill, signed into law by President Roosevelt in 1944; 7.8 million, about half, received some level of education under its benefits. By 1947 most colleges and universities had to contend with more than double their prewar numbers. These ambitious scholars were focused on their futures—doubtless, to most of them, communist conquests and communist spies were just black-and-white newspaper headlines at the background of real life and love.

They were not like prewar students. Older, seasoned by war, mated and with young children in many cases, living in slapdash married student housing tracts that had blossomed around campuses, they had little time for the juvenile, "rah-rah" aspects of student life, or for petty academic rules. Professors had to face docents who were serious but irreverent, ambitious but distracted by many worries, critical yet profoundly grateful for the opportunities afforded them in the America for which they had fought, and above all aware of the years that fight had spoiled and eager to make them up. Having won a hard but tremendous victory, and now making it through school, they were supremely confident that they and their generation could accomplish anything.

An interesting study that captures the flavor of that group's experience at Purdue University, John Norberg's *A Force for Change: The Class of 1950*, cites one of its members, Harold Michael, to this effect: "The legacy of the Class of 1950 was this: we were a group of people, many of whom had been in World War II, who came to college generally knowing what we wanted to do. And then we started working on the redevelopment of this country. And we still are."[4] John Hicks, who later became a vice president of Purdue, added, "You could say it was a good time to be young. If you got out of college in 1948, '49, or '50, I don't see how you could have helped but succeed. There were so many opportunities. . . They were good years, no question about it. We had faith and such a bright outlook on the future. . . ."[5] It was a great time to be starting out, and all in all a prosperous country with seemingly boundless resources.

Of course, there was the other half of the veterans, those who did not take advantage of the GI Bill to attend school. Indeed, many Americans, veterans or not, did not live in the conventional suburban home with two children and a white picket fence. Among those who did not were African Americans trapped by legal or de facto segregation in the inner cities or the rural slums of the Deep South. Other veterans were led by one consideration or another to return straight home to jobs on America's farms or in small towns and factories without pausing for school or new lifestyles. Some even chose to remain in the armed services, which was an increasingly bright career option as the country, by mid-1950, was preparing itself for Korea and the Koreas to come. All these worlds were also 1950.

For, even as the June commencements of 1950 seemed incredibly packed with future-oriented hope and glory, sinister forces of apocalyptic scope were also in the offing. Hardly was the hard-earned diploma in hand, the cheering over from graduation, then perhaps a June wedding and the brave young couple on the way to new home and job, than the news of the last week of June 1950 hit the radios and newsstands: War!

War in Korea, as Communist armies poured south across that Asian peninsula, American as well as South Korean forces under nominal UN authority attempted to stop them, and the world waited for a week of nearly unbearable anxiety to see if the Soviet Union would intervene with its newly developed atomic weapons and turn the world into Armageddon.

It did not, and the war eventually fizzled into stasis, but the anxiety lingered, for inward anguish coexisting with a "bright outlook" was endemic to 1950. When a nation or world is divided into two immensely powerful and seemingly almost equal powers, when all depends on who wins, or at least is able to contain the other, and it is not clear which the victor will be, anxiety and all its attendant evils are bound to arise and flourish like plagues everywhere. For some two decades now, since the bitter depression years of the 1930s, Americans had lived in a world divided and dualistic: rich and poor, fascist and free, Axis and Allies. Now it was the Soviet Union and its cluster of Communist satellites versus the United States and its supporters. Though they might have wished it otherwise, Americans were used to thinking in war terms. It did not take them long to make the so-called cold war like any other war, complete with defense industries, spy scares, loyalty tests, and military draft. And now that war too was becoming hot, at least in one far-off place where Americans would go to fight and die. The low point of the war came in the first week of December, when U.S., South Korean, and Allied forces were trapped in an enclave around the southern port of Pusan; this moment coincided with the founding of the National Council of Churches in Cleveland.

Culturally, 1950 in many respects was a sterling year. On April 9, Tony Awards for outstanding contributions to the theater went to *The Cocktail Party* by T. S. Eliot and *South Pacific* by Richard Rodgers, Oscar Hammerstein, and Joshua Logan. Both had opened the previous year but were much watched and talked about in 1950. The play by Eliot, the great U.S. expatriate poet of Anglo-Catholic religion and traditionalist bent, well reflected the world of sophisticated intellectuals of 1950 and their inner anxieties. Eliot put his set of witty but hollow people at a cocktail party, then considered the modish and up-to-date way to get together. The usual sort of clever talk about various infidelities and marriage breakups fluttered around the room, all taken none too seriously by people who did not believe in sin. Then, in midplay, comes a lacuna of a couple of years. In the last scene, when the same group gathers at another cocktail party about two years later, a new development becomes the subject of chatter. It turns out that a woman who had been at the first party had in the interim discovered "the kind of faith that issues from despair." She had consequently radically changed her life to become a missionary sister and had been martyred in a horrible manner—crucifixion beside an ant hill—on a remote island.

Though of lasting value, the play surely reflects the central theme of highbrow 1950 culture: the fashionable pessimism about the emptiness of modern life. The solution is found in the discovery of a highly traditionalist, churchly way out in becoming a religious, though only after an inward, existentialist finding of faith through despair. Religion in 1950 was not yet ready to go in new directions; rather, it sought to find what had been there all along in the traditional faiths, though it was willing to take into account the language of the reigning fashionable philosophy, existentialism. Many American playgoers in 1950 could also no doubt identify with the underlying tension in the play between urban sophistication and traditional pieties: having, many of them, come out of Depression-era or World-War-II rural backgrounds, they partly enjoyed their glamorous new lives in cities and suburbs, yet also harbored feelings of doubt and guilt about leaving solid virtues and old-fashioned faith behind. They may have hoped, with the help of prophets like T. S. Eliot, to find that surety again on a higher level.

South Pacific, perhaps the greatest of the "musicals" that enjoyed their golden age as an American art form around mid-century, gives us a popular-culture look at the values of 1950.

The drama and its memorable songs, like "Some Enchanted Evening" and "Bali Hai," suggest a people in a wistful, romantic mood. The great war as presented on the stage of *South Pacific* is already beginning to turn to archetypal myth: young people in faraway paradisal places where life and death, love and despair are intensely experienced, yet there is comic relief and the extremes of horror are excised. The war according to *South Pacific* was after all only one self-contained episode, following which one could move on to other lives and other loves, perhaps back home where one really belonged. Undoubtedly more than a few veterans yearned to see their wartime lives in this way: now past, and, in retrospect, intense, heroic, and occasionally even glamorous and fun.

There were other unforgettable themes in *South Pacific:* the wartime exposure of countless young Americans to the humanity of other races and other cultures, and the great romantic motif that there is one true love for each person, to be found at the predestined moment—after other false encounters, perhaps in some exotic wartime location, had been left behind. Right or wrong, this sentiment appealed to many who, after the upheavals of the wartorn years, were now very much ready to settle down. In this respect too the musical reflected the fundamental desire of America's then-youthful population to be optimistic: one of its songs assured hearers that if you have a dream, that dream can come true. The sweet mysteries of love, whether before one's eyes, phantom-like in one's dreams, or enshrined in timeless art, that so preoccupied some deep level of 1950 consciousness, were celebrated in other popular songs of the year as well: "Good Night, Irene," "My Foolish Heart," and "Mona Lisa."

Another popular play, *The Member of the Wedding* by Carson McCullers, carried romantic drama to the altar. The part of Bernice, the African American housekeeper, was subtle and uncondescending, and it gave Ethel Waters the role of a lifetime as she conveyed sympathetically the strength and pervasive influence of the black servant in the old-style Southern family.

Nineteen fifty was an important but relatively unrecognized year in the development of African American religion and civic life. Despite the commencement of integration in the armed services by President Truman in 1947 and some evidence of postwar shifts in attitude, Jim Crow still reigned in the South, and the North was by and large interested in other things. The traditional black churches seemed more concerned with accommodation or strictly religious roles than confrontation, and the Supreme Court's *Brown* v. *Board of Education* was still four years off. Yet those who would make the civil rights movement come alive were preparing for their roles behind the scenes. It was in 1950 that Martin Luther King Jr., then a student at Crozer Seminary in Pennsylvania, heard a lecture at Fellowship House in Philadelphia by the distinguished black churchman and educator, Mordecai Johnson, just back from a trip to India. Johnson extolled the power of Mohandas K. Gandhi's nonviolent resistance and suggested it might have application in the situation of American blacks. The young Martin King, deeply stirred, immediately went out and bought six books about Gandhi. It was also in 1950 that Malcolm Little, later known as Malcolm X, incarcerated in Massachusetts and recently converted to the Black Muslims, was energetically studying his new religion in every way he could, preparing to become a force on its behalf after he was released two years later.

Finally, what about the moral values so closely associated with religion? As the twentieth century ends, there are those who claim that moral standards have seriously declined in recent decades, and some seem even prepared to point to the 1950s as a sort of baseline against which to measure this decline. But would people in 1950 have seen their day as an apex of virtue? I doubt it.

The fact is that moral prophets—from those of the Hebrew Scriptures to medieval bishops to nineteenth-century revivalists—have ever idealized a supposedly virtuous and pious past against which to showcase the degeneracy of the present. This is what may be called the myth of the pious past, usually effective only as a sort of generalized assumption that will not withstand the close examination of any particular date or place in the past.

Nineteen fifty was no exception. People did not consider themselves especially virtuous; indeed, there was considerable talk about returning veterans who had learned much about the seamy as well as the heroic sides of life—who had come back with newly uninhibited views on smoking, drinking, and sex, as well as a determination to achieve "success" in the new postwar land of opportunity by whatever means it took. Newspapers carried lurid news of teenage sex clubs that had been discovered in certain elite communities. And people were still talking, whether with a wink and a leer or an expression of outrage, about Alfred E. Kinsey's notorious 1948 book, *Sexual Behavior in the Human Male*, which advanced astonishing claims, supposedly based on the most dispassionate scientific research: that 85 percent of the male population had experimented with premarital sexual intercourse, that 70 percent had had relations with prostitutes, that at least 30 percent had indulged in extramarital sex, and that the typical unmarried American male past puberty experienced coitus an average of once a week. Needless to say the companion volume, *Sexual Behavior in the Human Female*, was eagerly anticipated; it appeared in 1952. At the same time, one can perhaps understand why a 1950 *Reader's Digest* article was entitled "I'm Sick of Sex."[6]

Of course, there were some differences in views of particular evils between 1950 and century's end. Sexual transgressions were more concealed by pretense in 1950, though they certainly existed, and not only in Kinsey's eyes. As a high school senior out in western Nebraska that year, I was well aware that sexual activity occurred among my fellow students and in every other high school of which I knew anything, but if as a result a girl "got in trouble" she would probably leave on an unexpected nine-month vacation to visit her grandmother.

Homosexuality was likewise not unknown, but even more concealed. Once in a while an otherwise well-thought-of minister or male teacher might suddenly resign and vanish from town within twenty-four hours. At the same time, though their era was coming to an end, the traditionally unmarried women schoolteachers and nurses were still around and still highly respected for the dedication indicated by their single state, though some of them openly lived together in a way adult single professional males in a small town certainly could not: a reverse double standard.

Moreover, if one regards, as one certainly should, racial prejudice and discrimination—together with the humiliation, degradation, and lack of fair opportunity that accompany them—to be serious evils, one must set alongside midcentury virtues the fact that in 1950 racial segregation was still rigidly enforced by law in the South, as were laws against interracial marriage. More often than not, such laws were also observed de facto elsewhere. Not only that, but language and "jokes" that were blatantly and crudely racist and anti-Semitic could be widely heard. Restrictions, quotas, and "gentlemen's agreements" barred numerous Americans of many backgrounds from desired housing, education, jobs, clubs, and even recreation, and these bars could be enforced by mob violence in those years. Most women in 1950 also found themselves facing a narrow range of choices and were often virtually forced into one of a limited number of social roles—including choosing between marriage and a profession—in ways that would be intolerable to their granddaughters.

Even so, to many in 1950 the year was, after depression and war, a time that looked immensely liberating and hopeful as well as dangerous. But it was not a time they would have thought of as a moral beacon to later generations, unless in its determination to fight against Communism and for the American Way of Life. For this they probably did think later generations would give them thanks, and no doubt with justice: for whatever the wrongs done in the name of that cause, the world would indeed be a darker place had Communism in its 1950 form prevailed. And many in 1950, if they were not overly influenced by the sense of crisis and impending end of civilization that so affected some intellectuals, did think things were better than they had been. Another *Reader's Digest* contribution to 1950 was a condensation of Clyde Brion Davis's nostalgic but open-eyed book comparing life in the United States in 1900 and 1950, *The Age of Indiscretion*. Davis concluded, after discussions of the diseases still rampant in 1900 but now largely defeated, of the turn-of-the-century's appalling child labor, and of its uninspected and often-adulterated or contaminated food: "Yes, I know about taxes. I know about the A-bomb and the H-bomb. I know about the possibility of war. I know about the conflict of ideologies and the decline in railroad earnings. But we still never had it so good. Despite the prophets of doom, I am not disappointed in Americans."[7]

In the end, it may be that there is about the same sum total of good and evil in every year, at least in this age of the world, though it might be distributed somewhat differently from one year to another. So perhaps the year 1950 was morally and spiritually no better or worse than most. But it was definitely unique. And in American religious history it was more than just the year that, by calendric accident, happened to be the midcentury point. It was also a time that was pivotal in its own right, defining and setting in motion forces that were to dominate much of the rest of the century. Examining those specifics of 1950 will be the task of this book.

Heir of the 1930s and 1940s; Depression, World's Fair, and War

Let us now turn back to the 1930s, two decades before mid-century. Those years, like the war-torn 1940s to follow, are essential background to 1950. To get a sense of religion in the traumatic depression decade, here are a few items from *The Christian Century* of the year 1933, the year the great slump reached its nadir, and the year both Adolf Hitler and Franklin D. Roosevelt came to power.

The lead editorial in the first issue, "Wages and Human Desperation," tells us that "wage levels in many industries have now sunk to the point where they will scarcely sustain life." The garment trade in Massachusetts was paying from four to six dollars a week; children under sixteen were working in large numbers in Pennsylvania for two dollars a week; candy workers in Illinois, who earned from eighteen to twenty-five dollars three years before, were now receiving five to seven dollars a week. Not only that, but the "time schedules have also been inhumanly protracted. Girls in Connecticut sweatshops are working from 81 to 85 hours a week."

But these grim statistics spoke only of the fortunate people who had jobs. The article concluded "that millions will jump at the chance to get such jobs is a measure of current human desperation."[1] A later news item of March 1, 1933, "The Depression Enters a More Tragic Stage," tells of fifteen million unemployed—31.2 percent of all those who had been employed as recently as April 1930. The rate was 46 percent

Livorno, Italy, September 1944.

of those in manufacturing and mechanical trades. Of those unemployed, over a million and a quarter were homeless, wandering the country in a desperate search for work, their families disintegrating.

In that same week, Roosevelt became President. *The Christian Century* featured an editorial, much more conspicuously displayed than the one on 15 million unemployed, entitled "This *Is* Armageddon." But contrary to what one might expect, the apocalyptic reference was not to the Great Depression, nor of Hitler's rise to power in Germany a month before. The Final Battle was instead that which faced godly drys as they confronted the expected repeal of Prohibition under the incoming Democratic administration—a political issue that oddly took up more space in many 1933 media, and evidently engaged more passion among Americans who had work and enough extra money to buy newspapers than the economic catastrophe or the rising tide of fascism in Europe.

The last matter was not overlooked, however. In an editorial of February 8, 1933, just after he became Chancellor, *The Christian Century* had asked, "How Much of a Menace Is Hitler?" At that point, this liberal Protestant magazine, like many others, was concerned, but not yet urgently so, and held that the Nazi leader was in power only at the sufferance of other politicians. By March 15, however, in "The Third German Reich," it granted that Hitler was on the way to establishing a dictatorship, and by April 5 a saddened editorial articulated "World Wrath at Hitler's Attack on German Jews." Then on May 10, we were told that "Hitler Is Completely Triumphant within Germany." Other articles worriedly discussed the Nazi promotion of pagan religion, and asked (June 14, 1933), "Has Hitler Cowed the Churches?"

Returning to the situation at home, a January 4, 1933 editorial, "Is Security Gone Forever?" related the Great Depression to the fate of religion, stating that 1932 had been a hard year for the churches as incomes and contributions fell drastically. On a profounder level, it noted that family and home, as "shelter from the storms of life, security from the attacks of adverse fortune," as well as a foundation of church and religious life, were falling apart due to "worldwide dislocation of the economic order." The upshot was that we entered this new year, 1933, purged of the "false confidence" of the past. Victorian "easy optimism" about progress, about the "infinite and automatic perfectibility of human institutions," was now about vanished. We no longer accepted, "wide-eyed and open-mouthed," what science said, nor what the banker or the salesman spieled forth about endless prosperity.

Religion was the only hope left, America's premier Protestant magazine declared. Twelve million Americans and their dependents had no food because they had no money, which was because they had no work, and they had no work because organized society did not need their work. The logic of economics then says, cried the print preacher, "Let them starve!" But, he went on, "Religion says, Give ye them to eat." Thus, religion is "the sole bulwark between the nation and ultimate disaster because it, and it alone, decrees that our clumsy economics and our political ineptitude shall not lead to their logical conclusion."

But what kind of religion? Religion of the left, which would carry the social gospel tradition into Christian socialism or even communism, or religion of the right, which would point to the sin in all human institutions and decry identification of the gospel with social utopianism? Both voices were heard in the 1930s. By 1932 Reinhold Niebuhr, though a political liberal, had broken with pacifism and with Marxist or utopian blueprints for the social order, and said so in *Moral Man and Immoral Society*. In a January 1933 review of this book in *The Christian Century*, tension was painfully evident between the reflexes of the liberal religious progressivism with which that journal had long been identified and the repudiation of Victorian "easy optimism" the editors had been forced to make in the same issue. In his review, Theodore C. Hume called Niebuhr a "prophet of disillusion," with his message that man will never be purely reasonable and that there must be a place for coercion. But disillusionment, Hume contended, can never inspire men and women to do what must be done to rectify evil.

The same message of theological crisis over liberalism and its allegedly too-facile view of natural religion and human perfectibility was coming in from Europe, represented above all in the person of Karl Barth. To some, though not all, American Protestants, Barth's Neoorthodoxy, Dialectical Theology, or Theology of Crisis, as it was variously called, seemed the wave of the future. On January 18, 1933, Edwin Lewis asked, "What Is Barth Trying to Say?"

The answer was that the European theologian emphasized afresh the ultimate difference between God and humanity. Chastened by the horrors of World War I, Barth and his school realized the fatuousness in liberal claims of an easy continuity between the human and the divine. Humans cannot "find" God on their own; rather they must receive the Word of God through scripture preached with insight opened by faith. It was a new kind of message for a troubled time, one that very much recognized the sin all too evident in the world of the twentieth century.[2]

Yet there were models of other ways as well. The media of those years made much of Mohandas K. Gandhi and his nonviolent campaigns against British rule in India. The same January 3, 1933, issue of *The Christian Century* that reviewed Niebuhr presented Agatha Harrison's "88 Knightsbridge, London," which focused on the life of the Mahatma and his inner circle of disciples, all pictured as colorful figures in their own right, as they dwelt in the imperial capital attending the second roundtable conference on India. C. F. Andrews, Anglican clergyman and one of Gandhi's best-known associates and interpreters to the West, published "Lifting the Deadweight from Missions" in *The Christian Century* for January 25, 1933, calling for a new kind of missionary of whom Gandhi would approve, one without the terrible "arrogance of the Christian" but rather "the servant of all."[3] One wonders which of these the Barthian would appear to be in India?

In 1934 the situation was not much better so far as churches were concerned. Budgets were sharply reduced from pre-Depression figures, and ministers were restless. Kirby Page, a stalwart of religious pacifism, undertook a much-discussed survey of some twenty thousand clergymen, of whom he said that fourteen thousand were convinced that the time had come for the churches, as such, to declare their refusal to support the government in any future war. This, Page declared, was a marked increase over the 1931 level of support for pacifism. He also announced that the ministers he polled rejected laissez-faire economics. "Only one in 18 of these ministers proved ready to affirm that the 'rugged individualism' which governed life in the United States prior to 1929 was as consistent with the religion of Jesus as a cooperative commonwealth in which the service motive would be predominant."[4]

While the statistical representativeness of Page's sample may be questioned, no doubt such sentiments reflected widespread clerical thinking in the liberal Protestant denominations. As another writer indicated in "Protestantism for Such a Time as This," it was "a watershed in history" in which churches faced a "beleaguered capitalism." Unfortunately, however, religionists found themselves better at analyzing the problem than providing solutions.[5] Some—especially high-spirited ministerial students at New York's Union Theological Seminary—believed they had found the solution in the agenda of the left. Not a few UTS seminarians took part in demonstrations and joined union picket lines, and even—though perhaps as a stunt—flew a red flag on the chapel spire on May Day 1934. UTS President Henry Sloane Coffin squelched such radicalism with a firm hand.[6]

However, life gradually got better in the United States as the 1930s advanced, and it seemed increasingly unlikely that the red flag would be raised anywhere except at UTS. Jobs became more abundant; wages crept upward; more and more people bought cars and washing machines. Roosevelt, though bitterly hated by those he called "economic royalists," was widely popular. His buoyant spirit and New Deal programs injected cautious optimism into national life. All this was apparently healthy for religion. While church membership and attendance had declined in the early and middle 1930s, by 1938 and 1939 the numbers were on the rise again. According to the *Yearbook of American Churches* total church membership was 64,159,248 at the end of 1938, up by 915,414 from the 1937 figure.

A poll by the Psychological Corporation, a New York sales counselor, also showed a sharp rise since 1937 in positive answers to the question, "Do you think that religion is losing or gaining ground in the United States?" In 1937, 45 percent said religion was slipping, and 34 percent that it was gaining; in 1939 the numbers had been virtually reversed—to 45 percent voting for gaining, 32 percent for declining.[7] Charles Eugene Conover, writing in *The Christian Century* in 1939, said that one could "sense" a revival of interest in religion on campus, together with an increasing conservatism in social life.[8] The last year of peace and, after September 1, the first year of war, 1939 was one of the hinge years of history. It was moreover the last year of the depression-wracked 1930s and in some sense the first year of the future that had sustained hope in hard times.

For 1939 was the summer of the New York World's Fair, that celebrated event that defied ominous days and weeks to preview futuristic marvels. As befitted a hinge year, 1939, like 1950, looked forward, backward, and, as if in horror at some of what it saw in both directions, sideways into fantasylands. Top movies in the United States that year were the historical fantasy *Gone with the Wind* and the otherworldly fantasy *The Wizard of Oz*. Americans showed their devotion to the New Deal's kind of democratic idealism in their enthusiastic response to Frank Capra's *Mr. Smith Goes to Washington* and Robert Sherwood's Pulitzer Prize-winning play, *Abe Lincoln in Illinois*.

American religion in 1939 was, as in 1950, also caught between nostalgia, futurism, and fantasy. Indeed, the hard-bitten and "radical" 1930s were perversely reflected, as in a distorting mirror, in that much-different midcentury year a decade or more later, for 1950 used the 1930s to showcase its prosperity and wanted to rectify the sins of its 1930s' fathers. But back in 1939 American religion seemed uncertain as to the direction it should take in a dangerous and rapidly changing world. Wounds from the bitter battles between fundamentalists and modernists that had riven several denominations in the 1920s still festered. Other problematic issues as well hung in the darkening air.

First of all, American religion was, as always, divided into unequal parts. The center was definitely the "mainstream" Protestant churches of old Anglo-Saxon, colonial background, especially the Episcopalians, Presbyterians, and Congregationalists. Though numerically representing less than 5 percent of the total population, these three traditions received unequal attention on society pages, where not a few of the weddings worth writing about were solemnized in one of their flagship churches. Their leaders, before all others, would be reverently quoted by journalists on major issues. More important, a disproportionate share of the powerholders on Wall Street and in Washington, from President Roosevelt on down, still came out of an elite culture shaped by those churches, and the old denominations were well represented in the Ivied, East Coast educational institutions that formed many of the nation's leaders, both temporal and spiritual.

Respectable if not quite as prestigious were the larger mainstream Protestant denominations based in the South and Midwest. They owed their great numbers to postrevolutionary frontier religious ferment: Methodists (who had formed the United Methodist Church in May 1939, bringing together Northern and Southern Methodist denominations separated since the Civil War era), Baptists, Disciples, and others. Increasingly liberal and well-educated, they were, despite a few crotchets like passionate temperance concerns, increasingly assimilated into a wider Protestant hegemony that saw itself as something like the normative strand of American spiritual and moral life. That lineage was well defined by inclusion in the Federal Council of Churches, precursor of the postwar

National Council of Churches, which in 1939 embraced the northern Baptists, the northern Presbyterians, the Congregationalists, the Episcopalians, one Lutheran denomination (the United), one Eastern Orthodox church (the Syrian), the Reformed and Brethren churches, and African American Baptist and Methodist churches, all together representing some twenty-one and half million souls.

Definitely outside the circle were hard-core evangelicals, fundamentalists, and Pentecostals, regarded by Federal Council types as country cousins or worse. They frequently looked down on these stem-winding, Bible-pounding coreligionists with an open disdain that bordered on bitterness. The educated scorn was born from the passions raised by the 1925 "monkey trial" and other epic struggles for the American soul, a struggle the liberals of 1939 confidently believed they had won. Sometimes they seemed puzzled that the fundamentalists had not simply disappeared by now. African American churches were also outside the circle; despite formal representation in the Federal Council, their theology and modes of worship could not be taken seriously by the privileged in a nation still racist and segregated almost everywhere, whether by law or custom.

Roman Catholics (also numbering about twenty-one and a half million in 1939), Eastern Orthodox, and Jews were another issue. Though certainly not part of the historic circle, they were, like the elite, largely Eastern and urban, as though creating an alternative religious culture alongside theirs, altar against altar. A town like Boston was by 1939 two cities with two cultures, as sealed off from each other as if by a Berlin wall: one was Catholic, Irish (the large Italian population did not yet have a comparable influence), and Boston College; the other, what remained of the colonial past, was liberal Protestant, Yankee, "Brahmin," and Harvard. The former controlled politics; the latter thought they still ran intellectual and cultural affairs.

Though their election-time votes were mostly corralled by Franklin Roosevelt's New Deal coalition, Catholics, Orthodox, and Jews still largely found themselves in the role of new-comers and outsiders. In the larger cities they were based in ethnic enclaves centered around parish or synagogue; people at best left their subculture only to go to work. But the newly arrived were here to stay; the educational institutions they established, as well as generational change, were preparing them to enter the American mainstream. The upcoming war was to greatly accelerate that process. But in 1939 assimilation was still incompletely realized. Religiously, Catholics, Orthodox, and Jews had little if any significant dialogue with the older Protestant establishment. Positive ecumenicity beyond mainline Protestantism was by and large an idea whose time had not yet come. Though pockets of virulent nativism, anti-Catholicism, and anti-Semitism definitely remained in 1939, a lofty live-and-let-live attitude, noting that the religious facilities of such people ministered well to "their own kind," was more typical and was the best that even the most well-meaning establishment religionists could offer.

Interreligious relations were in a kind of stasis in 1939, for even more significant issues hung on the horizon. Of these, the most important were war and peace, forcefully brought home to the New World democracy by the immense, looming figure of Hitler across the Atlantic and Japanese militarism across the Pacific. The widespread religious pacifism of the 1920s and 1930s, engendered by progressive idealism and the horrors of the 1914–1918 conflict, was still a powerful voice in mainline Protestant churches. Though challenged by the "Christian realism" of Reinhold Niebuhr and others, as we have seen, Protestant spokespersons seemed generally sympathetic to the mood if not the letter of the pacifist cause.

The tension was reflected in continued uneasiness about Karl Barth, who though German was by now in Swiss exile and still one of the most talked-about Protestant theologians in 1939. With his untriumphalist view of Christianity in the world and his opposition to Hitler, Barth was a difficult as well as an important figure for American Protestants. Despite his role as theological guru to the anti-Nazi German Confessing Church, much of Barth's teaching flew in the face of the optimistic social gospel of numerous American pulpits and seminaries. In curious ways, the liberal mood so scorned by the prophet of Basel had been strengthened by the radicalism of the 1930s and at the same time sorely challenged by the decade's descent into poverty and incipient violence. But many Americans were still not ready to find Barthian neoorthodoxy's rejection of liberalism and rediscovery of sin to be helpful. Halford E. Luccock pointedly entitled his article in *The Christian Century*'s "How My Mind Has Changed" series, "With No Apologies to Barth." The author confessed that he had become a bit more orthodox of late, accepting a truly transcendent God revealed in Jesus Christ, but insisted he did not owe this change of heart to Barth and could not accept the "social inadequacy" of Barthianism. Instead he wanted it all: the traditionally open, progressivist spirit of American liberal Protestantism and the full-fledged God of the new European theology.

At the same time, a remarkably bitter editorial in *The Christian Century* said, after noting that Barth had been stripped by the Nazis of the doctor's degree given him by a German university:

> There is irony as well as honor in this bit of news, and it indicates that Barth has reversed his position. During the 1920s he propagated with great success among religious circles the sort of political neutrality which played into the hands of Hitler's rising movement. God is so "wholly other" that man, he proclaimed . . . can be saved only in spite of his deeds. From the standpoint of true religion, politics was irrelevant, incompetent and immaterial. If the nazi regime had not interfered with what he regarded as the indispensable rights of academic freedom, Barth— as would have been the case with Martin Niemöller had the church and its doctrines been let alone—would have continued to live in the third reich with as much happiness as his theology allowed. But the nazis interfered, and Barth went to Switzerland where he apparently came to make a second "existential" choice.[9]

Most American churchmen had nothing but contempt for the Nazi dictator, above all because of his persecution of Jews, or for the Japanese warlords. But they hoped the nations would avoid excesses of jingoism and diplomatic brinksmanship, which general opinion believed had provoked the unnecessary First World War. They were desperately eager to prevent another European war and, when it came in September, to keep the United States out of it. Not a few, influenced no doubt by the long and impressive tradition of Protestant missions in China, were profoundly disturbed by the brutal conflict already flaming in that ancient land as a result of the Japanese "incursion," and prayed it would be early resolved and would not spread.

But the widely heard slogan, "Keep America Out of the War!" was used by all sorts of people, from the pacifists to proto-Nazis. Veering toward the pacifist side was Henry Emerson Fosdick, the celebrated pastor of Riverside Church in New York. In June, John D. Rockefeller, builder of that church, had fifty thousand copies of a Fosdick sermon, "Dare We Break the Vicious Circle of Fighting Evil with Evil?" distributed to business and political leaders. It called for ending the drift to war by ceasing to "copy those we hate" by trying to cast out Satan with Satan.[10]

A. J. Muste was pictured in *Time* in July 1939 as "No. 1 U.S. pacifist." The outspoken Quaker, labor organizer, and sometime minister, was vice-chairman of the premier interdenominational religious pacifist organization, the Fellowship of Reconciliation. The accompanying article cited the issuing of a *Pacifist Handbook* by seven U.S. peace groups, stating that the book matter-of-factly described the courses of action open to conscientious objectors in event of a renewed draft and that it presented the main arguments against pacifism together with possible rebuttals. Another article on the same religion page of the newsmagazine noted it was now the third year of Pastor Niemöller's imprisonment in the Reich.[11]

In July the Moral Re-Armament movement of Frank Buchman held a great rally in the Hollywood Bowl. Twenty-five thousand attended; ten thousand more were turned away.

Searchlights stabbed the air, reminding some uneasily of the Nuremberg Nazi rallies, but the message was entirely in favor of Absolute Honesty, Purity, Unselfishness, and Love.[12] Perhaps the spectacle was an example of the "demonstrative democracy" sometimes called for in those days to counter the theatrical and emotional rallies at which the fascists were such virtuosi.[13] Buchman's largely middle-class audience was pleased to hear how Moral Rearmament had solved labor disputes, generally in management's favor, by letting Christ act as arbiter.

In the same neighborhood, the Rev. Allen Hunter, articulate pacifist pastor of Mt. Hollywood Congregational church, published *White Corpuscles in Europe*, a poignant if oddly named account of several heroic activists, both statesmen and religionists, who were fervently trying to stem the drift toward war.[14] A series of articles in *The Christian Century*, reprinted from a 1933 book by Ray H. Abrams, *Preachers Present Arms*, provoked uneasy discussion as it showed how eagerly U.S. clergymen had adopted militaristic and superpatriotic stands twenty-two years earlier once the country had entered World War I. Despite the previous pacifist or questioning attitude of some men of the cloth, once the bugles had blown very little dissent was to be found, and what there was, was brutally squelched.[15]

Also in the news, as leader of a mass movement and opponent of American involvement in war, was Father Charles Edward Coughlin, the baritone-voiced "radio priest" whose demagoguery reportedly drew 4.5 million regular and 15 million occasional listeners. On the air and in his periodical *Social Justice*, Coughlin attacked Jews, Communists, and "Jewish-Communist" machinations while, in November 1938, describing Nazi policies against Jews as understandable "defense mechanisms." In July 1939 the cleric revived a loose organization of his followers, the Christian Front. This dubious formation also functioned as a federation of like-minded groups; critics noted that they included the Christian Mobilizers, who were in turn allied with the pro-Nazi German-American Bund. Although Coughlin insisted that he was in no way directly connected with the Christian Front, *Social Justice*, using the same term with which its editor had defended Hitlerite anti-Semitism, described the Front in glowing terms as "a defense mechanism against Red activities and as a protector of Christianity and Americanism."[16]

New York meetings of the Front drew as many as thirty thousand participants shouting slogans like "Buy Christian," "Down with the Jews," and "Wait Till Hitler Comes Over Here!" After getting fired up in conclaves, Fronters might then demonstrate in the streets against Jews and alleged communists. These activities often led Coughlinites into street brawls. New York's radio station WMCA was a flashpoint. After airing the "defense mechanisms" apology for Nazi policies toward Jews, the station had refused to broadcast the radio priest's talks unless submitted in advance for approval. Christian Fronters retaliated by boycotting and picketing WMCA in large numbers, making for tense and often violent situations.

The liberal press was full of complaints that in these altercations New York's mainly Irish Catholic police showed partiality to Coughlin followers. Mayor Fiorello La Guardia denied the charges but tried to defuse the situation by limiting pickets at WMCA to four. After the beginning of war in September 1939, Coughlin mentioned Jews less, but this was partly because he was attacking Nazi Germany's present enemy, Great Britain, even more. Britain was almost as much a bête noire to Coughlin's followers as the allegedly intertwined Jewish-Communist world conspiracy, and the island kingdom was now perceived to be in league with the demons of the left against Hitler.[17] Coughlin carefully insisted, however, that he was not pro-Nazi as such; in October he loudly symbolized rejection of support from the Bund and its allied Christian Mobilizers by returning a donation of exactly 128 dollars raised by the Mobilizers.[18]

Then, in late 1939, the National Association of Broadcasters tried to curb the fiery prophet, whose rhetoric was wearing thin as news of European horrors poured in. A new code of broadcasting standards aimed at excluding Coughlin was adopted that barred "controversial" speakers unless they appeared with others taking divergent views. Coughlin and his followers were outraged. Some stations, under pressure from Coughlinites or out of their own management's predisposition, declined to abide by the protocols. But many, especially in the larger cities, seized the excuse to drop the opinionated priest.[19]

The leadership of the Roman Catholic Church generally did not like Coughlin, but they hesitated to crack down on him for fear of schism and did not silence him completely until 1940. Indeed, American Roman Catholics found themselves in awkward positions on several issues as they tried to reconcile their church's ancient traditions, its lingering suspicion of democracy, and the diplomatic obligations of its international character with U.S. society and the realities of 1939. Passionate anticommunism on the part of Catholics was real and understandable, and so was concern among a largely working-class constituency for the dignity of the church they loved. But not all anticommunists or professedly Catholic rulers were equally admirable. Catholics had at first effusively supported the Spanish Falangist strongman Francisco Franco, who completed the consolidation of his power early in 1939, because of his anticommunism and his expressed intent to restore the rights of the Spanish Catholic Church. However, though some Catholics were to defend Franco far too long, by midyear doubts had already arisen in many minds. The dictator often seemed more fascist than Catholic. Execution or concentration camps awaited defeated republicans, while SS leader Heinrich Himmler, despite his role as a foe of the church in Germany, was honored on a 1939 visit, and anticlerical Falangists lauded the new Germany and Italy with impunity.[20]

Roman Catholicism in the United States in 1939 had many facets. A church comprised largely of immigrants or their first and second generation offspring, the nation's largest denomination was haunted by profound identity concerns. Its members' Old World loyalties and deep-seated support for the papacy, all too easily exploited by anticommunist and anti-

British rightists, was paralleled by a no less passionate desire on the part of Catholics to present themselves as true democratic Americans, as much so as Anglo-Protestants of colonial background. That yearning could, as Coughlinism showed, produce bitter tension between democratic and ultrist definitions of "Americanism."

There was also the reality that many Catholics were of the working class, concerned with bread-and-butter issues; on these matters they were naturally inclined to be sympathetic to the unionizing movements of the thirties, and to labor's alliance with the New Deal and the Democratic Party. Catholic blue-collar districts were invariably represented in Congress by Democrats who were pro-labor and pro-New Deal but anticommunist; some prelates, like Bernard Sheil, auxiliary in Chicago, and Edward Mooney, Archbishop of Detroit, were outspokenly sympathetic to Roosevelt and unions.

But in 1939 the American church was becoming more conservative at the top under the pontificate of the cautious diplomat Eugenio Pacelli, elected Pope Pius XII on March 2 of that year. As it happened, the two most important sees in the United States, New York and Chicago, were also vacant in 1939. In the former city the new pontiff replaced Cardinal Hayes, a kindly pastor but bumbling financial administrator who had died in September 1938, with the hard-driving, efficient, and unquestioningly conservative Francis Spellman. In Chicago, Sheil, despite the hopes of liberals, was passed over in favor of the more hidebound Samuel Stritch, transferred from Milwaukee.

All these conflicting Catholic trends were to be refocused in 1950, indeed with enhanced burning power, like a beam of light concentrated by a magnifying glass. By 1950 Spellman, now a cardinal, was the dominant Catholic figure in the United States. He was still an apologist for Franco and various "Catholic" dictators in Latin America, and no less a fervent anticommunist and defender of Senator Joseph McCarthy. In these sentiments he was supported by a large segment of the Catholic press and people. Their anticommunism had by then only been exacerbated by Communist threats or takeovers in the ethnic homelands of millions of American Catholics, and their resentment of the Anglo-Protestant United States that McCarthy loved to bait had only grown with Catholic America's increasing education, prosperity, and sense that millions of boys of that faith had paid dues as real Americans through service in World War II. But the blue-collar, union-hall Catholicism of the 1930s was also still alive in 1950, as was a carefully defined Catholic intellectual liberalism represented by periodicals like the lay-edited *Commonweal*. Utterly unexpected as that outcome might have seemed in the 1930s or in 1950, the Catholic left was to surge forward with power in the 1960s after Vatican II and prevail for a season.

But that was well into the future. Let us return to 1939 and the rest of U.S. religion. Once European war began with the German invasion of Poland on September 1, 1939, the vast majority of U.S. church leaders appeared to favor strict neutrality and refused to see the conflict as a religious war. Henry Emerson Fosdick, Fr. Coughlin, the National Baptist Convention, and officials of the Federal Council of Churches, whatever their other differences, concurred in this. The National Council of Methodist Youth vowed to refuse to participate in "any war in which the U.S. may engage." A "Keep America Out of War Day" in San Francisco was supported by most denominations other than Roman Catholics, including Mormons, Buddhists, Christian Scientists, and Jews.[21]

The year 1939 was still part of the "Red Decade," and sympathy for communism and the Soviet Union remained an issue in the churches. Certain clergymen were well known for their pro-Moscow stance. There was the Episcopalian Bill Spofford, editor of *The Witness* and longtime secretary of the Church League for Industrial Democracy, a group that followed the communist line on labor and other issues. He was also vice-chair of the communist-sympathetic American League for Peace and Democracy, of which the Methodist Henry Frederick Ward was chair. Their overseas colleague, Hewlett Johnson, the "Red Dean" of Caterbury Cathedral in England, was also a favorite source of pro-Soviet journalistic quotes, such as his statement that "Communism has recovered the essential form of the real belief in God, which organized Christianity, as it is now, has so largely lost."[22] The faith of many Communist and Soviet sympathizers had been sorely tested by the Stalinist purges of the late 1930s, the cynical Hitler-Stalin pact of August 1939, and the two conquerors' subsequent division of Poland as well as the Soviet invasion of Finland. A remnant, however, was able to rationalize all such geopolitical maneuvers by the land of their utopian dreams and keep the faith.

Noncommunist dreams were flourishing as well. One was well represented by the global-oriented patriotism of Henry Luce, editor of *Time* and *Life* and probably America's most influential journalist in midcentury. He despised communism, fascism, and U.S. isolationism in equal measure, and more than any other single person, his vision shaped the wartime and cold war future of the nation. Always influenced by his childhood as the son of missionary parents in China, Luce kept a dignified Presbyterian Christianity near the center of his thinking, along with recognition of the importance of Asia as well as Europe to America. As war arrived, all these concerns came more sharply into focus.

According to *Time* magazine on September 25, 1939, "the greatest, most tragic failure of the Christian Church in modern times was that it was unable to halt the slow drift of Christendom toward World War II. The World Council of Churches [then in embryo; its birth was to be long delayed by war, finally occurring at Amsterdam in 1948] was born too late to help; it is not even yet operating officially." One here has a sense of Luce's personal world: informed by religion and the feeling that power wrought by good, whether temporal or spiritual or both, ought to be able to do anything it willed on the field of history. Also significant is the very idea that Christianity could have had such a world-historical role as preventing World War II.[23]

Luce also undoubtedly believed that the United States had a special vocation given by heaven to support the churches in their peacemaking task. His 1941 book *The American Century*, mentioned in the last chapter, was to make him a major apostle of American "exceptionalism" and its redemptive role in the world. That was a concept that, in 1939 as in 1950, could appear remarkably persuasive, for the nation seemed, like the Statue of Liberty's torch, a powerful beacon of liberty and sanity in a world gone mad with war and hatred. On a planet plagued by dictators whose captives only increased in number as the days went by, America was a land uniquely peaceful and free, and potentially still strong enough to reverse the tyrannical trend.

This worldview was severely tested in World War II after December 7, 1941, Pearl Harbor Day, and in the eyes of most Americans it tested successfully. The unity the nation felt in those terrible years was attributed in large part to its churches, temples, and religious heritage. Unfortunately, the end of the greatest war in history did not bring an end to the sense of crisis. An editorial in *The Christian Century* of January 3, 1945, asked, "Can the War Be Saved?" It expressed much concern about continuing Western imperialism as well as Soviet aggression, with its deprivation of freedom to eastern European countries as the Red armies pressed the Germans back toward Berlin. In a similar vein, Norman Thomas, Presbyterian minister and perennial Socialist candidate for president, warned on April 11 that the real victor in the war would be Russia, because of the shortsighted Allied policy of unconditional surrender and postwar plans to restore the British, French, and Dutch empires.[24]

The events of 1945, however, kept the current scene so overwhelming that it was difficult to look far ahead. By April 25 the tributes to Franklin Delano Roosevelt were pouring in: "He had been President of the United States longer than any other man in the life of the republic. A generation of new citizens have never consciously known any other President. His leadership was of the kind that caused them to think of him more nearly as Great White Father than any other president in our history. This long tenure makes it difficult at this moment to believe that the title of his office can really be bestowed upon his successor."[25]

And there were more terrible things to contend with. The German death camps, now opened to a horrified world, revealed "an evil beyond the power of words." A *Christian Century* editorial, however, considered that even so they were not entirely unique—there were also the rape of Nanking, camps in the Soviet Arctic, brutality in the Baltic states and East Poland, lynch mobs at home—making all too visible "the horror of humanity itself when it has surrendered to its capacity for evil."[26]

Then came the atomic bombs of August. The liberal Catholic journal *Commonweal* flat-out compared them to the bombing atrocities of the enemy—Rotterdam, Coventry, Pearl Harbor—calling Hiroshima America's "guilt and shame," a horror that showed how war in the end puts the "good guys" and the victors on the same level as the adversary, in the process teaching a grim and unwelcome moral lesson.[27]

The first response of *The Christian Century* was to move from outrage over Hitler's camps to "America's Atomic Atrocity," asserting that the use of the bomb "has placed our nation in an indefensible moral position," and claiming that the United States should have first given Japan prior warning, or a test demonstration of the new weapon's power.[28] Many letters to the editor, however, protested this position: non-pacifists argued that the bomb ended the war and so could not be called an atrocity; pacifists said that the evil was war itself, not any one weapon. The periodical was forced to retreat to the position that it was only the bomb's "impetuous" use that was objectionable, and the editorial voice now declared that it would accept atomic "military necessity" if it had to be employed to win a just war. Indeed, other religious leaders, including the Methodist Bishop G. Bromley Oxnam and John Foster Dulles, after initially condemning the flattening of Hiroshima and Nagasaki, had, following Japan's surrender, praised the A-bomb's power to end war.[29]

The long-term moral impact of the atomic experience was well expressed by Francis X. Murphy in the *Catholic World*. The priest said that the war, its sudden end, and above all the bomb had chastened the modern secular sense of inevitable progress and showed humans that they must deal with setting moral limits to raw scientific power. All this, he claimed, recalled the Christian concept of life as subject to God.[30]

A similar conclusion was reached by a Protestant report issued by a committee of theologians chaired by Robert L. Calhoun and sponsored by the Federal Council of Churches. It related that the bomb immensely enhanced the dangers inherent in humanity's God-given power of moral decision.[31] Such concerns as these fed directly into the antiscientific, antiprogressivist, and deeply if distractedly spiritual mood of the postwar years.

Yet religion generated its own disturbing tensions as well. A series of articles by Harold Fey, redoubtable writer on the editorial staff of *The Christian Century*, dealt with the question, "Can Catholicism Win America?" The trenchant tone and comments on alleged Catholic efforts to convert service personnel and that church's "invasion" of Protestantism's rural American heartland suggested that the ecumenical spirit had not yet warmed Protestant-Catholic relations in the United States. The stage was set for the bitter antagonism between the Christian faiths in 1950.

It was on deeper levels than denominationalism, however, that the epic 1930s and 1940s shaped American religion as it moved into 1950. Religion in its social role can reflect the surface features of an era. American spirituality did so in its depression and wartime social concerns, in the postwar burgeoning of suburban churches and temples, and in the public piety of the media. But religion can reflect an era's deepest dreams and anxieties as well, for it dwells in the realm of the symbols by which they are expressed. So it was that by 1950 religion was raising up monuments to postwar prosperity as though the future were nothing but glowing, while in its spiritual life it paraded the past, using the latest technology to advance the doctrines of medieval monks and pioneer revivalists.

Those years were thus trapped between horror and hope. As the 1940s advanced, hope increased as the true scope of postwar prosperity and technological advance became apparent, but so did the horror with the bomb, the unfolding of the cold war, and the great fear of communism at home. The postwar years were the time of the baby boom and archetypal suburban homes; they were also the years of the House Un-American Activities Committee's investigations of colleges and Hollywood, the "blacklisting," and the Chambers-Hiss hearings. Overseas were the Berlin airlift in 1948, the Marshall Plan, the Truman Doctrine (advocating "containment" of communism), and finally the ominous Soviet A-Bomb of 1949. In those years the American state had grown immensely in power, from the rather modest federal government of the period before the Great Depression to the postwar colossus that had mobilized a nation, lifted it out of economic stagnation, unleashed atomic energy, and begun a grim struggle against world communism. In the minds of those who feared "statism" and "mass man," it was a distant dynamo that so far had accomplished some good, or at least done some necessary tasks, but it was still like an ominous machine, in imminent danger of running out of control.

Perhaps the Catholic journal *Commonweal* put it best when, on January 6, 1950, it declared that the much-anticipated Man of the Half-Century about to be named by *Time* ought simply to be a "survivor." The real heroes of 1950, that magazine sardonically argued, were simply those who have managed nothing more than to survive all the half-century's wars, liquidations, hungers, and A-bombs. He, *Commonweal*'s Man of the Half-Century, "lasted for 50 years, if he exists, only because the history of his times never caught up with him. He is not a creature of his history, but is thumbing his nose at it."[32] Such was not quite an account of Winston Churchill, who became *Time*'s Man of the Half-Century, but it says as much as did the great Prime Minister's career about the dreadful years before 1950. So also was religion a survivor, both backward-looking and future-anticipating, in those gaudy and terrible years leading up to 1950.

Things Old and New: Intellectual Life in 1950

Religious thought in 1950, as well as religious institutions, had to face the challenge of a new postwar world. It was a world of unprecedentedly different lifestyles and technological possibilities than denizens of the 1930s and 1940s had experienced—in some ways the Future of the 1939 World's Fair and of wartime dreams of "after the duration" marvels had become reality. It was also a world contorted by almost unimaginable psychic trauma. As Norman Mailer put it in 1952, the concentration camps and the atom bomb wreaked havoc on the unconscious mind of almost everyone alive in those days, twisting the times into a kind of extreme neurosis. Writers, he claimed, who were productive beforehand scripted little of note after the war, and new penmen like himself emerged in the wake of war—Mailer had burst on the literary scene in 1948 with *The Naked and the Dead*, still one of the best novels of World War II.[1]

The assertion that the prewar and postwar literary casts were totally different was not entirely true, at least of theological figures like Reinhold Niebuhr or Martin Buber, who labored right through it all. But certainly something profound had happened. Many philosophers were left virtually numb after the great conflict, as after a deep grief, while others were stimulated to frenetic intellectual action to try to encompass it all within the circles of the mind, hard as that was.

R to L: Reinhold Niebuhr, Professor of Applied Christianity, Union Theological Seminary, New York City; Senator Herbert Lehman (D-NY) and Senator Hubert Humphrey (D-MN).

These trends created a situation of both crisis and hope for religious thought. As for hope, by the late 1940s and 1950 there was, at least within religious institutions themselves, an almost triumphant mood, a great sense that religion had been vindicated, that it was indeed the only hope for the world. It was science and progress that were on the defensive. It seemed modern alternatives to faith had all been tried and found wanting in the fires of Auschwitz and Hiroshima. Not a few secular intellectuals, whether with deference or distaste, sensed the same on their zeitgeist antennae. Yet crisis was also in the air; it was as though religion had returned, providentially, just in time to prepare the world for Armageddon. Not all religionists rejoiced in this role; some were sensitive enough to take no pleasure in general tribulation and the disconfirmation of others' dreams. And what they had to offer in this weary year was not vanguard faith but rather a look backward to premodern tradition, since it was modernity itself that had failed the world.

The general intellectual life of 1950 involved religion possibly more than any other twentieth-century year before or since. Books and articles of explicitly religious character by such spiritually oriented writers of gravitas and good intellectual pedigree as Reinhold Niebuhr, Aldous Huxley, T. S. Eliot, or Thomas Merton had exceptional standing in the 1950 world of ideas. Whether in agreement or disagreement, other savants had to acknowledge that the new cultured aficionados of religion, like the noisy existentialists of postwar Europe, were voicing something of profound importance to the soul of the year.

It was a time when "intellectual" designated a rather clearly understood status in national life. According to the common stereotype, intellectuals were adored by their own clique, which centered around New York and the great Ivyish universities, but were despised and ridiculed by the vast sea of "lowbrow" Americans everywhere else. Nonetheless this intelligentsia bravely took onto itself the task of maintaining "values" and "standards" in a philistine world. Becoming an intellectual was almost like joining a monastic order: one lived it, wrote in innumerable "little magazines," argued endlessly in the manner expected of intellectuals, and no doubt covertly congratulated oneself on one's role in the great conversation. And now religion was penetrating citadels of modern thought that "intellectuals" had long since considered impermeable to such remnants of the past.

That flagship of American intellectual life, the *Partisan Review*, early in 1950 presented a long series of brief articles under the general heading "Religion and the Intellectuals: A Symposium," in an attempt to come to terms with the unexpected phenomenon.[2] Writers included such literary, philosophical, and theological stalwarts as Allen Tate, Paul Tillich, A. J. Ayer, Sidney Hook, Philip Rahv, James Agee, W. H. Auden, Hannah Arendt, John Dewey, Robert Graves, Marianne Moore, and I. A. Richards. In its introductory "Editorial Statement," the *Partisan Review* declared, "One of the most significant tendencies of our time, especially in this decade, has been the new turn toward religion among intellectuals and the growing disfavor with which secular attitudes and perspectives are now regarded in not a few circles that lay claim to the leadership of culture."[3]

Interestingly, in their responses to this conundrum the select writers did not generally attempt any careful definition of religion, nor did they seem to doubt that the "new interest" was real (though some doubted that the interest was in "real religion," however exactly that was defined). For that matter, they did not question the expression "return to religion," as to some *status quo ante*, as a description of what was happening. The exegeses were instead of the times, and regardless of whether the intellectuals were personally for or against religion, they attributed the "return" to a widespread sense of world failure, to the inadequacy of science as a source of answers to a world of anxiety, to the fact that most people did not feel free even in freedom's heartland, to the still-fresh legacies of Auschwitz and Hiroshima, and to the cold war.

The world of science and progress had spun out of control,

we were told. The experience of recent years had given all humanity a vague but oppressive sense of sin and guilt, leaving the feel of an age near its end and ready to self-destruct. As that one-time prince of the apostles of modernity, the now-aging H. G. Wells, put it in the title of his 1946 book, it was judgment day for *Mind at the End of Its Tether.*

All this modern malaise called for a powerful counterweight. Philip Rahv in his *Partisan Review* contribution expressed it from an intellectual's point of view as well as any: "The back-to-religion movement among intellectuals is scarcely to be understood without reference to the permutation of the *Zeitgeist*—and the *Zeitgeist* makes fools of us all. In the 1930s the key-term was 'revolution' while now it is 'tradition.' And it is tradition which provides the leading motive, not belief in God."[4]

Rahr was thinking of the neotraditionalist likes of the Anglo-Catholic convert T. S. Eliot, whose acquaintance we made earlier, or the literary critic and Roman Catholic convert Allen Tate. Both had now come into their own. Not a few unimpressed fellow intellectuals attributed those religious transformations to the "extreme crisis" of radical secularism, but they had few other solutions to the "crisis" to offer. The *Saturday Evening Post* concurred, in a editorial later in the year, that "If People Ever Required Religious Faith, It's Now," pointing out that according to statistics, people should be happier now than ever—but they're not.[5] However, the writers at that solidly middlebrow periodical, contrary to their highbrow colleagues at *Partisan Review*, insisted that intellectuals were still drifting away from religion, and that the present revival of faith was largely a lay movement. It no doubt depended on whom you were looking at and what you were looking for.

In any case, many of those accounted intellectuals, and some others from the *Saturday Evening Post*'s Norman Rockwell country, despite the "Class of '50" optimism, regarded the nation and the world in 1950 to be in extreme crisis. Not seldom this view was joined with a general sense that Western civilization was in serious decline, failing at once in morals, vision, spiritual cohesion, and creative energy. Oswald Spengler's post-World War I classic, *The Decline of the West*,[6] despite its intellectual links to the murky world of Germanic antimodernism and "volkish" thought out of which Nazism had emerged, enjoyed a new vogue just after World War II, as though such great wars inevitably and understandably induced a sense that all good things were ending. People of intellectual pretensions liked to talk about pervasive decadence and the inevitability of some catastrophe that would shatter the West, if not the world. They enlivened their cocktail parties with Spenglerian praise of the timeless values of peasant cultures, and there was talk also of Arnold Toynbee's charts of the rise and fall of civilizations. That sense of the end was only exacerbated by the advent of the terrible new atomic weapons and the arising of the cold war out of the ashes of 1945.

Of course, religion (and the West, and the world) persisted and flourished after 1950. In the 1960s, Vatican II and its aftermath changed religion in ways that went far past what religious thinkers in 1950 would have considered "tradition." The terminal crises of secularism and the scientific point of view, not to mention the end of civilization as the Western world had known it, never quite played themselves out in the way 1950's pundits widely envisioned they might. As the world of the 1950s did in fact get better, due partly to new technologies and partly to a slightly calmer view of cold war realities in the Eisenhower era, the decline of the west gradually faded from consciousness, and a more optimistic take on the future, to be consummated in the Kennedy era, began. The technology-based but spiritually significant spaceflights of the 1960s culminating at Tranquillity Base on the moon in 1969, so remote from the intellectually fearful spirit of 1950, epitomized the new hope.

It would be easy to assert that the crisis mentality of intellectual life in 1950 was largely of the intellectuals' own making, constructed out of free-floating anxieties left over from the two tumultuous preceding decades, combined with a clearly uncertain and insecure future. In fact, we would like to be able to tell those midcentury doomsayers things were not as bad as they looked to them then: American and Western civilization carried on and in fact in some ways got better; World War III didn't happen; and "the bomb" wasn't used again, at least in the twentieth century. But of course rational as well as irrational grounds for extreme anxiety were quite apparent in 1950, and intellectual or spiritual crises are doubtless real if they really exist in the realm of mind and spirit. Furthermore, consider what the half-spent century had meant up to the intellectually fatiguing year of 1950.

The twentieth century had so far been the century of total war, sacrificing more dead to the gods of battle—and to whatever valkyries snatch civilian casualties and the victims of ruthless genocide—than any other in history. The survivors of the First World War hardly knew why it happened; the survivors of the Second World War, and those enduring the cold war, knew all too well. For those two conflicts merely manifested in tortured flesh a planet of highly divergent ideologies and their respective visions of the human future—ideas and visions that sufficient numbers felt were worth their own lives and the sacrificial lives of millions of others. It was also a time when the most efficient military technology in history was available to expedite the giving and taking of those lives.

Three fundamental beliefs ruled the world of 1939 and the 1940s, beliefs that more than any others seemed discredited to much of intellectual 1950 in the wake of all that blood. First, there was a belief in *ideology*. Human society was riven by firm doctrinal commitments that, for believers, gave not only meaning to one's own life and actions, but also, through an idealization of social progress as the end of human existence, offered sure hope for a utopian future, through democracy, Marxism, fascism, Catholicism, socialism, capitalism, or a thousand subsects of each. While each believer was likely to see his or her own faith not as ideology but as patent, usually "scientific," truth, a general affirmation of the power of ideology to shape history for good or ill presented itself. Each ideology tended to divide the world's peoples into circles that were "in" or "out" of the wave of progress, whether the lines were between favored and ill-favored nations or between the social classes. When ideologies were riding high, so were intellectuals, for the construction and maintenance of ever-improved intellectual products was their métier; and when the awful cost of the ideological division of humanity became apparent, they could hardly help but view themselves and their role as in crisis. For when the world is split into good and bad along race or class or belief lines, one could, as Eric Voegelin once remarked, rejoice at the entry of half the human race into the earthly paradise even at the cost of liquidating the other half—or one could stand back, finally appalled.

The boons of material well-being were accelerated by a second reality that also entailed belief: *technology.* Only since yesterday, it seemed in midcentury, had the advent of the automobile, radio, refrigerator, and other consumer technologies changed the nineteenth-century world to the "modern" version at a dizzying rate. It was imperative to believe that this was for the good—that because of technology human life was much better now than then, and even its application in war would, or should, work on behalf of the forces of righteousness. Even those who seemed to be intellectually antimodern, like romantic nationalists and existentialist philosophers, had their own uses for the equipages of technology.

Rapid and radical changes in the technological world only enhanced a third basic area of belief that, like the others, had been around at least since the Enlightenment but in the whirlwind 1920s and 1930s appeared to be gathering dramatic speed. This was belief in *progress:* that the world was, and almost had to be, getting better in every way, politically and spiritually just as much as technologically. The less tangible dimensions of progress—like the growth of democracy, social welfare or socialism, education, and health—were tied to the broader confidence in the value of the technological progress. Half-conscious doubts as to whether human development was keeping to its timetable were responsible in no small part for the blossoming of ideologies dedicated to assuring that the trains of progress would run on time, given the right social engineering and a spirited resistance to all opponents. But then the awkward paradox, put as well by the *Saturday Evening Post* as anyone, came home: if everything is better, why aren't we happier? Intellectuals of 1950 were asking not only whether "progress" was worth the ideological liabilities it seemed to entail, but also whether progress actually gave people an improved sense of well-being. Alarmists, of whom there were not a few, insisted that what was called progress might really be only accelerating the timetable of apocalyptic doom.

It must be emphasized, however, that beliefs in ideology, technology, and progress were really held in common by virtually all parties with any real power over midcentury events. It was only on the question of what master they should serve, and what ideology would best and most correctly bring humankind to the promised land, that divisions occurred: democracy versus fascism, capitalism versus communism. But those doctrinal games were deadly serious because both sides held high cards in the three areas that counted for strength of mind and might. All the great warring powers of those days were strong in their own ideology, in technological prowess, and in their particular vision of progress. Even the major world movement of the late, postwar 1940s—for independence by colonialized peoples left over from the eighteenth and nineteenth centuries' great empires—was driven by the assumption that only through independence could they harvest the full rewards of technology and progress, and only through the power of the right ideologies of nationalism, and in some cases socialism or Marxism, could those desiderata be attained.

In all this, midtwentieth-century religion was in an ambiguous position, as befitted something coming out of a far more distant past than virtually any other force at play. Yet religionists also saw themselves as, and wanted to be, major players in the emerging brave new world. Sometimes they could indeed take a freestanding position within the ideological spectrum, as when certain of them embraced pacifism, an important stance between the wars. Excessive otherworldly concerns, such as those of which Karl Barth was accused, might also put them apart from those who were merely ideological.

At the same time religious persons were of their times, and in one way or another they accepted the three basic principles of those times: ideology, technology, and progress. Their world of belief was part of the ideological spectrum, and more significantly they were likely to believe that it was convergent with, even a major component of, one of the great quasi-secular ideologies. Most Christians and Jews took it for granted that religion was an underpinning of democracy, fascism, capitalism, or Marxism. That would be not without some reason: Western democracy certainly had roots in religious belief in the infinite value of all persons before God; fascism was all too often Christian anti-Semitism in action; and it was often pointed out that Marxism was no more than a secular version of Judeo-Christian eschatology and, the likes of Hewlett Johnson would insist, of Christian ideals of social justice.

Religionists, like nearly everyone else, felt pressed to identify themselves with one or another of the regnant ideologies, partly no doubt with a desire to influence them, but also, recognizing their immense independent authority, to claim a share in their kingdom, power, and glory. A majority of American clerics undoubtedly embraced democracy, as represented by the New Deal spirit, as an ideology as well as a pragmatic way of doing society's common business. Perhaps there was an astringent bit of Niebuhrian criticism added in, and, as Kirby Page's poll in the 1930s indicated, a new depression-bred readiness to question the conventional values of American free enterprise and rugged individualism. But only a small number moved decisively toward the Marxist end of the spectrum; only a few, like Father Coughlin, moved to the anti-Semitic and crypto-fascist pole. (It is said that extremes meet; those two sides, which long saw themselves as enemies to the death, were more than a little disconcerted when the Hitler-Stalin pact of August 1939 forced Brown and Red into a shotgun marriage that lasted until the German invasion of Russia in June 1941.)

Religion also embraced technology; it was generally in no way backward in its enthusiasm for cars, trains, radio (e.g., Father Coughlin), the press, and all the other accoutrements of modernity. It was no less important for religion to be *seen* embracing them, for that would be a sign that it was as up-to-date as anything else. The matter of progress, though, was less determinate. Even though religion might stake a claim in the ideologies and in the new technological world, disturbing uncertainty lingered as to whether religionists were not intruding as ambivalent outsiders who could never really be at home in the new world being born. For at heart the ideologies and scientific technology appeared to be pointing toward a gloriously secular culture like that of the World's Fair, in which religion would be hopelessly outdated unless it was reborn in some dramatically revised form. A few ultraliberals might rejoice in that prospect, but most of the religious world felt caught between hope, fear, and rearguard defensive actions.

By 1950 many people were yearning for some kind of escape from ideology, progress, and technology. They wanted an alternative way of being in the world to those defined and dominated by such strict tutors. Where better to look for it than in the world as it was before the modern masters arose? The neo-Thomistic belief that greater wisdom than what the present knew could be found in the past was not limited to the Catholic academy. That past was still to be found in peasant communities around the world, and awareness of them was part of the "decline of the west" mentality. Oswald Spengler had predicated that as great, top-heavy civilizations rise and fall, the peasantry will survive and will bear into the future the fundamental values of human life. This idea was meaningful in 1950; people visited and were enamored of peasant life in, say, Latin America. They did not, as might later liberation theologians, ask *why* the peasants of Latin America were poor; it was enough to idealize their "rooted" though impoverished way of life, and above all their spirituality.

For 1950 was not so far from the premodern past that peasant life could not be remembered with nostalgia and even hope of recovery. That past was much closer in 1950 than it would seem in 2000, almost as though the preceding fifty years were five hundred. In 1950 peasant cultures still in spiritual continuity with the premodern past spread across much of Asia, Latin America, and even Mediterranean Europe. In the two latter cases, they were shaped by an immemorial folk Catholicism soon to be profoundly shaken not only by the Catholic traumas of Vatican II, but also—as in Asia too—by the massive urbanization, industrialization, and Protestant incursions in the last half of the century. All this was not clearly foreseen in 1950, despite some anxiety over the changes to traditional societies that were beginning to occur as a result of war, colonial independence movements, and, it was said, Marxist agitation.

In both Roman Catholicism and Anglo-Catholicism, the latter then at the height of its intellectual influence in 1950, a distinctively antimodern, neomedieval romanticism carried considerable spiritual vogue. It was of course closely connected to the Spenglerian anti-ideology, return-to-religion mood already marked. Neomedievalism was also related to the pre-Raphaelite spirit of the last century but—especially in America—even more to the spirit of the famous chapter in *The Education of Henry Adams* entitled "The Virgin and the Dynamo." Here that descendent of U.S. presidents contrasted what he saw as the vital, collective, organic culture that produced the Gothic cathedrals with the depersonalized industrial world he inhabited. The great gulf could be expressed by setting the spirit of the Virgin Mary against the dynamo, that symbol of the dehumanizing greed and technology of modernity.

But, Henry Adams went on to claim, the Middle Ages had no direct influence in America, itself a child of the Enlightenment. Medievalism's utility on this side of the Atlantic, he therefore implied, lay in the escape it provided from the increasingly harsh realities of the modern world. An inner spiritual, medieval realm was, for Americans, a place in which to locate the antimodern self we must all have for our own sanity as we live outwardly in the world of the dynamo.[7] Never was this charge taken more to heart than in 1950, a year that definitely wanted some inner alternative to its own forced modernism; the yearnings of the uneasy were explicitly medieval in much of Roman Catholicism and Episcopalianism that year. Others sought solace in the comparable pasts of the Reformation, the sawdust trail, or the Hasidic village.

What religion in 1950 wanted, therefore, was that which had the patina of age about it, which appeared to be grappling with issues on the level of soul and not simply of ideas, and which brought with it a time-tested spiritual practice that was difficult enough to seem serious and yet accessible to anyone who was prepared to be serious about it. But such religion could appear in many guises. One sign of its appeal was the remarkable success of Thomas Merton's *The Seven Storey Mountain*, which appeared in 1948 and astounded its publisher by selling some six hundred thousand copies that first year. This remarkable autobiography seemed to articulate the spiritual yearnings of a generation. It first portrayed the young Merton at Columbia University in the 1930s, when it almost seemed that everyone was a high-decibel ideologue of some sort—fascist, communist, Trotskyite, Protestant of various kinds, Catholic, Vedantist—all trying to shout down the others. Merton eventually chose the Catholic option, but for him it was far more than just the winning argument. In early December of 1941, just after Pearl Harbor, he entered Gethsemani Abbey in Kentucky, a house of the Cistercians of the

Strict Observance, or Trappists. Here he would follow a path of asceticism and silence, one as far removed as one could well imagine from the babble and brutality of a world at war, and for that very reason one that would exert a compelling fascination when that war was over and Merton's account of another way to live came out. By 1950 Trappist monasteries were bursting with would-be novices, young men wishing to join the white-robed ranks of those who, all through the tumult of modernity's many "revolutions," its battles over sex and fashion and political doctrine, had quietly kept their night watches and prayed for the world in their remote cloisters.

Merton's was not the only venue for 1950s' old religion made new. One could also mention *Behold the Spirit* (1947) and *The Supreme Identity* (1950) by Alan Watts, then an Episcopal priest, who in 1950 was to leave that calling to become the well-known 1950s and 1960s freelance mystic, writer on Zen, and, in his own term, "philosophical entertainer." But *Behold the Spirit* is an uneven yet unforgettable midcentury celebration of a deeply joyous, incarnational, and sacramental Christianity finely enriched by reference both to its own ancient mystics and congenial archaic souls in Taoism and Zen. With a characteristic light touch, Watts made his lively old masters more ready to laugh at the foibles of Western modernity than denounce them, but they too, like all the others, told us that what the modern world most desperately needed was a little quiet time with the wisdom of the spiritual past.

It was not only monks and solemn philosophers who shared spiritual 1950s' infatuation with the past and the decline of the West. Spengler also greatly influenced the "Beats," who were gathering in 1950 but would not burst visibly onto the scene until the 1957 publication of Jack Kerouac's *On the Road*. Kerouac and his set made much of Spengler and peasant life in their rejection of the alleged mindless materialism of the new postwar middle class. In 1950 Kerouac was already completing the adventure that went into *On the Road* and writing the book. In his journal for February 28, 1950, he said,

Time for action, time for a new life, my real life. I'll be twenty-eight in two weeks. Two meals a day instead of three. Much travelling. No stagnation. No more sorrows! No more metaphysical awe! Action . . . speed . . . grace . . . Go! Writing from true thoughts instead of stale rehashes. I'm going to express more and record less in "On the Road."

. . . .You have to believe in life before you can accomplish anything. That is why dour, regular-houred, rational-souled State Department diplomats have done nothing for mankind. Why live if not for excellence?[8]

It was inevitable that this mentality would give rise to a new intellectual conservatism, and so it did. Take the youthful William F. Buckley Jr.'s 1951 book, *God and Man at Yale*. Buckley had graduated from Yale University in 1950 and immediately set about writing a ferocious indictment of his alma mater, claiming that leading professors ridiculed religion and promoted "collectivist" and "statist" views verging on Marxism in such fields as economics and political science. Buckley, heir to a Texas oil fortune and (though he never mentioned it in this book) a Roman Catholic, met with a remarkable response; his jeremiad was talked about everywhere, even by the many who violently disagreed with him and with his values. Immature as this screed may have been, it popularized a new current, the postwar intellectual conservatism that was to find its voice in the *National Review* (founded by Buckley in 1955); it attracted its share of young rebels against what was perceived to be the "liberal establishment" in academia and government; and it found fulfillment in the Goldwater campaign of 1964 and the Reagan Administration of 1981–89. Other early classics were Peter Viereck's *Conservatism Revisited* (1949), B.I. Bell's *Crowd Culture* (1952), Eric Voegelin's *The New Science of Politics* (1952), Russell Kirk's *The Conservative Mind* (1953), and Whittaker Chambers's *Witness* (1952), which Buckley regarded as the most important founding text of all. But it all really began around 1950, when young Buckley was writing *God and Man*, and it ultimately reflects the polarized, apocalyptic worldview of the year of its publication. The book's most quoted and discussed lines were from the foreword: "I myself believe that the duel between Christianity and atheism is the most important in the world. I further believe that the struggle between individualism and collectivism is the same struggle reproduced on another level."[9] The widespread 1950 idea that the cold war was in its cold heart a religious war could hardly have been better put.

What else were religious people reading and thinking in 1950? Certainly not all were medievalist romantics, and not all really believed that Western civilization was at the end of its tether. But most were probably yearning for some kind of escape from whatever it was that had made the recent past so dismal. We shall now look at two important theologians and a religious philosophy: the Protestants Karl Barth and Reinhold Niebuhr, and the then-dominant Roman Catholic philosophy of Thomism. We shall consider three basic themes closely related to them that shaped the intellectual life of 1950 spirituality, besides the recovery of the spiritual past and the rise of antimodern conservatism: the individual versus mass society, existentialism, and religion and psychoanalysis.

Mainstream Protestantism was by no means prepared to give up the connection with modernity's institutions and intellectual life that was virtually its defining quality. Even there, however, challenge and change were afoot. The old theological liberalism, overall aligned with "natural theology" and a positive view of scientific progress, and seeking to bring religion into conformity with the best current science and philosophy, was very much on the defensive against the neoorthodoxy of theologians like Karl Barth, Paul Tillich, and Reinhold Niebuhr. Though by no means rejecting science and modernity in the manner of the fundamentalists, they emphasized the sinful imperfection of all human ideas and institutions; for them, religious belief was not a product of reason but of a "leap of faith" like the "existential choice" proposed by the then-fashionable existentialist philosophers.

Though updated in important respects, their outlook was presented as recovering the spiritual essence of the Protestant reformers; here was another past reappearing in the midst of the midcentury present.

Karl Barth, the great adversary of nineteenth-century liberal theology, was decidedly on the rise as a theological influence in Protestant America in 1950, especially among seminarians and younger clergymen. Rejecting rationalism and "natural" theology, which thought that God could be known through reason or the evidences of nature, as well as mysticism and its conviction that God can be known directly by human experience, Barth insisted that the Supreme Being is "wholly other" than humanity. Because of human sin God cannot be encountered by human means, but only through faith, which is a "dialectical" response to God's word in the Bible. Barth's credentials had been enhanced through his relation to the anti-Nazi "Confessing Church" in Germany, that struggle having lifted up the importance of faith based on transcendent reality and the biblical revelation "event" rather than on nation, culture, or human philosophy. In postwar America Barthian "crisis theology" and neoorthodoxy fit an intellectual spirit shaped by existentialism, with its stress on making free choices in an irrational universe. Barthianism suited the day's anxiety and crisis-borne sense that human sin, rather than human goodness or rationality, was the dominant reality in this beclouded world. A few years later, in an article on Union Theological Seminary, *Time* reported that among seminarians at that school, then at the height of its prestige as the intellectual bastion of mainstream Protestantism, the most radical men were the most orthodox—or neoorthodox—and for them, "sin is back in fashion."[10]

At the same time, Barth was no less problematic in cold war America because of his staunch refusal to equate the present struggle against communism with the anti-Nazi battle in which he had played such a compelling role. In "We Are Not Against the East," published in 1949, he had argued that the socialism of the East was not the same as fascism and not the same morally as Franco's Spain or "Imperialist Holland's war in Indonesia," the latter then fighting for its independence from that colonial power. In impassioned tones the Basel theologian declared that it would be hypocritical for Christians in the West to criticize the Communist world, and claimed that one could not mention in the same breath Marxism and the ideas of the Third Reich, or Joseph Stalin and such charlatans as Hitler, Goering, and Himmler.[11] (In regard to Stalin, it may be noted that on his birthday of that same year Bulgaria renamed a city, a mountain, and a school in honor of the dictator; Czechoslovakia erected a thirty-foot statue of him; and everywhere in the world under his sway he was praised in terms little less than divine.[12])

Barth went on to argue that the church does not need to denounce communism because Christians are not tempted to it because of its atheism, and Christianity's past social shortcomings do not give it the moral right to do so. With Hitler it was different, since the pro-Nazi "German Christian" movement represented a serious perversion of Christianity, not merely something non-Christian to which Christians can be indifferent or with which they can make whatever accommodations they must, if they live in Communist lands.[13]

This was the sort of talk that infuriated the likes of Reinhold Niebuhr, as it did most Americans of the time. He later said that Barth's position "prompts revulsion against every pretension to derive detailed political judgments from ultimate theological positions. When a man lacks ordinary common sense in reacting against evil, no amount of theological sophistication will help him."[14] Niebuhr also had been known to say that because communism could appear less heinous that Nazism, with its gloss of idealism, without the crude racism of the Hitlerites, it was actually more dangerous because it made totalitarianism more seductive to well-meaning reformers.[15]

The prestige of Union Theological Seminary owed much to that of Reinhold Niebuhr, who brought the perceptions of neoorthodoxy to ground in trenchant and highly influential writings on social issues in the United States. Niebuhr's eminence in 1950 had been boosted by the cover story *Time* had given him in its twenty-fifth anniversary issue in 1948, which was moreover the first feature-length story that newsmagazine had ever devoted to a theologian.[16] (This article was largely written by Whittaker Chambers, the former communist of deep intellectual and theological interests, now senior *Time* writer, who figured prominently in the famous Alger Hiss hearings.) Entitled "Faith for a Lenten Age," the piece brought out the background of neoorthodoxy's pessimistic, existential-faith-oriented view of human nature (as Chambers understood it) in Dostoevsky, Kierkegaard, and Barth, before coming to Niebuhr—although *Time* seemed a bit perplexed by Niebuhr's persistence in working diligently on behalf of non-Marxist "leftist" causes amidst all that debilitating pessimism and anxiety. The portrait did, however, manage to isolate in Niebuhr's thought two great themes, which are also major themes of religious thought in 1950: that humanity is in a permanent state of crisis, whether we know it or not; and that the anxiety engendered by this crisis is the cause of sin.

Actually Niebuhr's work for reform through democratic means was a radical and integral part of his theology. He held that humanity had a desire for transcendent goals and goodness, but a capacity on the social level for little more than justice; and together with this a sense that all human institutions are flawed by sin and therefore can never be absolutized but must be corrected continually through checks and balances. He said, "Man's capacity for justice makes democracy possible, but man's inclination to injustice makes democracy necessary." More of a theological social thinker than a theologian in the abstract sense, Reinhold Niebuhr triply enriched the religious life of 1950: he gave voice to the profound sense of crisis of the day; like the Luce publications whose favorite theologian he was, he supported the cold war belief that for all its faults America was worth preserving, was better than Marxist and other totalitarian alternatives, and had a world role; and finally, by his example he gave encouragement to those who believed that working for reform in America was still possible and was incumbent on responsible citizens.

Turning to Roman Catholic intellectual life, we must first observe the immense presence that institution was in the spiritual world of 1950, when it was dominated intellectually by neo-Thomism and institutionally by that conservative and fervently anticommunist autocrat, Francis Cardinal Spellman, Archbishop of New York. By far the largest, best organized, and most monolithic religious institution in the nation and the world, it also presented itself as the most authentic custodian and transmitter of those premodern values for which the age so much yearned. In 1950 that church appeared as an unchanging, self-assured bearer of definite and precise answers to all basic human dilemmas. There was, however, a leaven of yeasty intellectual life in 1950 Catholicism: in the school known as the Catholic Revival, in emergent trends in Jesuit thought, and in the sometimes freewheeling enthusiasm of intellectual converts, all to be discussed later in this book.

On a popular level, Catholic thought was well represented in its most appealing media spokesman, Msgr. Fulton J. Sheen, who had a popular radio program in 1950 and was to become a celebrated television personality in 1952. He had published *Peace of Soul* in 1949.[17] Sheen therein outlined all the voguish modern concerns to which popular psychoanalysis responded—anxiety, frustration, repression, remorse, and sex in all its complications—and then showed how Catholic Christianity with its "age-old wisdom" dealt with them better than anyone else through authoritative moral teaching, confession and forgiveness, and the "psychology of conversion." Sheen was well known for the collection of celebrity converts he had garnered, most of them drawn by the promise of a sure harbor amidst the tossing waves of the modern world.

The same motif of answers from an age of faith to an age of anxiety was presented on a more academic level by the neo-Thomistic philosophy regnant in Catholic universities. (Fulton Sheen had himself been a philosophy professor before becoming a media celebrity.) This school was simply a modern rearticulation of the scholasticism supremely expressed in St. Thomas Aquinas's thirteenth-century *Summa Theologica*. The hallmarks of this school were its ability to combine faith and reason as means of knowledge, as in Thomas's famous arguments for the existence of God; his belief in the possibility of absolute and objective knowledge; and his consideration therefore that the true nature or "essence" of things—God, humans, the universe—can be known through their phenomenal appearance.

The most important twentieth-century neo-Thomist philosophers, both active and well known in 1950, were the two Frenchmen Jacques Maritain and Etienne Gilson. Maritain taught that the contemporary world had fallen into a deep malaise owing to its excessive skepticism about the possibility of finding truth in any of the main areas of human concern, from theology to art, morality, and political life. That was because modernity had in effect given the truth-finding task over completely to science, which is not equipped to find more than one narrow range of truth. Only by recovering the medieval confidence in pure reason, in mystical experience as knowledge, and in the mediation of God through the universe could the world recover wholeness on a deep level. Gilson also wished to recover the sense, which he found in Augustine and Aquinas, that the universe is an unfolding of the mind of God within time that has no meaning apart from this transcendent point of reference.

In 1950 the philosophical vogue for existentialism was at the height of its popularity in Europe and much debated in America as well. Clearly it was another way of turning inward, into individual subjectivity, where one might find some alternative to ideology, progress, and technology, all as surely soul-destroying according to the existentialist as the (traditionalist) religious canon. As befits such a highly individualistic movement, even a definition of existentialism is elusive. A major theme was the idea that one finds the world absurd and apparently meaningless; in this situation the only virtue one has is the absolute freedom to make choices, above all the freedom to decide who one is to be, which must be expressed in acts and way of life as well as by ideas. One simply finds oneself existing, hence the name; from there one can freely decide what one is to become. As the eminent philosopher of the movement J.-P. Sartre said, existence precedes essence. Like the later beatniks and hippies, existentialists quickly became associated with dress, beards, and rebellious lifestyles as much as with ideas, to the delight of the young and the scandal of their elders. But though short-lived in its counter-cultural phase, existentialism more broadly understood had a lasting impact on letters and theology in the 1950s.

Existentialism was divided into two wings: the atheistic, for which the universe was so absurd as to lack even a God, and the Christian. The latter, following the thought of Søren Kierkegaard, the Danish theologian and "father of existen-tialism," was in uneasy alliance with the "crisis theology" of Karl Barth and his followers. For they too predicated that because of human sin the universe as one experienced it was absurd, and the only response one could make was not by means of reason or natural theology but by "existential choice"—the "leap of faith" made in response to the word of God. Even Catholic philosophers like James Collins, in *The Existentialists*, took the movement seriously, though arguing that Thomism represented the fullest expression of what the existentialists were seeking.

The individual against the collective was a major theme of 1950s' thought, both academic and popular, and was broader than existentialist protest alone. Indeed, the matter some-times seemed almost obsessive; the more the 1950s imposed conformity on some levels—standard brands, standard TV shows, the "blacklisting" of alleged subversives in Hollywood, universities, and government—the more it decried "mass man" and "mass society" and exalted individualism in princi-ple. It was commonly assumed that Americans were once more individualistic than now. This was the burden of an influential 1950 book, *The Lonely Crowd* by David Riesman.[18] This work proposed a postwar change in American character from "inner-directed" to "other-directed"; the latter derive their way of life from the example and values of others rather than from within, but other-direction can never assuage the inner loneliness a member of such a mutually emulating crowd will feel.

William Whyte, in another 1950s' sociological classic, *The Organization Man*, put it memorably in a sentence that expresses much about early 1950s' folk and their values: "They sense that by their immersion in the group they are frustrating other urges, yet they feel that responding to the group is a moral duty—and so they continue, hesitant and unsure, imprisoned in brotherhood."[19] The same theme was pursued on more theoretical levels by such thinkers as the increasingly popular Carl Jung, who frequently dilated on the evils of "mass man." Others used the contrast as a staple of anticommunist rhetoric.

As suited its basically inward look, intellectual life in 1950 was also much preoccupied with psychology. It is not surprising that, as it reacted against ideology, progress, and technology—all fabrications of the outer social or mechanical world—1950s' intellectual life turned to the even more complex and fascinating workings of the mind. Freudianism was in its heyday, and since it was well known that the atheistic Viennese doctor regarded religion as no more than an "illusion," that naturally created problems for an increasingly religious year. Books like R. S. Lee's *Freud and Christianity* and Benjamin Gilbert Sanders's *Christianity after Freud* were much read and discussed.[20] Their basic theme was that psychoanalysis offered an accurate picture of the world of fallen humanity, with its neuroses and anxieties, and also made clear enough that, as the neoorthodox and Catholics like Fulton Sheen declared, there is no way out by ordinary human means. With Freud they also acknowledged that much ordinary religion is infantile, of no real help, and just sin in another guise. But here the religious physician of the soul went on to call down true divine grace, which can help as much as the talking cure though it may entail deep confession.

At the same time, in the popular mind the dominant Freudianism was being increasingly challenged by the analytic psychology of Jung. Jung's timeless "archetypes" drawn from myth, dreams, and religion—the great mother, the wise old man, the maiden and the hero, and the shadow—interpreted on the deepest possible level what was going on in modern history and modern lives, and at the same time gave greater credence to both tradition and religion than the atheistic Freud. In 1949, the young mythologist Joseph Campbell had published his influential book *The Hero with a Thousand Faces*, which offered much the same message from the vast warehouses of ageless myth. The present is incomplete, these wise men said, and can hardly be understood or rightly lived without its past, above all its psychic past, that still contains the golden key to the meaning of human existence.

This idea was not new, but it was profoundly at odds with the most advanced message of modernity and progress: that the human story is a tale of human emancipation from the past; that if we can finally and entirely let go of it, we can live a free and unimaginably rich new kind of life bestowed by the new gifts of science and democracy. Despite a few liberal holdouts, 1950s' religion chose to affiliate itself with the recovery of the traditionalist side of this divide, and indeed to hold that humanity's great religious institutions were by far the deepest and most accessible reservoirs of those riches.

Finally, what books were in the hands of "mass society" in 1950? A *Saturday Review* editorial, "The Novel Goes to Church," began with a nod to the *Partisan Review* symposium, declaring that "the explanation of the growth of a new religious ardor in the United States does not require the investigations of philosophers or intellectuals. When the people became convinced that there was no certain hope in politics or science or academic learning it was inevitable that the moment must come for a return to the Church." As part of this revival, it added, "there can be no doubt either that the religious novel and autobiography have returned in a manner that would have startled publishers twenty or so years ago."[21] It went on to mention such popular hits as the already mentioned *Seven Storey Mountain* of Thomas Merton and *The Cardinal* by Henry Morton Robinson, the latter the 1950 top fiction bestseller. This opus was the occasionally clumsy yet unforgettable tale of a priest who finds his way through doubt and temptation to both serenity and a cardinal's red hat; it was widely thought to be modeled on the career of Francis Cardinal Spellman.

What about other best-selling books? The *New York Times* best-seller list for October 1, 1950, presents an interesting contrast of titles in the nonfiction category. Harry Overstreet's *The Mature Mind*, which was number one for nine weeks, presented a typical psychoanalysis-oriented approach to what was then called "mental hygiene," at a time where there was considerable evidence of immature minds abroad in the nation and the world. It shared the list with *Dianetics* by the science fiction writer L. Ron Hubbard, who was soon to use it as the fundamental text of his controversial Church of Scientology. Dianetics, the science of becoming "clear" by removing "engrams," psychological blocks created by traumas in this or previous lives, through confession-like self-expression, was a brief vogue in psychology-conscious 1950 despite being castigated by most orthodox psychologists.

Alongside *Dianetics* on the list was *Worlds in Collision* by Immanuel Velikovsky, another controversial work that was immensely popular, though labeled pseudoscience by academics. It claimed that such ancient biblical miracles as the parting of the Red Sea and the fall of manna could be explained as the result of catastrophic astronomical events—planets moving into new orbits and the like. This bizarre work responded to what seemed a widely felt need in 1950—justifying traditional religious beliefs through superficially scientific means. University science departments and associations threatened to boycott textbooks by Doubleday, the publisher of the unlikely best-seller, in moves that smacked of academic censorship at the same time the House Un-American Activities Committee and McCarthy were harassing academic freedom on anticommunist grounds. The backlash threatened to do more lasting harm to free inquiry than Velikovsky's quickly forgotten crank theories.[22]

There was more. Also on the best-seller list was *Behind the Flying Saucers* by Frank Scully, an early sensational account of crashed saucers in the Southwest. It was later revealed that the book did no more than immortalize a hoax played on the respected though gullible reporter Scully. Nonetheless this bizarre bit of pseudoscience suggests what was to be an interesting—and in some ways significant—1950s' theme: a virtual religion of UFOs (in Carl Jung's phrase, "technological angels") as saviors in the traditional mold of transcendent figures descending from above, but now, in the gestating space age, riding flying saucers rather than clouds of glory.

Finally, one finds books on the list that seemed to want simply to recall in tranquility and almost nostalgia the horrific days of the two previous decades. *Anybody Can Do Anything* by Betty MacDonald describes with humorous sparkle job-hunting in the depression 1930s. *The Story of Ernie Pyle*, whose dispatches virtually created the GIs of World War II for many stateside readers, was told by his close friend, Lee Graham Miller.

All together these books give an interesting picture of the popular mind in 1950: nostalgic, eager to relive the tumultuous past viewed through a safe and romanticizing lens, seeking sensational new theories of the world to counter a drab and anxious time, wanting generally to be somewhere else than in the present time and wanting peace of mind and soul. That last urge was certainly suggested by the continuing popularity in 1950 of several 1949 books of more explicitly spiritual character: Thomas Merton's *The Waters on Siloe*, on the history and life of the Cistercian order; Fulton Oursler's *The Greatest Story Ever Told*, a fictionalized and some thought sentimentalized life of Jesus; Norman Vincent Peale's *A Guide to Confident Living*, which was not quite the best-seller his 1952 *The Power of Positive Thinking* would be, but which already established him as the master of the upbeat affirmative living that so many in 1950 seemed to want and to have so much difficulty finding; and Fulton Sheen's *Peace of Soul*, already mentioned, which offered what were presented as eternal Catholic verities as the answer to what was widely known as the Age of Anxiety.

At least since Augustine, autobiography and the autobiographical novel have been favorite forms of religious literature, perhaps because they can engage life in all its intricacy far more directly than more abstract treatises. A much-noted 1950 work was *I Leap Over the Wall*, by Monica Baldwin, a niece of British prime minister Stanley Baldwin who left a convent with the blessing of the church and returned to lay life in wartime London. In the same vein were *The God that Failed*, edited by Richard Crossman, a widely read and at least covertly religious set of narratives by ex-communists, including Arthur Koestler, whose experiences were later presented in thinly fictionalized form in his *Darkness at Noon*; and *Dream and Reality*, the Russian Christian existentialist Nicholas Berdyaev's 1950 spiritual autobiography.

To sum up the intellectual flavor of 1950: it was a year in which the life of the mind felt oddly trapped, unable to move forward though able to explore in profound, psychological subtlety the coils of its own constrictions. It was, however, able to move backward with elegance and sideways into fantasy-like alternatives to the present horrendous times with charm and naivete. But on the great issues the mind of the year was overburdened by the past, by its fear of systems and of innovations because of the "once-burned" syndrome, having suffered through far too much ideology and "progress." It allowed itself instead to be hampered by the self-foreclosing nature of both existentialist and psychoanalytic thought, with their disdain of reason and of anything but subjective knowledge, or by too-perfect systems from the past like Thomism or Spenglerism. It was a time that could be brilliantly critical, in the manner of Maritain or Niebuhr, but that was not ready for new constructions.

4

Lies, Spies, and the Junior Senator from Wisconsin

It was a time when things were often not quite what they seemed. Events had double meanings, and people lived double lives. In 1950 a series of three articles in the *Saturday Evening Post* by Matt Cvetic (as told to Peter Martin) related how "I Posed as a Communist for the FBI." With a slightly simplified title those revelations then became the classic cold war movie, "I Was a Communist for the FBI."[1] Communists in turn, it was known or believed, had "posed" as moviemakers, State Department officials, teachers, or almost anything else—under orders straight from Moscow. Spies, subversives, double—even triple and quadruple—agents were on everyone's mind.

The wartime experience was of course part of the backstory. The "Brown Scare" over fascist sympathizers in the United States and constant security precautions against German or Japanese espionage had done much to accustom Americans to the murky world of spies and infiltrators. Nor did it take much to persuade people to switch that fear from Brown to Red.

The fear was not groundless. There really were "card-carrying" communists in the United States who concealed their identities and passed on various sorts of information, most notoriously about the making of atomic bombs, to Moscow. The most striking case was that of Klaus Fuchs, the German anti-Nazi nuclear physicist who became a Communist in

Senator Joseph McCarthy (left) with Roy Cohn during Senate hearings on Communism.

1932, fled to England the next year when Hitler came to power, and worked as a scientist with both British and U.S. nuclear weapons programs. His service included time at Los Alamos, very profitable to his unofficial labors on behalf of the Soviet allies and, he believed, also on behalf of peace. Fuchs transmitted vital information to his Soviet controllers in a ring that involved several other notorious names from the period, among them Julius and Ethel Rosenberg. His arrest in London was announced February 3, 1950.

The exposure of Fuchs led quickly to the detention of the Rosenbergs, the New York couple whose trial and execution attracted public attention around the world. In his confession, Fuchs had mentioned Harry Gold, a courier for Soviet spies; Gold then cited the small-time operative David Greenglass, and Greenglass in turn pointed the finger of accusation at his sister Ethel Rosenberg and her husband Julius, a committed Communist. Julius was arrested in July 1950 and Ethel a month later. In a trial marred by the defense's incompetence and conducted in 1951 when cold war anticommunist hysteria was at its height, the two were found guilty and sentenced to death. Despite worldwide protests, the executions were carried out June 19, 1953. Although undoubtedly involved in some level of espionage, the extreme price they paid must be attributed to the times. On the other hand, even in those times the Rosenbergs were the only U.S. citizens actually to suffer the death penalty for Communist activities for work on the behalf of the Soviet Union.

(In retrospect, Fuchs called his state of mind at the time of the espionage on behalf of the Communist cause "controlled schizophrenia," saying that, "In the course of this work I began naturally to form bonds of personal friendship and I had to conceal from them my inner thoughts. I used my Marxist philosophy to establish in my mind two separate compartments."[2] Nonetheless, after his release from prison in 1959 he went to live with his father in East Germany.)

Other quests for Communists were broader in scope than the

precise and accurate trans-Atlantic investigations that had led to the detention of Fuchs and the Rosenbergs. As early as October 20, 1947, the House Un-American Activities Committee (HUAC) opened hearings on Communist influence in the motion-picture industry. Before an entranced audience and surrounded by huge klieg lights, anticommunist witnesses like Robert Montgomery and Ronald Reagan pointed to pro-Soviet propaganda in certain films and talked of Communist actors and writers in Hollywood. (However, Reagan, then a Democrat, defended screenwriters and denied that the Screen Actors' Guild, of which he was president, had been infiltrated by Communists.) When the accused—narrowed down to the so-called Hollywood Ten, mostly writers—were called in, they pleaded the Fifth Amendment repeatedly against being forced to testify against themselves, again to much publicity and head shaking, to the extent that "taking the fifth" became a ubiquitous joke.

It was not a joke to the Ten. Although never formally convicted of anything in a court of law, the "blacklisted" writers and others were fired, deprived of their passports until 1958, and accounted nonpersons in Hollywood for more than forty-five years. Credits to their names were erased on pre-1947 films, and never placed on the films—some of them well-known—they were able to write after that year.

Then, in 1948, the investigation moved to Washington. On the testimony of such ex-Communists as Elizabeth Bentley, several high-ranking officials, including Lauchlin Currie, of the Department of Commerce, and Dexter White, a former Assistant Secretary of the Treasury, were called before the HUAC to explain alleged pro-Communist actions; they asserted their complete innocence. It was in the same years that inquisitions began on a number of college and university campuses against professors who were reported to be members of or sympathizers with the Communist Party. These investigations now enabled state legislators and even campus administrators to share the limelight with the grand inquisitors of the HUAC. Several Reds were flushed out, although in no case was it ever proved that the instructor's political persuasion had affected his fairness as a teacher, or had unduly influenced his students.[3]

But these shows were nothing compared to the sensation of the HUAC hearing in 1948 concerning Alger Hiss, against whom charges were brought by Whittaker Chambers, a senior writer for *Time*. Chambers, a highly intelligent but troubled individual, had gone from childhood in a very dysfunctional family through Communist Party membership in the 1920s and 1930s to revulsion against his Soviet masters at the time of the Moscow "purge" trials in 1938. He then embarked on a spiritual search that ended in his becoming a passionate Christian of a rather existentialist, neoorthodox sort, and a member of a Quaker meeting. That was the story he told in his anguished and uneven best-seller of 1952, *Witness*, a book that remains an essential document for getting at the heart of the years around 1950. That eight-hundred-page autobiographical opus combines embarrassing exaggeration and vindictiveness with remarkable inside information on communism and the New Deal, together with sometimes brilliant disquisitions on the modern soul and such writers as Kierkegaard, Dostoevsky, Barth, and Niebuhr. Many conservatives, including William Buckley, considered *Witness* the most important book for their burgeoning movement. But Paul Hutchinson, presenting it in *The Christian Century* (June 11, 1952), exclaimed in exasperation, "Only God knows enough to review this book."

Chambers's foil was a character who could not have contrasted more effectively with the ex-Communist's awkward but somehow sincere testimony, or with Nixon's brash on-the-make Republicanism. Hiss was a poised, suave, articulate icon of the East Coast liberal "establishment," a former State Department official who, in 1948, was president of the Carnegie Endowment for World Peace.

Chambers claimed that he had known Alger Hiss as a fellow Communist agent in the 1930s. Both had lived in the Washington area when Hiss was with the State Department and Chambers was a full-time organizer for the Communist Party. Chambers had then gone on to his apostasy from the Party and his brilliant career in journalism, and Hiss to the presidency of the Carnegie Foundation for International Peace. But it was in their capacities in the 1930s that Chambers claimed to have known Hiss as a Communist. Hiss long held his own in flat-out denial, but finally as further circumstantial evidence began to surface indicating his acquaintance with Chambers and his involvement in espionage, he wavered, though he never confessed. Hiss was finally tried, not for espionage as such, but for perjury; the first trial resulted in a hung jury, but in the second he was convicted and sentenced on March 1, 1950. In the end he served forty-four months of jail time.

The drama made the career of Richard Nixon, the young congressman from California who relentlessly pursued Hiss, and who capitalized on these endeavors in his highly anti-communist Senate campaign in the fall of 1950 against the liberal Democrat Helen Gahagan Douglas.[4] Hiss/ Chambers meant in American life something like what the Dreyfus case had meant in France; it was claimed that even after the original issues in Dreyfus had been forgotten, the same people who had been on opposite sides in that tragic trial were no less on opposite sides in the great Left versus Right issues of decades to come. The same can be said of Hiss vs. Chambers and Nixon in the United States. It was the "Red Decade" of the 1930s against the conservative middle-American values that had come back into their own amid cold war and postwar prosperity. It was the confrontation of two sides of American life: the elegant, Ivy League, eastern internationalism of Hiss and the small town, America-first patriotism of Nixon and other Chambers's supporters.

Hiss's conviction was traumatic for liberals. Some among them perhaps had deep doubts as to whether Hiss was really telling the full and complete truth, or reserving memories from the Red Decade that, in his view, simply could not have been rightly understood or assessed in the very different world of postwar anticommunism. But such qualms stuck in the throats of his supporters; if true, that would have meant Nixon and even McCarthy were right, which was unthinkable.

Up to then many (though not all) liberals had wanted to believe that the Communist threat in the United States was mostly a bugbear in the imagination of such unsavory persons as Chambers, Nixon, and McCarthy; that such Communists as there were in this country, however deluded they may be about Russia, were fundamentally idealists working for the same goals as all progressives. It was hard for them to accept that a person with the respectable credentials of an Alger Hiss could act criminally on behalf of a foreign power while working for the U.S. government, especially when that government was itself liberal. Now, if they wished to continue in denial, they would either have to reject evidence that had been tested in a court of law, or minimize its importance and persist in asserting that the sins of the anticommunist "witch hunters" were worse than those of their side. Fortunately for them, the flagrant investigative excesses of Senator Joseph McCarthy soon gave them justification for that contention.

On the other hand, those conservatives who allowed Chambers his purple rhetoric and wide-ranging accusations would have gagged on acknowledging openly that 1930s' activists like Hiss possessed genuine idealism, however misguided, and moreover, unlike the atom bomb spies, were not in a position to do much serious harm. So it was that Hiss/Chambers also presented a dilemma for conservatives. They naturally felt vindicated in their view that the New Deal, and the whole eastern establishment that Hiss epitomized so well, was riddled with Communists and Communist sympathizers, or at the least was unduly tolerant of them and influenced by them. But now, to make that case they had to show that Hiss was not just an isolated figure but part of a vast conspiracy. To uncover that submerged monster was the McCarthy agenda. Its excesses and eventual failure left conservatives in turn discomforted and the McCarthyist cause discredited in the eyes of all but a small coterie of ultrists.

Both protagonists fulfilled a larger-than-life symbolic role, and 1950 was the pivotal year in a great contest among American archetypes. That drama was nothing less than a religious passion play. In the theater of the world the struggle between communism and the West became not so much competition between rival systems to see which could best meet practical human needs for food, housing, and security as a battle of ultimate significance between diametrically opposed faiths. So it was, of course. For the concepts of human nature and of the state, not to mention of God or ultimate reality, in the two parties were very different, even if the ordinary human dimensions of the cold war may sometimes have been forgotten amid all the theology. Whittaker Chambers's *Witness* reflected a mentality characteristic of 1950, for the ex-communist illustrated the fundamentally theological way in which the conflict between communism and the West was typically painted:

> Communism . . . is not new. It is, in fact, man's second oldest faith. Its promise was whispered in the first days of the Creation under the Tree of the Knowledge of Good and Evil: "Ye shall be as gods." It is the great alternative faith of mankind. Like all great faiths, its force derives from a simple vision. Other ages have had great visions. They have always been different versions of the same vision: the vision of God and man's relationship to God. The Communist vision is the vision of Man without God.[5]

This was the faith Chambers had once had, and which he now saw as the latest embodiment of the eternal adversary of the true faith. He put his own conversion plainly enough: "My need was to be a practicing Christian in the same sense that I had been a practicing Communist."[6] Chambers' problem was that it was not always easy to move from theology to practical politics. His criticism of the Roosevelt era was not that its actual programs, such as social security, were necessarily wrong; it was just that the New Deal had somehow failed to put God first. Chambers was always strengthened and anguished by God, who interested him much more than everyday politics. In the end he was to quarrel with his fellow conservatives over their lack of pragmatic flexibility and their tendency not to treat divinely given human rights with his scrupulous care. (He shocked many of them by arguing in 1959 that Alger Hiss should be given back his passport on human rights grounds.) But in 1950 Whittaker Chambers was a larger-than-life player in a drama that amounted, in the title of Alister Cooke's book of that year about the affair, to "a generation on trial."[7]

The early months of 1950 were important for the unfolding drama. In January came the conviction of Hiss for perjury and President Truman's decision to develop the hydrogen bomb. Early February brought the arrest, confession, and conviction of Klaus Fuchs in London. Then came Senator Joseph McCarthy's bombshell speech on February 9, in which he extended the conservative anticommunist crusade to flush out a huge treasonous network he asserted still existed among the sons and daughters—some highly placed—of that "generation on trial." In Wheeling, West Virginia, the Wisconsin lawmaker told a Republican women's group that he held in his hand a list of Communists who had infiltrated the State Department. "While I cannot take the time," he said, "to name all the men in the State Department who have been named as members of the Communist Party and members of a spy ring, I have here in my hand a list of 205 that were known to the Secretary of State as being members of the Communist Party and who nevertheless are still working and shaping the policy of the State Department."

This was the essence of McCarthyism. His lists were usually invisible and changing. But in the atmosphere of the day that was hardly the crucial point. By then the nation was basically in the grip of an imagined religious war between light and darkness on a cosmic, apocalyptic scale. Events to date had largely confirmed, not belittled, belief that there had indeed been Communists in government, and suspicion that what had come out so far was only the tip of a vast conspiratorial iceberg did not seem unreasonable. If so, people thought, it will be war, and religious war at that. Wars of the spirit call less for footnotes than for prophetic zeal, and that the senator from Wisconsin seemed, for the moment, well able to provide. His speech in the Senate on February 20, 1950, set the tone for engagement on this religious level and deserves to be cited at some length, for it is crucial to the spiritual understanding of 1950:

> Today we are engaged in a final, all-out battle between communistic atheism and Christianity. The modern champions of communism have selected this as the time. And, ladies and gentlemen, the chips are down—they are truly down.
>
> Unless we face this fact, we shall pay the price that must be paid by those who wait too long.
>
> Six years ago, at the time of the first conference to map out the peace—Dumbarton Oaks—there was within the Soviet orbit 180,000,000 people. Lined up on the antitotalitarian side there were in the world at that time roughly 1,625,000,000 people. Today, only 6 years later, there are 800,000,000 people under the absolute domination of Soviet Russia—an increase of over 400 percent. On our side, the figure has shrunk to around 500,000,000. In other words, in less than 6 years the odds have changed from 9 to 1 in our favor to 8 to 5 against us. This indicates the swiftness of the tempo of Communist victories and American defeats in the cold war. As one of our outstanding historical figures once said, "When a great democracy is destroyed, it will not be because of enemies from without, but rather because of enemies from within."
>
> The truth of this statement is becoming terrifying clear as we see this country each day losing on every front.
>
> At war's end we were physically the strongest nation

on earth and, at least potentially, the most powerful intellectually and morally. Ours could have been the honor of being a beacon in the desert of destruction, a shining living proof that civilization was not yet ready to destroy itself. Unfortunately, we have failed miserably and tragically to arise to the opportunity.

The reason why we find ourselves in a position of impotency is not because our only powerful potential enemy has sent men to invade our shores, but rather because of the traitorous actions of those who have been treated so well by this Nation. It has not been the less fortunate or members of minority groups who have been selling this nation out, but rather those who have had all the benefits that the wealthiest nation on earth has had to offer—the finest homes, the finest college education, and the finest jobs in Government we can give.

This is glaringly true in the State Department. There the bright young men who are born with silver spoons in their mouths are the ones who have been worst.[8]

The apocalyptic structure of this speech is evident enough. One is caught up in its almost biblical tone as it points to traitors from the ranks of the privileged—like Hiss, then on everyone's mind—and proceeds to extol the faithful who are not from among the mighty of the nation. Indeed, they may be from despised minority and underprivileged classes but nonetheless have remained true to the country in a way those born with silver spoons have not.

The speaker begins with the alarming portrayal of the crisis, which was real enough. (However, McCarthy ignored the efforts of the Truman administration since 1945 to deal with it. These were actually very impressive: the Marshall Plan; NATO; the Truman Doctrine; the Berlin airlift; substantial aid to Greece, Turkey, and Italy; atomic rearmament.) Finally the senator's discourse comes to the inevitable quest for blame. It is sought not in the complexities of the outer world, but at the door of infiltrators within the government itself.

They could be presumably identified and given comeuppance, and administering to them the vengeance they richly deserve would be satisfying because they are overprivileged and ungrateful Americans, not ordinary people like those to whom and for whom the solon was speaking.

All this is secondary, however, to the fundamental mythological, eschatological worldview behind this oration: the vision of "final, all-out battle between communistic atheism and Christianity," making the picture essentially more religious than political. This Armageddon-like scene is what McCarthy's many followers responded to, above all those Roman Catholic and evangelical Protestants who were accustomed to polarized religious views of the world in the first place—and who, in their own eyes, were decent people in the opposite camp from those privileged young men who had been treated well, but who had, they were assured, betrayed that trust. The nation's Catholic population and conservative Protestants from the South and West often saw themselves as hardworking and patriotic but treated as second-class compared to the silver spooners—why, for example, was it the latter and not they who got the striped-pants jobs at State, and who apparently unlike them could be elected President? Right or wrong about communism's influence, McCarthy had struck a social nerve at home.

McCarthy's fellow Roman Catholics were not alone in putting the cold war in ultimate religious terms. One could compare the perspective of the evangelical *Moody Monthly*, in a striking editorial of September 1950, after the Korean war had begun:

> *When will America wake up?* In the political arena, the rumble of sixty-ton tanks and the rattle of machine gun fire, the discovery of American soldiers tied together and shot through the head are beginning to cloud the dreams of a united world. And it is time, before our nation, our freedom and our opportunities are gone, that we awake to the danger that such an attitude has brought us.

What happens when America with its Christian heritage and its reputed character goes into conference
with the Soviet Union? Because Vishinski says, "We
never pray," the representatives of our country forget
their need for God in being nice. The conference is held
without a word of prayer and we wonder at the confusion that results. . . .

And America will fall and fall unless, with superior
conviction, greater skill, more determination and militant faith she matches the power of the enemy. . . .
Where are the men who will stop being merely nice and
stand on their convictions? Where, above all, are the
men who will call America back to the faith that has
made her great?[9]

Here, clearly, are reiterated the basic themes of Chambers,
McCarthy, and others for whom anticommunism was above
all a religious passion: condemnation, in the light of the
Marxist evil, of the liberal, progressivist view of human nature
as shallow and naive; denial that the enemy can be seen in
merely human terms, without the backdrop of demonology
and a theological concept of sin; call for spiritual armament—
prayer—as the supreme weapon in such a conflict, for "it takes
a faith to fight a faith"; assertion that this sort of faith was in
greater store in the past than in our present reprobate time,
and so is a faith to which we must be called back; affirmation
that it will take persons of unshakable conviction to turn the
nation around.

Earlier, in May 1950, the *Moody Monthly* had, in referring
to the threat of the H-bomb, spoken of the present as a time
of the changing of power among the nations, as was the time
of Jeremiah, and had called for a new prophet of his stature,
for "we are living in a day when it looks as if judgment is about
to fall."[10] Was McCarthy that Jeremiah?

McCarthy knew where to direct his charges. One of his
first attacks, in March 1950, was against Owen Lattimore, the
distinguished scholar of Asian history at Johns Hopkins Uni-

versity who had been President Roosevelt's personal envoy to Chinese ruler Chiang Kai-shek during the war. Lattimore was now accused of a being a Communist agent who held great responsibility for the recent "loss" of China. Despite his denials, the academic had to endure five years of hearings in Senate committees and the Justice department before his name was cleared. (In the end, it has been generally accepted that the charges against Lattimore were false; though a liberal, he was no Communist nor part of any conspiracy.[11] He was fingered because he fit the symbolic needs of nascent McCarthyism so well: a liberal, an academic at an elite eastern university, a prominent New Deal figure associated with just-lost China.)

The Lattimore hearings climaxed with testimony by Louis Budenz, former editor of the Communist *Daily Worker*, who had left the Party and returned to his natal Roman Catholicism in 1945. Now a fervent believer, he denounced the Communist Party in the United States as no more than a vast Soviet espionage apparatus, and offered charges, usually unsubstantiated, that such prominent persons as Hiss and Lattimore were part of that insidious network. Critics suspected the Catholic Budenz to be as capable of managing the truth on behalf of ideological ends as the Communist Budenz had been, but he became a conservative hero. In any case, Budenz—like Chambers and many others—had followed the well-known short path from commitment to one totalistic system to equally fervent commitment to another at an opposite ideological pole. By April 1950 the jittery mood stirred up by McCarthy was having an effect. The House was set to pass the Mundt-Nixon antisubversion bill; the FBI budget was boosted, with $4,000 added to Hoover's own salary, and seven hundred additional agents brought on; and the HUAC got an additional $150,000.

Much, though certainly not all, of the energy behind the anticommunism of the 1950s came from McCarthy's own Roman Catholic Church. The Catholic support was based on anticommunism as firm policy of the Vatican under Pius XII, and over the past five years diocesan and national Catholic periodicals had run story after story on the persecution of the church by Communists in its East European strongholds and fertile mission fields like China. For millions of American Catholics, these earthshaking catastrophes for the church and its faithful were not just far-off events, however terrible, as they might be for American Protestants of different origin, but matters of ethnic and even family importance.

On top of that, anticommunism was an ideological position with which Catholics of all stripes, liberal and conservative, concurred in 1950. Like Buckley in *God and Man at Yale*, Chambers in *Witness*, or McCarthy in his Senate speech, they were prepared to see the cross and the red star as symbols of two ultimately and eternally opposed principles, the cold war amounting in the end to nothing less than the current version of God versus the serpent in the Garden of Eden saying that men could be as gods. Catholic lay organizations like the Knights of Columbus and the Catholic War Veterans held large and well-publicized anticommunist rallies, though they carefully avoided official endorsements of McCarthy.

Not a little of Catholic anticommunism was sparked by Francis Cardinal Spellman, Archbishop of New York and then generally seen as unofficial spokesman for Catholicism in the United States. His opposition to communism was pure and simple; his rhetorical portrayals of life in Communist countries remind one of nothing so much as traditional Catholic visions of hell, and for him the Communists presiding over those realms of the earthly damned were closer to demons, or vermin, than human beings. Though known for his intemperate denunciations of films containing any suggestion of sexual salaciousness, the Cardinal went so far as to endorse *One Lonely Night*, a novel by Micky Spillane, notorious for the pornographic violence and extralegality (*I the Jury*) celebrated in his works. *One Lonely Night* contained lines about Communists like these: "Don't arrest them, don't treat them with the dignity of the democratic process . . . do the same thing they'd do to you! Treat 'em to the inglorious taste of sudden death."[12]

More measured Catholic positions were also submitted. The question was whether the Communist menace was chiefly to be sought coiled and concealed within the structures of American life itself, or whether such a quest would only make America more like the adversary in the name of opposing him. Bishop Bernard Sheil, outspoken opponent of McCarthy, later put it plainly enough in an April 9, 1954 speech to the United Auto Workers-Congress of Industrial Organizations: "It is not enough to say that someone is anticommunist to win my support. As I remember, one of the noisiest anticommunists of recent history was a man named Adolf Hitler."[13]

Finally, a piece of what might be regarded as urban folklore regarding the origins of McCarthyism: The story began circulating in 1950 that on January 7 of that year Senator McCarthy had dined at the Colony Restaurant with Father Edmund A. Walsh, SJ, founder and dean since 1919 of the famous School of Foreign Service at Georgetown University in Washington. The Wisconsin Republican had mentioned to Walsh and a couple of other prominent individuals at the table that he needed an issue to help him get reelected, and the Jesuit had suggested that McCarthy seize on the question of Communist infiltration in the U.S. government.

This story seems to have originated in a March 14, 1950 column by Drew Pearson in the *Washington Post*, who gave the essentials of the alleged conversation but added that after McCarthy began his campaign Walsh was "not happy at the outcome" of his advice. Indeed Donald Crosby, after investigating the matter, concluded in his study of McCarthyism and Catholicism that the Colony Restaurant story is dubious. Pearson was not noted for scrupulous accuracy, and Crosby felt the suggestion would have been out of character for

Walsh, who though firmly anticommunist was quite sophisticated and more a New Dealer than a conservative.[14] Or perhaps he did make the suggestion to the senator in some
off-the-cuff, unguarded way, but was, as Pearson acknowledged, distressed at the direction McCarthyism took the
nation and appalled by the senator himself. In any case, the
Colony legend can be said to symbolize the intimate yet
ambivalent—and to many disturbing—relation between the
1950s' anticommunist crusade and Catholicism.

The McCarthyist episode of 1950 came at a time when several major American religious traditions were undergoing
postwar redefinition, and it played an important part in that
process. Prewar Catholicism had often been severely afflicted
by tensions between its various ethnic strands; anticommunism provided a powerful ideological cement that brought
Catholics together even as ethnicity was beginning to lose
force for immigrant families moving into their second and
third, and much more "Americanized," generations. Far more
Catholics were receiving higher education than ever before;
in Catholic colleges Thomism combined with anticommunism to produce a briefly important vision of a spiritually
based, integralist "Catholic civilization." Finally, the burgeoning opposition to McCarthy within the church offered a
preview of the intra-Catholic liberal-conservative struggles of
the 1960s, in which the integralist ideal of a Cardinal
Spellman-style church—conservative, authoritarian, and passionately anticommunist—would give place in the hearts of
the majority of Catholics to a more changing and open vision
of the people of God. But the McCarthyist experience was
apparently a tunnel through which the church had to pass in
order to get to what Vatican II meant to American Catholicism.

The impact of McCarthy on American Protestantism was
also important. First, it must be recognized that as many
Protestants as Catholics were in McCarthy's camp, even if the
senator did not receive the same level of support from mainstream Protestant leaders and periodicals as he did from

some, though not all, Catholic equivalents. But numerous Main Street Protestants in American Legion halls and the more conservative churches—like those to which the *Moody Monthly* catered—certainly had no problems with the ideology behind what he was doing, and usually not with the man himself. Indeed, the crisis seems to have effected a watershed change for many Protestant evangelicals and fundamentalists. Heretofore, strong anti-Catholicism had been a major foundation of their religious position. But, as Warren Vinz put it, "Fear of the Roman Catholic Church miraculously vanished with the rise of Roman Catholic Senator Joseph McCarthy and his anticommunism crusade."[15]

Now, suddenly, conservative evangelicals found that they agreed so strongly with McCarthy and Catholic anticommunism that theological differences could be set aside when it came to political issues of such import. The tacit anticommunist alliance of conservative Protestants and Catholics was to be perpetuated in future crusades of the religious Right, such as opposition to abortion, to the civil rights movement, and to radical feminism. On the other hand, liberal Protestants found in their opposition to McCarthy not only new alliances with liberals in the senator's own church, but confirmation of their long-standing suspicion of the ideological antecedents of militant anticommunism, and the seeds of support for the civil rights movement and the New Left in the 1960s.

In "The Great Lie," an April 17, 1950 editorial, the politically liberal, Union Theological Seminary-based journal *Christianity and Crisis* interestingly set McCarthy alongside John T. Flynn's anticommunist and anti-New Deal book *The Road Ahead*, which had notoriously targeted the Federal Council of Churches as Communist-tinged. Liston Pope, author of the editorial, accused both those Irish-named rightists of being, like the Fascists, Anglophobes.[16] A later *Christianity and Crisis* editorial by John Bennett, "The Self-Defeating Attitudes of America's 'Reactionaries,'" continued the ad hominem defense by claiming that the extreme anticommunists were so blinded by their hatred and opposition to everything that had come about in the United States since 1933 and the New Deal that they could not see that democratic liberalism was the best bulwark against communism.[17]

However religious and apocalyptic in its own ideology, McCarthyism was a forge that was reshaping American religious contours along lines that were really as sociopolitical—one might even say secularized—as they were theological or denominational in character. What liberal and conservative meant in American religious discourse would become more political and cross-denominational after 1950 than before.

McCarthyism had its effect on American Judaism as well, and one that was far from welcome to many Jews. The case of the Rosenbergs, which seemed almost entirely to involve persons with Jewish names and backgrounds, had raised the specter of anticommunism becoming anti-Semitism. They could recognize the disproportionate number of Jewish names among the senator's targets, despite his discreet avoidance of that issue, the fact his chief counsel was a Jew named Roy Cohn (who had been an assistant prosecutor in the Rosenbergs' case), and his pretense that the Communist infiltrators were old Yankee elites born with silver spoons in their mouths. But the community was well aware that not a few Jews had been Communists or Communist sympathizers in the decades after the Russian revolution; after all, Jews had good reason to hate the old czarist regime, and their own experience of marginality in "Christian" societies, together with their religion's passionate pro-labor and social justice concerns, made some susceptible to the appeal of Marxism and communism.

Though most American Jews were not Communist, there were those among them who had memories of grandfathers or uncles who read *Freiheit*, the Yiddish Communist newspaper, and argued about it around the dinner table; communism was a familiar presence in a way it was not for Catholics or most Protestants. Nonetheless, McCarthyism did not become the pogrom that many Jews, all too well-acquainted with Old World demagogues of the Right, dreaded that it might. The McCarthyist experience was also a catalyst for change in Judaism. The community tended increasingly to divide between Jewish neoconservatives like Roy Cohn and the crowd that would be associated with the conservative Jewish magazine *Commentary*, and those who remained loyal to the Left—a divide that would reach epic dimensions in the 1960s.

Religious journalism from America offered highly varied, though fairly predictable, perspectives on the issues. *The Sign*, not the most extreme Roman Catholic editorial voice but a trenchant one, asked in response to McCarthy's critics, "Why not guilt by association?" It pointed out that in everyday life people are often judged by the company they keep, and rightly so, and concluded that "particularly after the Hiss case, the Coplon case, and the case of scientist Fuchs, Government employees should be investigated if they have a fraternization record."[18] On the other hand, the Methodist *Christian Advocate* wrote a tongue-in-cheek editorial about witchcraft, concluding that "the American mode of dealing with witches is not to sink to the level of witchcraft." To make the point perfectly clear, they added that "if you want to substitute 'Communism' for 'witchcraft' in the foregoing, that is all right."[19] Others in the moderate-to-liberal Protestant camp spoke no less openly of "hysteria" and "pathological fear" in the nation's Capitol. One poignant sign of the times: the Episcopalian *Living Church* reported that a distinguished professor of history at Harvard had recently jumped from the window of a Boston hotel, leaving a note saying, "I am depressed over world affairs. I am a Christian and a Socialist."[20]

A far more robust observer than this obviously disturbed individual was Milton Mayer, who wrote for *Motive*, the magazine of the Methodist Student Movement, which in 1950 still continued the liberal campus Christian tradition. Mayer did not hesitate to declare

> I don't know why, exactly, but I would rather be Alger
> Hiss than Whittaker Chambers. I would rather be
> Harry Bridges than Louis Budenz. I would rather be
> Owen Lattimore than Joseph McCarthy. And I would
> rather, far, be stranded on a desert island with Judy
> Coplon than with Elizabeth Bentley. . . . I guess I had
> my belly full of the Red menace, which always was a
> fraud, still is, and always will be.

Mayer was no Communist. He acknowledged that "communism is a rotten, red-handed institution out of which no good has ever come or ever will." But, he insisted, "I will not engage in the national pastime of lynching communists, probable communists and possible communists." He connected the "guilt by association" attitude with those who condemned Christ on the grounds of those with whom he associated.[21]

Presbyterian Life published an editorial defending Secretary of State Dean Acheson in saying that as a Christian he would not turn his back on Alger Hiss, whether the latter was guilty or not.[22] That provocative position was printed in the same issue as the second part of an article by William Lindsay Gresham, "From Communist to Christian." Here that fairly well-known literary figure recounted his pilgrimage from the Party to the Church. The statement was supported by an attractive photo of Gresham, accompanied by his wife, Joy, and their two sons, on the way to a Presbyterian service. (Interestingly, Joy, who had also traveled from communism to Christianity, left William Gresham a few years later largely because of his alcoholism, went to England with the two boys, and finally became the wife of the celebrated Christian apologist C. S. Lewis.) The Acheson article received much negative letter-to-the-editor comment, the gentlest of which accused Acheson and the editorialist of confusing sentimentality with Christian principle. The denominational magazine responded in a semi-defensive vein, saying that "it is not expected that all readers will agree with all [editorial] writers."[23] The Gresham article, on the other hand, received lavish praise from readers.

It was indeed an upsetting and edgy time. For Independence Day *The Sign* wrote, "[O]n July 4, 1950, there is genuine worry in the hearts of many an American. Worry not about our form of government, our democratic way of life, or our average public servant in Washington. But deepseated worry about the extent to which betrayal from within has penetrated the various branches of government." And this was because, in this magazine's view, "Senator McCarthy has stumbled upon a hornet's nest more angry than he knew when he made his initial charges."[24] The plot was thickening and the adversaries separating to do battle as the year advanced.

Anticommunism of the McCarthy, Chambers, or Spellman type in 1950 had features of an embryonic dualistic or millennialist religious movement. But the religious vision behind it needed to be developed. To become a real religion, a vision needs to become a church, and better yet a state church. This virtually seemed to be happening for a few years around 1950, when an apocalyptic scenario involving Western "gods" and Communist demons took on the quality of Chambers's and Spellman's drama of a world divided between light and darkness. The usual accoutrements of millennialism were present: charismatic prophets; symbols of the righteous, like the flag and the cross; the discovery and expulsion from their sacred community of "pollutants" (i.e., impure, demonic persons in the guise of Communists); the management of truth to produce a seamlessly consistent religious worldview. But the anticommunist state church was not to last. Within four years McCarthy made the mistake of hounding alleged Communists not in the unpopular State Department but in the U.S. Army, and those televised hearings revealed for all to see the obnoxious character of the man. Public opinion turned against the high priest of anticommunism as a state church, and that cause was lost. An editorial

in the Episcopalian journal *The Living Church* put it percep-
tively:

> If there is any one place where a Congressman has the
> right and duty to investigate Communism, it is in
> the army. There is therefore something ironical about
> the fact that the public has become upset about the tac-
> tics of the junior Senator from Wisconsin only when he
> began to look into something strictly within the lines of
> his authority and responsibilities.
>
> The secret of the public upset is this—we have all
> known right along that witch-hunting tactics were not
> really security measures, but rather a grisly form of pub-
> lic entertainment. But we do not choose to have those
> on whom our lives and safety depend made the butt of
> the show. When investigation of Communism really
> comes close to our security we want it done in a intelli-
> gent and skillful manner, not for emotional effect.[25]

With realizations like this, McCarthyism as psychodrama
of national inquisition was largely finished, for when a liturgical mystery is seen for what it is— an act of theater and the
manipulation of special effects—its days are numbered. With
it passed the brief lifespan of the possibility that the country
would embrace anticommunism as a sort of national religion,
a state church in the sense suggested by Chambers, Spellman,
Buckley, and McCarthy around 1950, rather than just a matter of secular policy. Not long after, in the fall of 1957, two
momentous events pushed the country further in the direction of secular, and pragmatic—rather than sacred—anticommunism. Sputnik, the tiny Soviet satellite intruding into
American skies, raised the terrifying prospect that *they* might
be ahead of us in science and technology. The majority
response by that year was not that we need more spiritual
purity and expulsion of demons, but better education and science programs of our own—a conviction that culminated in
the moon walk twelve years later. And that same fall the Lit-

tle Rock school-integration crisis forced white America to recognize, if Montgomery and other racial crises had not, that in the great conflict the angels could be tarnished as well as the demons, that social justice would not wait for victory over the ideological foe but rather was an essential part of that struggle.

5

The Protestant Establishment

The year 1950 saw the beginning of a golden age for the "mainline" Protestant denominations of the United States. They were growing at a faster rate than the burgeoning U.S. population, and at the same time the traditional prestige of the Anglo-Protestant denominations of colonial or frontier background—Episcopalian, Presbyterian, Congregational, Methodist, Baptist, and (though not strictly Anglo) Lutheran—though challenged, was still basically intact. Overall during 1949 the U.S. population had grown by 1.5 percent—itself a high rate of increase at the height of the baby boom, representing 15 percent for a decade—but religious bodies overall had grown by 3 percent in that single year, and the upward trend was continuing in 1950. Many mainstream Protestant churches, for a change, were benefiting as much as anyone, often keeping up with the evangelicals and Catholics.

At the same time, mainstream Protestantism was changing as it endeavored to define a role for itself in the postwar world. It was no longer the activist 1930s or even the wartime 1940s. Instead, Protestantism now faced a season of conservative, anticommunist reaction against the "social gospel" mentality of the previous Protestant generation. When Horace Donegan was installed as Episcopal Bishop of New York in November of 1950, he found it appropriate to acknowledge that he was "aware of the menace of communism to religion

---

The face of mainline Protestant ministry, circa 1950.

and its threat to our American way of life," and he was not alone among quintessentially mainstream religious leaders.[1]

On the other hand, an ecumenical spirit was very much in the air and had to be answered. Cooperation to meet wartime exigencies, and the example of the formation of the World Council of Churches in Amsterdam in 1948, pressed American Protestants to follow through with plans to consolidate the old Federal Council of Churches and several other ecumenical agencies into the National Council of Churches in 1950.

Closer to the grassroots level, the church now had to minister to the needs of new suburbs overflowing with young families, the husband and father perhaps an "organization man" in a gray flannel suit and, at least for the moment, more interested in corporate conformity and reaching higher levels of Norman Vincent Peale "success" than in reforming the world. At the same time, enlivened by idiosyncratic voices such as those of Reinhold Niebuhr, Karl Barth, and thousands of 1930s-style pastors still in pulpits across the land, mainstream Protestantism was far more ready to offer liberal challenges to the new anticommunist conservatism than were evangelicals like Billy Graham or Catholics like Cardinal Spellman or Fulton Sheen.

Nonetheless, old-style religious pacifism was floundering in the world of Korea and the cold war.[2] The decline had begun during America's engagement in World War II, which almost all clergy supported after Pearl Harbor. This conflict had seemed to oppose a level of evil that went far beyond the old pacifist image of wars as simply engineered by corrupt statesmen or arms-selling "merchants of death." On the use of the A-bomb or H-bomb, religious leaders in 1950 were decidedly more circumspect in weighing just-war and pacifist ideologies than their predecessors had been in the days of Kirby Page's survey, and more in the mood of the 1945 and 1946 post-Hiroshima voices presented in chapter 2. A commission on the issue was appointed by the Federal Council of Churches, predecessor of the National Council. It was chaired by Episcopal Bishop Angus Dun of Washington, D.C., and boasted such eminent names as John C. Bennett, Reinhold Niebuhr, Paul Tillich, and Georgia Harkness, among others. Following in the footsteps of the Calhoun commission of 1945, this body issued a 1950 report on "The Christian Conscience and Weapons of Mass Destruction."

These representatives of the Protestant mainstream deplored modern warfare but rejected pacifism, saying "most of us find ourselves called to follow a course which is less simple and which appears to us to be more responsible because more directly relevant to the hard realities of the situation." War may be less evil than surrender to "some malignant power," the commission said, but must be as limited as possible. However, there are no absolute rules; one could not say that "Christians can approve of using swords and spears, but not guns"; in the same way, no absolute rule could be drawn between conventional warfare and nuclear arms. In lines reminiscent of Reinhold Niebuhr, these ethicists argued that "for the United States to abandon its atomic weapons, or to give the impression that they would not be used, would leave the non-Communist world with totally inadequate defense. For Christians to advocate such a policy would be to share responsibility for the worldwide tyranny that might result."

Dissenting statements came from Robert L. Calhoun and Georgia Harkness, who said they felt that while the report might be defended on political grounds, it did not offer a sufficiently distinctive Christian response to war. Harkness added that "Christian pacifism as an attempt to eliminate war through international reconciliation is less simple and more responsible than is here suggested."[3] The pendulum was swinging to the right on the war issue, and all but a tiny number of real Communist sympathizers among churchpersons saw little but menace in the Soviet power. But there remained those who were willing to look for other means than military might as a way of containing it.

Turning to the grassroots, we may note that in 1950 mainstream Protestants, seeking to catch the wave of the religion "boom," were engaged in evangelistic campaigns almost in imitation of Billy Graham. In 1949 a project called Religion in American Life came into being under the chairmanship of Baptist layman Charles E. Wilson, president of the General Electric Company and soon-to-be treasurer of the newly formed National Council of Churches. Jewish as well as Protestant organizations were among the sponsors of Religion in American Life. The project supported speakers in more than three thousand communities in an effort to boost church attendance and contributions, and was promoted by billboards, radio announcements, and newspaper ads donated by the Advertising Council. A year later the campaign was declared a success, with towns from Elmira, N.Y., to Ripley, Iowa, reporting increases in attendance and pledging up to 30 to 35 percent.[4]

At the same time, thirty-eight denominations combined institutionally in a separate campaign called United Evangelistic Advance. Among its activities was the sponsorship of united Reformation Sunday services. We were told in 1950 that three years before fewer than a dozen such services were held; now they could be found in more than five hundred communities. An important feature of Advance was that it was promoted chiefly by laymen; in 1950 some 350,00 had been enlisted.[5]

Local mainstream evangelistic crusades continued this work at the grassroots level. In Washington, for example, the Federation of Churches placed full-page newspaper ads declaring, "It's God's Hour for Greater Washington!" The organization imported a "preaching team" of thirty ministers and laypersons to evangelize the nation's capital during a six-day session. The campaign consisted of a kick-off "Festival of Faith," which brought an overflow crowd to the ten-thousand-seat Uline Arena. That event was followed by some three hundred breakfasts, luncheons, dinners, lectures, and services; a total of seventy-five thousand attended. The Rev. Bryan Green, a Church of England evangelist whom some considered a more genteel Billy Graham, came over to preach in Boston and elsewhere.[6] The "sales approach" was reinforced in a much-discussed book by William A. Pleuthner, *Building Up Your Congregation*.[7]

The growing interest in religion was undeniable. Members of the Associated Press Managing Editors Association, meeting in Atlanta toward the end of the year, agreed on this. But their explanations were diverse. In polling on the subject, most of the editors gave psychological insecurity as the chief cause, with the Korean War and the threat of world war a close second. But several credited aggressive tactics on the part of religion for its success; "Religion was been doing a good selling job," said E. N. Jacquin of the Champaign, Illinois, *News-Gazette*. The sales approach, new to a previously staid mainstream Protestantism, clearly was having an effect.[8]

Even Reinhold Niebuhr had to acknowledge that something was going on. In an article in the *New York Times Magazine* the great but hardheaded theologian commented on the alleged religious revival: "There are certain marked tendencies in both cultural and popular interests that seem to prove its reality [though the evidence is not] conclusive." He referred to "mass conversions under the ministrations of popular evangelists," namely Graham, and a new receptivity to religion in the world of culture, "in marked contrast to the indifference or hostility of past decades." But now intellectuals have been forced to face the fact that, whether they like it or not, religion today is more than just "escape," and from the point of view of human existence the historical religions are really quite sophisticated, giving place to the complexity and subjectivity of experience, in contrast to the simplistic "credulities" of science or Marxism.[9]

How did religion in mainline Protestant churches in 1950 play out on the local level? "Out there" not everyone was an evangelist or a neoorthodox theologian, or even a denominational bureaucrat. But the growing numbers who filled the pews must have had some reason for going to church rather than staying home.

Not all church members were torn by psychological *angst*

or were worried to a frazzle about war, although no doubt nearly all had some internal share in the anxieties of the day. Many were convinced by churchmen and politicians that having a "faith" and a religious institution, no matter what it was, was an important part of being an American and that it was especially urgent in these perilous times of war and conflict with atheistic communism. Many had other concerns as well. Young parents in new suburbs far from home and extended family were concerned about finding the support networks all young parents ought to have. The upwardly mobile knew, or hoped, they could make important contacts in the right churches. Finally, millions undoubtedly really believed in religion and found worship a vital part of their lives, and would have gone to church whether it was fashionable or not.

One great resource for awareness of what church life in some of its diversity was like in 1950 is a series of articles published throughout the year in *The Christian Century* on "Great Churches." The limitations of this series no doubt casts a significant light on mainstream Protestant mentality of the time. Perhaps, given publication in this liberal Protestant periodical, it would be unfair to note that none of the "great churches" were Roman Catholic or Eastern Orthodox, not to mention of Jewish or other non-Christian faith. But it is also the case that none were African American, Asian American, Episcopalian, Unitarian, or Pentecostal, and only two or three decidedly conservative evangelical. Nonetheless, the churches, selected by polling to represent the major sections of the country and various sizes of community, are cumulatively fascinating. We find rural, small town, and urban churches, churches of several denominational and ethnic backgrounds, churches all of which have interestingly distinct histories, emphases, and personalities. Here are a few examples of grassroots American religion in 1950.

To begin, there was Mount Olivet Lutheran Church in Minneapolis. It had grown from 338 members in 1938 to over 5,000 in 1950. According to the "Great Churches" report, this congregation had no "secret of success," no novel "technique" for church growth. It simply combined continuous activity, strong leadership, and solid but unsensational worship and preaching, and was in the right place at the right time. Certainly it was a positive factor that the edifice was located in a growing community, a new suburb made up largely of young families whose breadwinners held good, middle-class, white-collar jobs. Nor did it hurt that this was Minneapolis, and Mount Olivet was an Augustana (Swedish) Lutheran parish, though by 1950 less than half its members were of that denominational background. Other churches with similar advantages, however, did not do as well as Mount Olivet.

Much of the credit must go to the tireless labors of the Rev. Reuben K. Youngdahl, pastor. No doubt some were attracted to him and his parish because his brother, Luther Youngdahl, was Republican governor of Minnesota. But Reuben Youngdahl did not rest on anyone else's laurels. He was a powerfully built man over six feet tall who had been a star athlete at Gustavus Adolphus College and who now devoted all his energies to the church. It was his life from early morning until late nearly every evening. After spending the day in his office or downtown on behalf of several community service projects in which he was involved, Youngdahl made fifteen-minute calls from five to eight P.M., and after that he and his wife were "at home" to members of the congregation three nights a week. On Sunday, he delivered well-organized biblical sermons at no fewer than three hour-long services, all conducted in a dignified Lutheran liturgical manner.

Mount Olivet also emphasized lay evangelism, and no doubt Youngdahl would have claimed that much of the credit for the church's success belonged to congregational efforts rather than to himself. From our perspective, though, the overridingly important point seems to be that this parish exemplifies what many Americans in 1950 were looking for in local church life: a church doing what it had always done and doing it well, with all the advantages of modern methods and technology, but without radical innovation in the message or its liturgical medium.[10]

Another example of a 1950 mainline Protestant church, this time in a rural rather than suburban setting, was the New Knoxville, Ohio, Evangelical and Reformed Church. That parish, embracing a majority of the souls in the tiny community and the surrounding countryside, had a membership of a thousand. The chiming clock on the bell tower of the noble brick edifice regulated the life of a spic-and-span village representing the heartland at its best. Unlike many such country communities, which had been losing population since the 1930s, New Knoxville then seemed prosperous and stable. All around, rolling green fields supported fat livestock and the town's two main industries, a feed mill and a sawmill.

The Evangelical and Reformed Church in New Knoxville, based on German immigration that started in the 1830s, emerged from the German Reformed Church; some services had been in German until World War II. Recently, the church had sent Dr. D. A. Bode, the pastor, to the one-thousandth anniversary festival of the church in the town of Ladbergen, Germany, from which the ancestors of many in the congregation had come. (However, in 1950 church leaders emphasized that in the recent war over a hundred young men from this church had been willing to fight against the Nazi-dominated fatherland.)

The dignified and respected Dr. Bode taught a simple faith well grounded in the Calvinist Heidelberg Catechism of 1563. This church could be said to represent the solid continental European ethnic roots, in this case German Reformation, of much of rural American Protestantism outside the orbit of the old-line Anglo-colonial denominations with their now-liberalizing tendencies. One thinks also of midwestern Lutheranism as it was in 1950. In that year Evangelical and Reformed people in New Knoxville were not enthusiastic about the then-impending marriage of their denomination with the Congregationalists to form the United Church of Christ, probably because of the different ethnic and cultural backgrounds of the two faiths and the more liberal tone of the

New England-based partner, but they were resigned to accepting it.

New Knoxville congregants also seemed uneasy about alleged attempts of Roman Catholicism to infiltrate and propagandize their staunchly Protestant community, despite the small number of Catholic families residing in it; the spirit of the Reformation and attitudes formed in centuries-old church wars seemed to live on in this highly homogeneous parish. On the other hand, relations were reasonably good with the only other church in town, a much smaller Methodist body.

Prospects for some growth seemed favorable in 1950. The feed mill and sawmill were both expanding and hiring. New families would be moving to town. They would soon learn that in New Knoxville they would, like the previous residents, be expected to pay their bills, live upright lives, and join a church, which would be either Evangelical and Reformed or Methodist.[11]

Near century's end, Randall Balmer visited all of *The Christian Century*'s "great churches" to ascertain their status nearly fifty years later, and published the results in a fascinating book, *Grant Us Courage: Traveling Along the Mainline of American Protestantism.* The account of the New Knoxville E. and R., now First United Church of Christ, is not entirely sanguine. The German identity was rapidly fading; the town is now one that young people want to leave; and church numbers were down considerably from 1950, especially in the Sunday school. The theological and social tone was much more conservative than is typical of the United Church with which the New Knoxville parish is now uncomfortably aligned.[12] But it has carried on.

The First Church of Christ (Congregational), in West Hartford, Connecticut, was a suburban church, but one with a different heritage from Mount Olivet. Although suburban neighborhoods were becoming new melting pots in 1950, as families of many ethnic and religious backgrounds moved out of urban ghettos into them, by and large they were still predominantly Protestant. Some, however, looked on the traditional Protestant church merely as a social convenience, and churches needed to find new rationales for their existence in the new kind of community.

First Church had been founded back in 1713 when one had to be a member of a Congregational church to vote in Connecticut. Thereafter, First ministered from its situation on the "Green" to what was for more than two centuries a quiet New England village. Particularly in the snowy winters, with its tall steeple and Corinthian columns, the edifice looked like the classic New England church of Christmas cards or calendar art. However, the present building is not colonial, but little more than half a century old, for a major event in the congregation's long history occurred on January 3, 1942, less than a month after the United States entered World War II, when the old church burned to the ground. The local Jewish temple Beth Israel invited the congregation to worship in their premises until it could rebuild, refusing to accept any financial reimbursement. When a new church was erected in 1943, a memorial plaque was placed by First Church in both edifices, the Jewish and the Christian, commemorating the kindness and stating that, "in a day sadly clouded by inhuman prejudice we experienced in the fellowship of Jew and Christian the joy of true religion."

Unhappily, First Church had itself been severely riven by factionalism in the 1930s, one issue being whether a new church should be gothic or colonial. First Church did the best thing it could do under the circumstances when in 1937 it called a new pastor who was able to bring the congregation together and lead it into a new era with a new kind of ministry. That was Eldon Mills, who was not even a Congregationalist in background but an Indiana Quaker who had served in midwestern Friends churches, but was willing to accept the challenge of an ancient but fractured New England church on the Green. (*The Christian Century* article commented that New England Protestantism had long seemed unable to produce ministerial candidates in sufficient numbers to supply its historic churches, and in fact many of them are pastored by clergy from the hinterland.)

Mills maintained faith with his own tradition by keeping five minutes of silence for meditation during his services, but otherwise was an unquietist whirlwind of activity. He supervised the erection of a new church after the fire, and even more importantly, made the church available for activities that brought people into it and met the community's needs. After 1945 First Church suddenly found itself in the midst of a bustling postwar suburb. By 1950 membership had reached nearly two thousand, even though seventy-five to a hundred inactive names were pruned off the rolls every year. The locally famous Sunday school had a waiting list. A striking fact about First Church in 1950, furthermore, was the extent of male participation. The crowd at the average service was half men, which we are assured was a very unusual circumstance in New England churches.

At the same time the Women's Guild boasted more than five hundred members, divided into fourteen circles, three of which met in the evening so that employed women could attend, or young mothers could leave the baby with the father. The circles had a combined all-day meeting once a month. Moreover, these West Hartford women insisted on doing all the cooking and serving for parish dinners —about thirty a year—rather than trusting caterers in their sparkling kitchens, as did some other affluent congregations.

One is aware at century's end of how much the foregoing reflects 1950-style concepts of women's lives and roles. In *Grant Us Courage*, Randall Balmer found that, in this day of two-career families and different lifestyles, the number of circles in the Women's Guild was reduced to six, and they all met in the evening.[13] (Overall, in Balmer's account, First Church has declined since Eldon Mills' leadership in the yeasty years around 1950, but seemed to have recently begun to reverse falling membership and attendance.)

What of the weaknesses in 1950? Eldon Mills, who himself once took off six months to work with Arab refugees in

Gaza with the American Friends Service Committee, regretted the lack of serious, organized commitment to social action in First Church. It was not that the church was entirely indifferent to social problems. It hosted a flourishing chapter of Alcoholics Anonymous, and in 1950 was making plans to sponsor a family of Displaced Persons from Europe (still an important concern in 1950) in the community. The parish gave generously to local, state, national, and world Councils of Churches, but had no members who actually served on the boards and programs of those bodies. *The Christian Century* also made the intriguing point that, if First Church had organized, as the pastor wished, a council for social action, "It might, for example, make a study of salaries paid the thousands of clerical workers in near by Hartford's insurance companies, and bring the results before the company executives who live in West Hartford."[14]

However, it cannot be denied that the emphasis on spirituality, and on ministry to individuals and families rather than to "social action," represents a 1950 attitude much more widespread than the lingering Quaker, or Reinhold Niebuhr, concern for church and society. At a 1950 interseminary conference in Rock Island, a seminar on prayer led by the distinguished Quaker Douglas V. Steere was by far the most popular offering, and one on church and world order the least. Steere himself, a man strong in the conviction that prayer must find expression in practical good works, resisted the interpretation that students were rejecting social concerns, and proposed instead that spirituality was simply where they felt they needed most help.[15] Nonetheless, a sense that even the erstwhile liberal mainline churches were socially exhausted and needed some quiet time with the inner life, and with new postwar kinds of ministry, is hard to avoid.

To many white, middle-class Americans and their churches—though certainly not to African Americans or other minorities, or to still-exploited ranks of laborers, housewives, and children—it seemed that by 1950 nearly all the big battles for social justice had been won. The terrible evils represented by the Axis side in the victorious but exhausting war had been defeated; social security was in place; and wages were rising. Even in regard to race, many told themselves, slow progress was being made. It was now time to turn inward and see how newly affluent people could live full and fulfilled spiritual lives.

After all, the new postwar affluence, such persons might have thought in 1950, must represent some sort of rough and ready social justice. So many have so much more than before; so many are getting so much more education than before; so many are living in better homes than ever before, with washing machines and air conditioning and, soon, even television. Perhaps the best one could do now in church life was help people correlate material with spiritual affluence on a personal basis. Perhaps the stubborn evil that remained was just the basic sinful human condition the current theologians were always talking about, with their radical new existentialist or neoorthodox discovery of sin, and had to be dealt with individually.

On top of this was the consideration that since Americans were locked in a life-or-death struggle against communism, this was a time to close ranks rather than excessively criticize and destabilize American social order. Some reforms might have to wait until after the victory over communism, just as during the late war citizens were told they had to wait until V-day for new cars and televisions. For now, they were tired of fighting, whether physically or spiritually, and needed all the fight left in them for the remaining war against communism. And Americans wanted to enjoy the fruits of the previous struggle. But they were confused and sometimes demoralized by all the changes; they were plagued by individual demons like alcoholism (the new suburbs produced prodigious statistics for both church attendance and liquor sales); and maybe most basic of all they needed to know that their new way of life was good and serviceable in the eyes of God.

Here is where a last 1950 vignette of mainline Protestantism comes in: The Rev. Norman Vincent Peale of the

Marble Collegiate Church in New York. He was the best-selling religious author of the early 1950s, who stood firmly for laissez-faire, at least according to his lights, on social and political issues, but who was the supreme pontiff of attaining and sanctifying individual success through the power of faith. Born in 1898, Peale came out of Boston University and mid-western Methodism at the time that denomination was breaking out of old-fashioned evangelicalism into a populist, middle-of-the-road Protestantism. Peale's confident, anec-dotal preaching brought the world of the Main Street, prayer-filled salesman and Golden-Rule liberal to the heart of Manhattan. There his upbeat, achievement-oriented message played well to urbanites' nostalgia for America as they imag-ined it had once been, while at the same time giving them assurance that its values were just as valid as ever in the big city's stock exchanges and sales conferences.

Like the theological liberals, Peale translated the gospel into the jargon of the day, though his usages were those of the boardroom rather than the classroom. Religious commitment became "confidence-concepts," "faith-attitudes," and "spirit-lifters," and he insisted that Christianity was an "exact sci-ence" offering formulae capable of producing "proven," "guaranteed" results.

It was not critical liberalism, but certainly not sawdust-trail evangelicalism either. More than anything else, of course, it was in the tradition of nineteenth-century "New Thought," the doctrine that thinking affirmative, positive thoughts pro-duces corresponding realities. Peale's fundamental, easy-to-understand message, preached over and over with the help of homey anecdotes and simple slogans, was well expressed in the title of one of his books, *You Can If You Think You Can*. You set goals, believe you can accomplish them, and work till you do, not giving way to the "mental drainage" of self-defeating, negative thoughts along the way. You do this, and success is assured. Millions in 1950 were moving briskly toward eagerly sought personal goals in an open-ended, expansive America; in their world, Peale's confident faith struck the right note.

The year 1950 was two years before Peale's most famous book, *The Power of Positive Thinking*, but his 1948 work, *A Guide to Confident Living*, was still selling well, with chapters like "How to Think Your Way to Success" and "Prayer—The Most Powerful Form of Energy," all full of excellent advice on holding to affirmative attitudes and persevering through the rough times. In 1950 Peale and his friend, the psychiatrist Smiley Blanton, published *The Art of Real Happiness*, which contained more of the same, strewn like all of Peale's books with anecdotes about the anonymous "business executive," "chemical engineer," or "military officer" who had found he could solve his problems through the principles of positive living and peace of mind. It is hard to determine which part is Peale and which Blanton—it all sounds like Peale—though this volume does deal a little more systematically than others with specific psychological issues like depression, problem drinking, and marriage difficulties.[16]

In Peale's autobiographical *The True Joy of Positive Living*, 1950 is covered in the chapter, "The Message Goes Nationwide." That section relates the story of a 1950 financial crisis at *Guideposts*, the magazine edited by Peale, which was resolved with the help of visualizing and praying for the one hundred thousand readers needed to make the venture viable. They came, and so did many more, so that the periodical quickly reached millions and attained success. We are told it also received help and publicity from De Witt Wallace and Fulton Oursler, publisher and senior editor respectively of Peale's model magazine, the *Reader's Digest*.[17]

Peale's political outlook was staunchly right-wing Republican, and he seemed unable to sense the realities of life for laborers, minorities, and others outside the businessman's world with which he connected so well. On occasion he brought embarrassment to himself by endorsing causes he had naively thought were merely conservative but turned out to emanate from the extremist anti-Semitic, anti-Catholic, or crypto-fascist Right.[18] Though he endeavored to be active in the Protestant Council of New York and the National Council of Churches, he was stung by the severe criticism he received from colleagues who cared neither for his politics nor his version of the gospel—and who enjoyed nothing like his crowds of worshipers, his phenomenal book sales, his audience through *Guideposts*, or his status as a household name across mainstream and Main Street religious America.

Norman Vincent Peale and Reinhold Niebuhr came from very different directions, but both represent essential parts of the mainstream Protestant religious world of 1950, as do the "great churches" of Minneapolis, New Knoxville, and West Hartford. For it was a world of existential anxiety and naive optimism, of "Christian realism" and unbounded idealism, of uprooted suburbanites and tight ethnic communities. There was a lot for churches to do in handling such a complex mix; the remarkable thing is that, by and large, despite serious shortcomings, they dealt with them reasonably well. Mainstream Protestantism and its heritage did much to keep America on an even keel and away from permanent infatuation with extremist solutions in the dangerous days of Korea, McCarthyism, and the rest.

When they arrived in the new American churches, ancient spiritual traditions had to wear the garb of 1950. They had to seem serious, authentic, and set over against the world outside, yet at the same time they had to put on business suits and wear the advertising trappings of Madison Avenue. But once that was accomplished, it was not difficult for a religious institution to be successful in 1950. The main thing seems to have been for that church to do what it had always done, and to do it well. Indeed, it was important to connect by means of conspicuous yet appropriate symbols to the rural roots and various ethnic and denominational "heritages" still important to millions of Americans. At the same time, the church had to be up-to-date, helping people make the social transition from those roots to suburban and corporate reality. The "great churches" and many others did it in a variety of ways, from social occasions that enabled people to meet new neighbors to counseling and childcare services.

We might add that some Protestant churches in the 1950s, especially in denominations like Presbyterianism and Methodism, showed a novel tendency toward liturgical worship and gothic architecture and atmosphere. In the Methodist church, for example, the Order of St. Luke promoted frequent communion services, elaborate altars, vestments for clergy, the use of historic orders of worship, and other "high church" practices. This trend, though eventually to be somewhat eclipsed by the radical changes in religious life the 1960s were to bring, was of a piece with the 1950s' desire to honor tradition and recover spiritual values from the past. In Protestant churches of nonstate church background—which heretofore had shown little but contempt for the folderol of "high," established church liturgical practice— the liturgical movement, controversial though it was, may have indicated a half-conscious sense that all of mainstream Protestantism was now becoming a sort of unofficial public if not state church, and thus required the symbols of solemnity, tradition, and stability to go with the role. The movement wanted indications that its buildings, like the cathedrals of Europe, represented the best that a wealthy society could offer for divine worship. And it desired its clergy to be institutional and educated rather than raw charismatics, so it wanted the robes and academic or liturgical dignity expected of that status.[19]

The climactic event for the Protestant establishment in 1950 was the establishment of the National Council of Churches in Cleveland in late November 1950, which embraced twenty-nine Protestant and Eastern Orthodox denominations representing some thirty-one million members. The week culminated in a service on November 29 officially inaugurating the new organization. The National Council succeeded the old Federal Council of the Churches of Christ in America, a looser organization, and seven other ecumenical bodies, such as the United Council of Church

Women, the National Protestant Council on Higher Education, and several missionary conferences.

The National Council of Churches began literally under a cloud. Cleveland was devastated by a blizzard as the delegates began to gather. Schools and offices were closed; cars were buried; and on Sunday, reportedly, there were more empty churches in the city on Lake Erie than at any time in its history. Out of 600 voting delegates, only 475 actually arrived, and of the expected audience of 6,000 only a few more than half were present. Many of those who did make it had to walk from the train station to their hotels through two feet of snow. Just as grim as the weather was the news from Korea. A Chinese Communist offensive had just begun; allied forces were reeling; and neither President Truman nor Secretary of State Dean Acheson, who had hoped to visit the ecumenical undertaking as a major speaker, were able to come. (Acheson addressed the delegates by radio in a revised speech that branded Red China an aggressor.)

Despite the circumstances, the inauguration of the new National Council was auspicious in the context of 1950. It encouraged an ecumenical, interdenominational spirit that an increasing number of Protestants supported. According to Gallup polls, 50 percent of U.S. Protestants favored overall church union in 1950, compared to 40 percent in 1937,[20] and mainstream periodicals were full of church merger plans on both local and national levels. Lutherans were talking; Presbyterians were talking; Unitarians and Universalists were talking; Congregationalists and Evangelical and Reformed congregations were getting together; the northern and southern Methodists had reunited in 1939; and interdenominational "community churches" of mainstream bent were growing in numbers. Some leaders, like Charles Morrison, editor of *The Christian Century*, put forward elaborate plans for the unification of all Protestants.

At the same time, it must be acknowledged that the National Council drove divisive wedges into American religion. It exacerbated splits in Protestantism that had been

growing wider since earlier liberal versus fundamentalist battles. It clearly separated the "cooperative" denominations, as
they liked to call themselves, from the virtually equal number
of Protestants, not to mention thirty million Roman
Catholics who were not part of the Council. The excluded
Protestants consisted of a few denominations, largely Unitarians and Universalists, that were too liberal for the Council,
with its affirmation of basic Trinitarian beliefs, but most were
evangelical or other Protestant conservatives, from Missouri
Synod Lutherans to Southern Baptists and Pentecostals. The
attitude of the "cooperative" denominations and their leaders, as well as those of the National Council, to those separated brethren was admittedly often condescending and
unecumenical. The rural evangelicals were at best regarded as
unsophisticated and unenlightened cousins without benefit of
world-class theological education, at worst as bigoted zealots.
A little later, in 1959, Eugene Carson Blake, Stated Clerk of
the Presbyterians, while president of the National Council
commented on the "cultural crudities" of evangelical "sects"
and urged his ecumenical colleagues to help conservative
Christians overcome their "theological isolation and personal
provincialism."[21] But as we shall see, evangelicalism was
changing and growing in both spiritual and intellectual power
behind the scenes at the same time the new National Council and its kind of churches held the center of public and
media attention.

On the positive side, the National Council gave voice to
moderate and authoritative voices within American Protestantism just at the right time, at the height of despair over
McCarthyism and Korea. The tone on national and international issues was implicitly set by the selection of Henry Knox
Sherrill, Presiding Bishop of the Episcopal Church, as first
President of the National Council. On the war crisis, he,
together with most other leading clergymen in Cleveland,
was against dropping the bomb under present conditions, but
stated that morally there was no real difference between the
A-bomb and other weapons. Bishop Sherrill pleaded for

realism, saying that "absentmindedness is too often mistaken for spirituality." This prelate was a broad-minded, warm-hearted administrator and religious leader whose kindly, unruffled manner was a reassuring presence in those troubled times.

The soon-to-emerge charges from the extreme Right that the National Council was pink (if not Red) seem odd in view of its initial officers. The eight vice presidents included Harold Stassen, former Republican governor of Minnesota and perennial presidential candidate, and Mildred McAfee Horton, former president of Wellesley College and one-time head of the Waves; the treasurer was Charles E. Wilson, president of General Electric; the president of the standing committee on business and finance was Harvey Firestone, of Firestone Tire & Rubber Co. A special laymen's council of eighty to promote the Council was headed by conservative oilman J. Howard Pew and included such stalwarts of that persuasion as Noel Sargent of the National Association of Manufacturers and Charles P. Taft of Cincinnati.[22]

On the other hand, as early as December 20, *The Christian Century* pointed to the high percentage of delegates to the NCC inauguration in Cleveland who were denominational officials and from New York. The periodical asked, in the title of the article, "Where Were the Grass-Roots Representatives?" This observation highlighted a problem the new church council was never fully to overcome: the sense that, first, it disproportionately represented the Northeast where some of the major "cooperative" denominations had their greatest strength and where most were headquartered; and second, that it represented denominations, and more specifically denominational hierarchies, rather than the "grassroots" local churches and their people. The *Century* insisted then and later that until the Council was, and was seen to be, a truly popular body that directly spoke for ordinary Protestants, it would meet with only limited success. And so it was. On top of this, the cleavage down the middle of Protestantism that the distinction between "cooperatives" and outsiders indicated was as much a matter of social class, styles of education, and even regionalism as it was of strictly theological issues, and most people were half-consciously aware of this. That symbolic division did nothing to unite either church or country.

In the end, the National Council of Churches, like the World Council of Churches, was a more significant presence in the 1950s than in the following decades. That was certainly because both fitted in well with what mainstream Protestantism was in those days, or saw itself to be: institutionally and intellectually significant bodies whose leaders were the equals of other elites in government, business, education, and society at large. Looked at another way, cooperative Protestant congregations included, together with their millions of ordinary worshipers, those same classes at prayer. The mainstream not only had important ministries in its thousands of churches but also was perceived to have a unique spiritual role as custodian of the nation's profoundest moral and spiritual values. All this was changing rapidly in the volatile postwar world, but it was still the perceived reality in 1950. The supreme significance of the mainstream denominations in 1950, however, lay in their participation in the religious revival on the same level as others while providing a counterweight against the tendency to extremism of the less privileged religious traditions.

6

The Church of
the Triple Crown

In 1950 the Roman Catholic Church appeared to most of the
world to be an institution that was invincible, inflexible, and
perfectly ordered. Catholic apologists emphasized, as a mark
of the true church, its marvellous unity and sameness everywhere. Throughout the nation and the world, one could find
the same Latin mass, the same doctrines and sacraments, the
same papalist loyalty and fervent anticommunism. To enter a
Roman Catholic church in 1950 was to enter a virtual
medieval wonderland of saints, glittering candles, rows of
well-used confessional boxes, and a vast and monumental
altar against the sanctuary wall. At mass, the richly vested
priest would stand and genuflect at the altar, his back to the
congregation, as he muttered the sacred words in an ancient
tongue. He faced the altar because he was speaking not to the
congregation but to God on their behalf, and he spoke in
Latin because God in his omniscience understood that language as well as English and because the use of the same
sacred words throughout the world proclaimed the supernatural institution's extraordinary oneness. People said, whether
with pride or disparagement, that Roman Catholics were
always the same and would never change. Nor, by and large,
did the Roman Church in its perfection then have much time
for ecumenism. Its relations with different religions or
denominations were mostly limited to polemics or necessary,
if distasteful, political negotiation. Catholics were not

Pope Pius XII.

supposed to visit the services of other faiths; Catholic prelates and politicians contested forcefully for all they could get in such matters as funding for parochial schools.

Nineteen fifty was moreover a keystone year in what one sociologist of religion has called "the golden age of the American Catholic priesthood."[1] In a church once largely composed of poor immigrants often ill adapted to the New World, the priest was even more a central figure than usual in Catholicism. He was an educated natural leader, an advocate, and the cornerstone of the churchly institution that was at once a sentimental link to the distant homeland and a center of community life in a new place. His parish would educate the children of immigrants for a new and better life and link them to a powerful and regal institution in which they could take pride. The Catholic churches in the older ethnic neighborhoods of America's great cities were in 1950 imposing edifices and mighty institutions; parishioners, often of humble circumstance, took an understandable compensatory satisfaction in their church's splendor, as they also did in the quality of the priest's car and residence. He was idolized to the extent that parishioners would gather at the station to see him off on trips and greet him on his return, and the parish celebrated his birthday and ordination anniversary with great festivity. The British novelist and Catholic convert Evelyn Waugh had this to say about the matter in a remarkable 1949 article on his impressions of Catholicism in America:

> It is one of the functions of an upper class to remind the clergy of the true balance between their spiritual and their temporal positions. In most Catholic communities in the United States, so far as there is an upper class at all, the clergy themselves comprise it. From one year to another they never meet anyone better informed or more eloquent than themselves. The deference with which they are treated on purely social occasions would tend to spoil all but the most heroic humility.[2]

To be sure, some legendary priests of that era, such as Father Flanagan of Boys Town and not a few World War II Catholic chaplains, were certainly worthy of such adulation. No less important in creating the sacerdotal image of the times were Hollywood idealizations of the priest in such films as *Boys Town, Going My Way,* and *On the Waterfront.* Worthy or not, however, the senior pastor ruled the parish and his subordinate priests with unquestioned authority. He was rarely if ever seen without the black suit and clerical collar that indicated his status, and the clerical culture kept any hint of priestly scandal very quiet.

Waugh noted how much Roman Catholicism seemed at odds with fundamental features of American culture—with its dislike of titles, resentment of dogma and discipline, and repudiation of monarchy and aristocracy. Yet, "the language of the Church is largely that of the court; her liturgy was composed in lands where honorific titles of royalty were accepted naturally. . . ."[3] Nonetheless, this church, though certainly opposed with a vengeance that approached hysteria by some Protestants in 1950, seemed to be rapidly placing itself at the center of American life, and perhaps would soon be in a position to change America in some significantly Catholic way. In 1950 the expectation, hopeful or fearful depending on whether one was inside or outside the supposed monolith, was that the Roman Church would soon exercise unprecedented political and social influence without itself much changing. By the end of the century one would have to say that in fact it was the Roman Catholic Church that, largely in the wake of Vatican II, itself changed in the direction of flexibility, democracy, and "Americanization" to an extent that would have been almost unimaginable in 1950.

Many writers have attempted to capture the flavor of American Catholic life in the years around 1950. Books have ranged from bemused and nostalgic reminiscences of fish on Friday and parochial school nuns to furious indictments, like James Kavenaugh's 1960s' screed *A Modern Priest Looks at His*

Outdated Church, or to the splendid short stories of J. F. Powers, particularly in their portrayal of priestly life.[4] Two themes come through. First, one senses the tremendous pride and assurance of 1950s' Catholics in being Catholic, rejoicing in the things that made them different from their Protestant neighbors. They were proud even of their sacrifices, like getting up early for mass and doing the stations of the cross for penance, because it meant that their religion was obviously more serious—and so closer to God—than that of their easy-going fellow citizens. Second, one also senses the immense inner preoccupation with sin, above all sexual sin, that haunted not a few Catholics; one sometimes wonders if they were ever really thinking about anything else.

The novelist Whitley Strieber, writing autobiographically, put it well in a passage that reflects the interaction between the church and the intellectual life of the times:

> Still, my faith was a burning fire in me. I loved Christ and Mary especially, and used to pray with great fervor whenever I was trapped into going to church.
>
> But when I brought up Einstein with my mother, she said, "We are Catholic, Catholics are absolutist." She and I would spend hours together sitting on the front-porch steps talking. We discussed everything from general relativity to the price of tennis shoes. I used to try to talk her out of her religiosity, but she was a Catholic intellectual in the heady days of the fifties, when the mass was still full of mystery and there were many fascinating and subtle potentials for sin.[5]

However, even in 1950, the church was not quite what it seemed. Although outside observers often spoke acerbically of the standardization and uniformitarianism of American Catholicism, Waugh commented instead on "the exuberant variety of external religious forms among the American Catholics": New Orleans combined fervent devotion with skepticism, lassitude, and even witchcraft; the English-type old Catholics of Maryland were "very much like the old

Catholics of Lancashire"; the immigrant Italians and Irish and others brought all their national traits over with the faith.[6] On Sunday, June 9, 1950, Cardinal Spellman gave the papal honor *Pro Ecclesia et Pontifice* to three African American Catholic laymen, saying, "St. Patrick's Cathedral has been the scene of many ceremonies and I have taken part in many of them. But none has given me more pleasure and satisfaction than this one today." At the time there were some forty thousand black Catholics in the New York archdiocese, out of some six hundred thousand total Catholics in all the parts of the city covered by Spellman's jurisdiction.[7]

Nor was diversity only cultural and not intellectual. Already in 1950 the Jesuit order, the intellectual heavyweights of the church, had begun a cautious tilt toward the Left, as if to counterbalance the general rightward swing of the church. Jesuits such as John Courtney Murray, who was to present a Catholic rationale for separation of church and state; Gustave Weigel, a pioneer of Catholic ecumenism; and John La Farge, advocate for social and racial justice, were being heard, and they would be heard more widely as the 1950s advanced.[8] On the other hand, some Jesuits more resembled Fr. Walsh of Georgetown, alleged confidante of McCarthy. Indeed, as the McCarthy controversy gathered steam, and the Jesuit magazine *America* was caught in the middle of it, certain Jesuit houses were reportedly so deeply divided that any discussion of the senator had to be forbidden in the common room.

Diversity did not stop with modest advances in Jesuit thinking. In February 1950 Sally Whalen Cassidy wrote in the Paulist intellectual periodical *The Catholic World*, "The Church in this country receives plenty of criticism from its own members, or to put it more fairly, there are ardent if highly articulate groups who are not afraid to snap at any likely target in America." She mentioned magazines like *Integrity*, *The Catholic Worker*, *The Grail*, and *The Catholic Interracialist*, which lashed out at what they considered the superficiality of much Catholic concern for the worker, the meagerness of Catholic intellectual life, the lack of "initiativeness" in Catholic institutions of learning, the lack of interest in problems like race and housing, and the church's "unenviable reputation as one of the major authoritarian groups in America." The commentator noted that "Catholic America does not lack its revolutionaries," mentioning particularly the Catholic Worker movement, "which is looked upon with awe by Europeans."[9]

The Catholic Workers, co-founded by the convert Dorothy Day (whose case for sainthood is now being advanced and whose autobiography, *The Long Loneliness*, was published in 1952), was indeed one of the most remarkable developments in American Catholicism. Centered in New York, it was at the height of its contrarian fame under its founder in 1950. Followers of the movement established houses in desperate working-class districts of the great cities, where like the early Franciscans they ministered to the poor, the exploited, and the marginally employed or unemployed and lived in poverty themselves, not hesitating to promote pro-labor and other radical causes in their periodical ("never sold for more than a penny") *The Catholic Worker*. Its positions often ran quite contrary to the increasingly conservative outlook of the hierarchy, yet Dorothy Day and *The Catholic Worker* were not silenced. For one thing, she insisted that her position was true Catholic Christianity, which had nothing to do with communism or secular socialism. She was not, she said, a liberal Catholic but a radical Catholic, which simply meant one who tried to live the gospel seriously and completely. Francis Cardinal Spellman, the conservative autocrat of the New York archdiocese, though he might seem to embody everything in the church of 1950 that the Catholic Workers criticized, appeared somewhat in awe of Dorothy Day and insisted on leaving her alone. When once asked why, he replied simply, "She might be a saint."[10]

Spellman was the dominant figure of American Catholicism in 1950. Named Archbishop of New York in 1939 as one of the first major appointments of the new Pope Pius XII, he was not raised to the cardinalate until 1946 because of the war. The pattern of his episcopate was already in place and well known by 1950. He ran his diocese with an iron hand, insisting on obedience from his priests, down to their short clerical haircuts and clean-shaven cheeks. He also demanded administrative efficiency of them, especially in fundraising, at which he was himself a master. In the yeasty postwar years his archdiocese was the largest single non-governmental building contractor in New York as innumerable new churches, schools, convents, hospitals, and other works arose, usually debt-free upon their completion. Chief of Catholic chaplains in the armed forces during World War II and after, Spellman was especially devoted to the military, perhaps admiring them as fellow devotees of obedience, efficiency, and dedication to a great cause. His Christmas visits to the troops in far-flung locations from Europe to Vietnam became legendary.

Cardinal Spellman was an uncomplicated patriot who believed fully in the righteousness of America, and of its way of life as he understood it—life centered around the traditional, godly family, or, for the heroic military man or celibate priest, around a career embodying soldierly virtue. The American way of life rejected all foreign "isms" except Catholicism—though Spellman would insist above all that Catholicism was not foreign but as American as the proverbial apple pie, and that it was here to stay, grow, and prosper. No cause was dearer to him than making this clear to other Americans, whether it was news they wanted to hear or not. Thus, if Catholic children are as American as any other, he contended in season and out, the parochial school education to which they are religiously obligated ought to be supported by the state on the grounds of their families' religious freedom as surely as that of children in public schools, which are covertly Protestant or secular anyway.

Spellman's support of the official Catholic position in another heated issue of 1950, the appointment of a U.S. diplomatic envoy to the Vatican to replace Myron Taylor, the President's "personal representative," was, however, perfunctory. Privately, he was jealous on behalf of his own role, supported by well-maintained personal lines of communication with key Vatican insiders, as chief conduit of influence between America and the Holy See, and he feared that an embassy would diminish it.

The New York cardinal was fervently anticommunist, considering opposition to that atheistic system basic to Americanism and Catholicism alike, and he allowed himself in the name of patriotism to support the likes of Francisco Franco in Spain and Joseph McCarthy at home. He loved playing on the political stage, sensing (not always rightly) that, with New York's Catholic vote in his pocket and his unique influence through bishop-protégés in the rest of the country, and his excellent connections in Rome, he could deal from a position of strength with highly placed persons in Washington, including Presidents Roosevelt and Truman, and with innumerable city and state politicos in New York. Sometimes it almost seemed he sent his memos, made his phone calls, and conducted his whispered conversations at public functions just for the sake of the game, but in the end two concerns were primary: personal power and the power of the Roman Catholic Church as a force in the nation and the world.

Cardinal Spellman had a sentimental side as well, which somehow existed alongside the ruthless manipulation of power known all too well to the priests, bishops, politicians, contractors, and union officials with whom he did daily business. Not only did he give leeway to the fierce holiness of Dorothy Day, in 1950 he was, together with everything else, writing a novel, *The Foundling*, a cloying but sometimes moving story of a child at the Foundling Hospital he had himself established in New York.[11] He arranged for all royalties from the book to go to the hospital, and he liked to be photographed beaming with his cherub's smile surrounded by cute children. But his headquarters continued to be known as the Powerhouse.

Spellman's character, both in its irascibility and in the bathos that oddly complemented his pugnacity, came to public attention in the summer of 1949, in the shape of his famous controversy with Eleanor Roosevelt over the simmering issue of public funding for church schools. The former First Lady had written in her "My Day" column that schools supported by taxes should be free of any private or religious control, for the sake of separation of church and state. Spellman, passionately on the other side of the issue and eagerly wanting for the church the billions of dollars at stake, as well as hating the kind of liberals who liked Mrs. Roosevelt, issued a public response to his adversary that revealed the temperamental, vindictive side his close associates had long known. He accused her of being anti-Catholic, taxing her with not being able to find it in her heart "to defend the rights of innocent little children," and spoke of the sacrifices "America's Catholic youth" had made in the war. The prelate reminded her that she must have seen those wounded bodies on her many wartime hospital visits, and he then asked her, "how was it that your own heart was not purged of all prejudices by what you saw, these, our sons, suffer?"[12] He went so far as to call her "unworthy of being an American mother."

Eleanor Roosevelt issued a dignified reply, disavowing any prejudice against the Roman Catholic Church, mentioning her work for Al Smith's presidential campaign in 1928. While denying that she was attacking Spellman personally, she reiterated her belief that those who chose private or religious schools for their children should pay for them and not expect the taxpayers to do so. She said that when she visited the army hospitals, she did not even ask the wounded their religion. While Spellman had defenders in the controversy, a great many Americans were offended at the excesses of his letter. The bitter exchange finally had to be resolved by a personal envoy of President Truman, who brokered an uneasy truce. The matter exacerbated the Protestant-Catholic tensions characteristic of 1950, when Spellman reigned in New York but was increasingly mistrusted and disliked by Protestants— as well as, covertly, by some Catholics who would have preferred the church wear a more liberal and irenic face.

Catholic-Protestant relations were only worsened in 1950 by the fallout from Paul Blanshard's explosive 1949 best-seller *American Freedom and Catholic Power*. The book was a wholesale attack on the Roman Catholic Church's alleged intolerance and authoritarianism, its political influence in the United States, and its attempts to enforce Catholic values in such areas as medicine, law, and education through undue pressure, including boycotts. Blanshard also cited its disturbing closeness to European and Latin American dictators.

The book provoked heated responses from Catholic and some independent reviewers, whose words on the subject, sometimes together with responses from Blanshard, rippled through intellectual and religious periodicals all through 1950. Critics charged that Blanshard's documentation was selective if not incorrectly interpreted, and his conclusions shaped by preconceptions about Catholicism. One interesting consequence was the removal of the liberal magazine *The Nation* from public school libraries in New York City following its publication of a series of articles by Blanshard in 1947 and 1948, characterized in 1950 by the Jesuit magazine *America* as "cheap anti-Catholic propaganda." The Jesuit editors argued that banning *The Nation* was not a suppression of legitimate free speech because the Blanshard articles registered a religious point of view and so its availability under the auspices of the city's schools violated separation of church and state. Denominational and other religious publications were usually not found in public-school libraries either.[13]

For Roman Catholicism, 1950 was a year that epitomized

what the Pius XII, pre-Vatican II church meant in America and the world. At least from an external point of view, it was an age of devout parish life, parochial schools taught by white-coifed nuns, docile church colleges, and rapidly growing numbers of churches, institutions, and members. The intellectual tone of Catholic colleges and thinkers in this apparent heyday of a monolithic and authoritarian church was theologically, though not always politically, conservative, Thomistic, and seemingly confident of a Catholic future for America. Catholic intellectuals were eager to press the claims of "Catholic civilization" on the still basically Protestant nation, yet on some deep level they seemed still defensive about Catholicism's place in the Republic. Of Catholic colleges in this era, Evelyn Waugh had written that they were not meant to be Harvards, Oxfords, or Sorbonnes, but "their object is to transform a proletariat into a bourgeoisie, to produce a faithful laity, qualified to take part in the general life of the nation, and in this they are manifestly successful."[14] Others put it more bluntly: their purpose was to keep their docents virgin in both mind and body.

If the appearance of worldly success meant anything, Roman Catholicism in 1950 had it. Seminaries were growing dramatically as returning veterans and youth affected by the expansive mood in religion and especially Catholicism flocked to offer themselves to the sacerdotal life. In 1938 there were 209 seminaries preparing men for the priesthood; by 1950 the number had grown to 388, training no fewer than 26,322 students. In retrospect one sees that this upsurge was ephemeral. Within twenty-five years 259 seminaries would close their doors, though many of them were sparkling new buildings erected during the postwar, Cardinal Spellman-era construction boom. Moreover, of all those who were housed in them in 1950 many did not stay to be ordained, and of those that were, as many as 50 percent left the priesthood during the turmoil of the 1960s and 1970s. An exact percentage is hard to assess, but certainly less than 10 percent of those in

1950 seminary classrooms were to be priests at the end of the century, still ministering in a church and world extraordinarily different from that of their youth.[15]

Monasteries and convents were also in a dramatic growth cycle in 1950, partly inspired by the example of Thomas Merton's surprising best-seller *The Seven Storey Mountain*, still near the top of the lists on the eve of 1950. In 1949, fourteen Trappistine nuns had arrived from Ireland to establish the female wing of the famously ascetic Cistercians of the Strict Observance, or Trappists, in the United States. Other monasteries in the contemplative mode that many might have thought alien to the American spirit were also being founded in this day of monastic renaissance: the Carthusian order received a remarkable level of publicity for a society of hermits who, apart from their celebrated liqueur, Chartreuse, were known only for praying as much as fourteen hours a day in remote, isolated cloisters. But the successful endeavor of Fr. Thomas Moore, a former psychiatrist, to plant a Carthusian house in Vermont strangely thrilled the traditionalist, half-inward religious imagination of 1950 and was national news.[16] (The Carthusian story in *Time* was set alongside an equally typical item on the sales approach to church growth.)

It was an age of celebrity converts to the church, among them Thomas Merton, of course; Henry Ford II; Fulton Oursler, who had come to the church in 1943 while preparing his celebrated life of Jesus, *The Greatest Story Ever Told*; and Clare Booth Luce, wife of the publisher of *Life* and *Time* and a potent literary and political figure in her own right. The presence of eminent converts, especially intellectuals, in the church of 1950 was a proud and yet disturbing matter for other Catholics. It seemed to vindicate their loyalty to the faith to see thinkers of the first rank perceive in it the marks of the true church, yet at the same time the converts were not always predictable in what they said or did. For they were not as accustomed as "cradle Catholics" to the everyday practice of the religion or to thinking in conformity with the church on all issues.

The converts generally were seeking security and tradition, wanting the strength and comfort of the past, and often felt aesthetic frisson at the beauty and power of Rome at its best. But theirs was not always an easy path. The drama of a conversion like John Henry Newman's or Merton's, or of a deathbed scene like the set piece in the convert Evelyn Waugh's wonderful novel *Brideshead Revisited*, is one thing; but some converts found that the day-to-day life of the church they glamorized did not always put it to best advantage, nor was its authority always as easy to accept as when they had first sought out the rock of Peter. Intellectual converts, if traditionalist, were for that reason used to going against the grain in a liberal world and unaccustomed to clerical censorship. Whether intentionally or not, converts could hardly help but be more highly individualistic in their relation to the church than those born to it, for they had come to the faith in their own way, from out of a morass of non-Catholic connections, and they usually lacked the benefit of a thoroughly Catholic education. The hierarchy celebrated them in principle, but was at times wary of the provocative witness of a Dorothy Day or the later Thomas Merton.[17]

Many intellectual converts of the 1950s and before had come in under the influence of the movement known as the Catholic Revival, which affected Catholic thinkers after World War I. That watershed event had led to a new outburst of Catholic thought, especially social thought; one early fruit was the establishment of *Commonweal* magazine, intended to be a vehicle for fresh ideas and connections between United States and European Catholic intellectual life. An idea that excited some American Catholics, including converts, was what was termed Distributism. Its origins lay with such English Catholic thinkers, themselves largely converts, as G. K. Chesterton, Hilaire Belloc, and Eric Gill, who rejected capitalism in favor of an economic ideology that called for the redistribution of land so that urbanites could return to the soil and feel an organic connection with the earth. Its aficionados, like most romancers of rural and peasant life, favored folk crafts, decentralization, regional variations, and dialects.[18] In America, the movement established natural ties with the Southern Agrarian movement, which held to broadly similar ideals and was popular with some Southern writers and philosophers. Favoring Southern regionalism (and dialect), the movement was both conservative and radical; it combined support for a traditional, decentralized, rural way of life with a harsh critique of modern industrial capitalism worthy of a Marxist. Dorothy Day was in some sympathy with the movement; her preconversion lover, Forster Betterham, had been a Southern Agrarian. Those of the Distributist or Southern Agrarian schools who became Catholic naturally valued the church's roots in European rural peasant society, wished for it to have a similar role in America, and held that it was in any case an irreplaceable social and cultural treasure, the foundation of any truly rooted and refined society.

A case in point was the distinguished literary critic Allen Tate, who entered the church in 1950. Long associated with Southern Agrarianism, and a close acquaintance of Dorothy Day, he was expected to become the sophisticated man of letters who would give tone to the Catholic intellectual revival of the 1950s, putting its vision of Catholic civilization on the larger stage, and for a time he did this. But for him as for others the convert's role was not easy, and in the next decade Vatican II meant a difficult passage for most pre-1960s converts, above all intellectuals like himself. After the Council the church they had once joined was no longer there, nor was their own intellectual status the same; even if they had been looked on as 1950s Catholic liberals, that was in a pre-conciliar context that after John XXIII and Paul VI seemed as hopelessly dated as Distributism or Southern Agrarianism. Nothing is more passé than a radicalism whose time has come and gone, unless it is a reactionary conservatism of similar vintage.

The Catholic Revival and the excitement of 1950s' Catholic intellectual life, with its neoscholasticism and its visions of a traditionalist yet radically Catholic, share-the-wealth civilization, had something of both. But it was radical and conservative in ways that meshed poorly with the 1960s versions of radicalism and conservatism, not least because the church in which it was based had upended its vision of the relation of religion and world.

None other than the mentor of more 1950s' converts than anyone else, Fulton Sheen, complained that all the Council had done was buy into the secular worldview, as though Catholicism could no longer be anything other than the shadow-religion of a secular world. Others, of course, insisted that now for the first time in centuries the church was truly up-to-date (Pope John's *aggiornamento*) and open to the world it was supposed to serve. Pre-conciliar Catholic Revivalists had dreamed of the church as a high-towered stronghold set against the modern world; the new wave saw the church instead as thoroughly in the world without pretense and accepting all that could be accepted, the humble servant of all in the name of Christ. All this was symbolized by new mentalities, by the doing away with many symbols of Catholic separateness, and by new ways of worship. Tate's own Catholic commitment languished after the Council, though it was never repudiated.[19]

Msgr. Fulton Sheen, the charismatic radio priest whose even more successful television program would commence in 1952, had long conducted a well-known instruction class for converts, and was famous for his success in this field. In many ways Sheen's thought, reflected in his 1949 book, *Peace of Soul*, represented the spirit of Catholic 1950 as well as any source. As we have seen, it presented Catholicism as the answer to the issues raised by the popular psychology of the day: anxiety, frustration, marital instability, and the rest of the demons haunting the American mind. To be sure, there were those who thought that the conjoining of confessional and psychoanalytic couch was too easy, and in the words of New York psychiatrist Fredric Wertham in an article provocatively entitled "The Air-Conditioned Conscience," it was likely to lead to strange phenomena in "the suggestive twilight of abnormal psychology and supernatural revelation."[20] Consciously or unconsciously, however, what most people, including Catholics, really wanted in 1950 was assurance that the traditional teachings of religion and the latest products of science, not least depth psychology, were truly compatible. What was best of all, in fact, was what Sheen declared: that psychiatry did a good job of indicating problems in modern language for modern people, but the church's traditional teachings and sacraments were ultimately the best cure of all.[21]

In 1950 Sheen arrived in New York to be made director of the national office of the Propagation of the Faith, the vast organization that raised money for foreign missions. Cardinal Spellman was convinced that Sheen's charisma and popularity would increase donations but also expected that the presence of the well-known priest in his bailiwick would redound to his own prestige, and that he would, as usual, keep control of the money and policy from behind the scenes. He also appreciated the radio personality's fervent anticommunism, though Sheen was, overall, not as politically conservative as the archbishop.

The personalities of the two stellar Catholic figures seemed to contrast well. Sheen was a handsome, articulate, and gifted public speaker, deeply grounded in the mystical life of the religion, but not very interested in administration or church politics. Spellman, on the other hand, was barely competent in the pulpit and only conventionally pious, but he was a consummate administrator and church politician whose forte was fund-raising and string-pulling on a person-to-person basis.

Before long, however, the two prelates began to clash; both were accustomed to center stage and celebrity status, and New York was not big enough for two international ecclesiastical stars. Conflicts arose over their relative authority and prestige in the Propagation of the Faith organization, and over the distribution of its largesse. However, the problems did not surface openly until after 1950 and Sheen's 1951 elevation to the episcopate—in Rome, because, he told friends, he did not want Spellman to officiate.[22]

Rome. Above all 1950 was a year of Catholic loyalty to a pope who expanded the scope of doctrinal orthodoxy while setting his face firmly against the evil spreading from the east. Pope Pius XII had been elevated to the chair of Peter in 1939, on the eve of World War II. Before then, he had spent many tumultuous years as papal envoy in Munich and Berlin, followed by service as Secretary of State to Pius XI. His preparation for the supreme office had been chiefly in the Vatican's foreign service, and there were those who considered his response to the evils of fascism and Nazism couched too cautiously in the language of the diplomat rather than of the pastor, much less the fiery prophet. But as if to make up for past weaknesses, his cold war stand against communism was unbending, and his image was increasingly that of world pastor and defender. In numerous photos and flickering newsreels one saw his lean, ascetic figure robed all in white, arms stretched out as though to embrace the earth, eyes raised to heaven. He seemed already more spirit than flesh, yet he could turn his attention to this world when the duty of his office called, and so it did in the great struggle to which he dedicated himself. The exigencies of that titanic conflict seemed to call for the church to postpone any significant reform until another day, probably after the passing of that last pope named Pius.

For that pontiff's church was the final epoch in the chronicles of the rigid, antimodern style that Catholicism had acquired, especially since the nineteenth-century reign of Pius IX, he of the notoriously antimodern Syllabus of Errors and the loss of the temporal power. The manner had been reinforced by the narrow piety and painfully divisive antimodernism campaign of Pius X early in the twentieth century, and it had not been significantly eased by Pius XI, despite his social justice encyclical *Quadragesimo Anno* (1931) (together with the great *Rerum Novarum* [1891] of Leo XIII, the inspiration of all Catholic social liberals in 1950) or by his confrontations—and accommodations—with Mussolini and Hitler. All this was the ultramontane, monarchical style of papal centralism in what has been called the "Pian Age" of Roman Catholicism. After the death of Pius XII in 1958 there would be no popes of that name in the twentieth century, and his successor, John XXIII, was a different kind of churchman altogether.

For Pius XII in 1950, as for most of his followers, the anticommunist conflict was holy and total war. On June 13, 1949, the pope, through the Holy Office, had promulgated a decree excommunicating Catholics who willingly adhered to the doctrines of atheistic communism. An article on "Communism," written in 1950 by John F. Cronin, assistant director of the Social Action Department of the National Catholic Welfare Council, acknowledged the social evils of early capitalism that had given rise to Marxism, as well as to Christian reformism, but pointed out that Marx differed from the latter by holding mere reform inadequate and unscientific. Unlike Christians, Marxists believed revolution to be both necessary and inevitable, and they called for the complete abolition of private property in productive goods. The church had to oppose communism, and also socialism as it defined it, because of its "atheism, materialism, and denial of basic human rights."[23]

Papal authority over the entire church was reinforced by the encyclical of August 1950, *Humani Generis*. This wide-ranging document confirmed papal decision as the definitive word on doctrine. Theologians had freedom to debate undecided issues, it allowed, so long as they were prepared in the end to accept the judgment of the church voiced by its supreme pontiff; when Rome has spoken, the case is finished. This letter to the faithful also reinforced the supremacy of

Thomism as the church's reigning philosophy, and dealt with certain contemporary "false opinions which threaten to undermine the foundations of Catholic doctrine." Among those was excessive adherence to modern science, including the theory of evolution "which has not been fully proved even in the domain of natural sciences," but which has been used to "audaciously support the monistic and pantheistic opinion that the world is in continual evolution," or the false opinion called "polygenism" that contends that humans are not all genetically descended from Adam and Eve. No less unwise is the related idea of "historicism," making doctrinal teachings contingent on their cultural and historical setting, or any "eirenism" that imprudently minimizes religious differences. In all of these matters, the church, while valuing human reason, must always fall back on the fullness of revelation and the ecclesiastical teaching magisterium.[24]

The Pian Age and the spirit of *Humani Generis* seemed to be mystically complemented by the 1950 promulgation of the dogma of the Assumption of the Blessed Virgin Mary bodily into heaven, that supreme act of solitary papal authority and of a distinctively Roman Catholic Thomistic theological style. In the Apostolic Constitution *Munificentissimus Deus*, the pope announced, "We pronounce, declare, and define to be a dogma revealed by God that the Immaculate Mother of God, Mary, ever virgin, when the course of her life on earth was finished, was taken up body and soul into heaven." The entire declaration was a document running to some six thousand words, the original on twenty-six pages of parchment made from the whole skins of six sheep.[25] This solemn definition was pronounced in a great ceremony in St. Peter's Cathedral, Rome, on All Saints Day, November 1, 1950, in the presence of thirty-six cardinals and 480 archbishops and bishops.

The climax of a trend toward greater formal doctrinal authority on the part of the Roman pontiff, the definition of the Assumption as dogma was the first and thus far only exercise of papal infallibility, in the strict sense of a formal pronouncement on faith or morals spoken *ex cathedra* by the Vicar of Christ, since that infallibility was itself formally defined by the First Vatican Council in 1870. It was, however, the second and thus far the last in the tradition of modern papal definitions of dogma, the first having been Pius IX's *ex cathedra* pronouncement of the Immaculate Conception in 1854. This dogma, not to be confused as it often is with the Virgin Birth of Christ, states that the Mother of Jesus, though conceived in the normal manner, was uniquely preserved from the original sin ordinarily transmitted to all human flesh through conception.

The Assumption definition was a significant advance in the consolidation of papal authority, though it should be emphasized that this does not mean that the Assumption was a "new" doctrine, in the way that many non-Catholics seemed to take it to be. On the contrary, the point of a papal definition is simply to state formally that the whole church has long since come to consensus on a matter, and therefore it must be regarded as part of the official faith of the church. The Assumption had been universally taught in the Roman Catholic Church, and celebrated on its feast day of August 15, for centuries. A few theologians, mostly in northern Europe, were disturbed in 1950 by the dogma's lack of clear scriptural or traditional warrant, or felt, mainly because of the damage it would do ecumenical relations, that the timing of the definition was inopportune. It was against them that the paragraphs in *Humani Generis* on final papal authority were in part directed. But the formal definition actually made no practical difference in the faith or worship of the vast majority of Roman Catholics.

Protestants on the other hand were seriously critical of the "new" doctrine. Article after article from that camp emphasized the lack of scriptural or historical basis for belief that the mother of Jesus, after dying in the normal manner, had been taken body and soul into heaven in a kind of reflection of the resurrection and ascension of Jesus, there to reign as Queen of Angels and supreme intercessor on behalf of mortals here below. An editorial in *The Christian Century* said that the definition put the church "in opposition to all the canons of historical scholarship as that discipline is today understood," and claimed bitterly that it would only drive intelligent and educated persons away from Christianity, thereby aiding those in the Kremlin and elsewhere who wished to attack religion.[26] Certainly the Assumption did nothing to alleviate the icy Catholic-Protestant relationships characteristic of the day.

In fact, an informal survey of the media in 1950 leads one to the surprising observation that the definition of the Assumption caused more excitement among non-Catholics than among most Catholics, who took it in stride. At the same time, some non-Catholics and Catholic converts saw the dogma has having profound positive significance. The great analytic psychologist Carl Jung, son of a Protestant pastor, went so far as to call the definition "the most important religious event since the Reformation." In terms of the archetypes of the unconscious that were so fundamental to Jung, it meant that the heretofore all-male Trinity was now completed as a Quaternity by incorporating female nature into the highest heavens, all of profound symbolic significance for the human psyche. With only slightly more reserve, *Life* magazine (edited by the staunch Presbyterian Henry Luce, whose wife was the convert Clare Booth Luce) called it, "for Catholics the most important theological event of the century."[27] While no doubt extreme, such assessments of the dogma's importance in the year of its proclamation reminds us of how profoundly introspective and intrapsychic were important segments of the intellectual world of 1950, deeply tinged as it was by existentialism and depth psychology, and how important events in the Vatican were to a world dominated by the clash of absolutes.

The distinguished novelist and Catholic convert Graham Greene, in an interesting article, set the definition squarely in the context of the present world struggle of the Christian faith and its values against foes near and far, especially communism. After a lengthy rehearsal of the many apparitions and miracles attributed to the Virgin Mary in the course of the modern battle for Christianity, Greene opined that "sometimes it seems as though the supernatural were gathering its forces for our support, and whom should we expect in the vanguard but Our Lady? For the attack on the Son has always come through the Mother. If you wish to discredit the divinity of Christ you discredit the Virgin Birth; if you wish to discredit the manhood of Christ you discredit the motherhood of Our Lady." Recourse to her has always been especially fervent in time of crisis, we were told, such as when the Turks seemed on the point of conquering Europe in the sixteenth century, and Pope Pius V countered by instituting the Marian Feast of the Most Holy Rosary. Now the world faced an even heavier threat from the east. The dogma of the Assumption, Greene considered, was an especially appropriate response to the kind of apostasy the church now faced: "Today the human body is regarded as expendable material"—no other conclusion could be drawn from the twentieth century's grim annals of war, holocaust, exploitation, and callous indifference to suffering. But the Assumption, in glorious contrast, affirms the resurrection, and hence the eternal worth, of the physical body as well as the soul.[28]

It was inevitable that, in the year 1950 when the world's two great powers were locked in a struggle with immense theological dimensions, the cold war significance of the definition would be assessed by worldly and worshipful observers alike. Although the bodily rising of the Blessed Virgin Mary into heaven might seem a rather recondite churchly matter, people naturally asked if an ideological or even political rationale for making its definition as dogma precisely at this time lurked in the back of the papal mind, as the Korean war raged and many expected World War III at any moment. Some

Catholics insisted with Graham Greene that the recent Marian doctrines, the Immaculate Conception and the Assumption alike, argued in the church's own way against the faith's modern enemy, the Enlightenment and all its works, including Marxism and communism. Claiming that human nature is merely material, historical, and at best rational in only a this-worldly sense, the eighteenth century and its aftermath denied the reality of both sin and grace. But the emergent doctrinal model of Mary, in the face of modernity, subtly asserted the reality of evil and the potency of its antidote. It was real sin that required her suffering and that of her Son; it was supernatural grace that, in her, overcame sin from the moment of her conception and made her an image of the triumphant sovereignty of the grace that all beings here below can receive.

All this was brought home to ordinary Catholics as 1950 became a Holy Year—a "Year of Pardon" when the faithful could receive special plenary indulgences (full remission of the punishment of sins in purgatory) by making a pilgrimage to Rome and there performing certain religious rites. More than that, a Holy Year was also an occasion for Catholics to celebrate the faith and reaffirm loyalty to the Roman See. Nineteen fifty was a particularly auspicious and important year to do this. There was much for which to be thankful—the end of the war and the remarkable growth of the church in the United States—and much for which to pray in the terrible persecution of the church in other parts of the world. There was also reason in such perilous times to gather around the papal throne in loyal devotion as the struggle against atheistic communism accelerated. Looking forward to the sacred year, Percy Winner in late 1949 viewed it as a symbolic celebration and consolidation not only of spiritual values but also of the Holy See's growing postwar political power. Thanks in part to active papal initiatives, Catholic-oriented statesmen or parties held office in much of Europe west of the Iron Curtain and in Latin America. Spain and Portugal lay peacefully

under church-friendly dictators. Moreover, Catholics offered
potent democratic alternatives to communism in France and
Italy (the latter still feeling the divisiveness of its political
defeat of communism in the traumatic elections of 1948, in
which the United States and the Vatican unabashedly inter-
vened), as well as holding power in Belgium, West Germany,
and Austria. Probably no other Holy Year since the Middle
Ages has had quite the political as well as spiritual significance
of 1950.

The season of grace was opened on Christmas Eve 1949
by Pope Pius XII, who, according to *Newsweek*, "seemed
pale, gray, and tired with his 73 years, and staggered under
the tremendous weight of his cope." Nonetheless the pontiff rose to the auspicious occasion, emphasizing in his
Christmas message the "effrontery with which the united
front of militant atheism advances." But his main point, in
the face of this, was to invite humanity to return to God and
the church of Rome. He called 1950 the "decisive year" for
communists, Jews, dissidents, schismatics, pagans, sinners,
and atheists to come back to forgiveness and reconciliation.
Pilgrims to Rome in this year would, he prayerfully hoped,
be "the faithful vanguard in the crusade for peace. . . .From
far and near, every continent and region, from every country and by every route, crossing the ocean or flying through
the air, come here to Rome which opens to you its ever-
maternal arms."[29]

Certainly the Roman and papal significance of the Holy
Year was profound, and the occasion came at a time when that
emphasis was especially beneficial to the Vatican in its world
struggles. Publicity out of Rome never failed to exalt the Holy
Father as Vicar of Christ, absolute ruler of the Catholic
Church, and putative leader of all Christendom. Newspaper
and magazine photos and cinema newsreels of the colorful
doings in Rome inevitably focused on the pontiff in magnifi-
cent vestments, enthroned while cardinals kissed his hands
and abbots his feet. Ironically, none caught the feel of papal-
centric Rome like that nemesis of the church's politics Paul

Blanshard, *The Nation*'s correspondent in Rome during the Holy Year.

> Its most interesting feature is the Pope himself. He fits into the ceremonial atmosphere perfectly. His thin ascetic face, his luminous eyes, his kindly smile, his long graceful hands combine to make him a natural idol for the faithful. His reputation for personal piety is unchallenged. The sight of him in robes of white or of scarlet trimmed with gold, with a triple tiara or a white skull cap on his head, waving his hands in graceful benediction from his gestatorial chair, which is borne on the shoulders of two rows of stalwart guards dressed in scarlet uniforms, fulfills every pilgrim's dream. For good measure, at canonization ceremonies the Vatican jeweler carries two extra tiaras, and behind the Pope's chair are fan-bearers with huge Oriental fans.[30]

In the end, over three million of the faithful made it to Rome during the Holy Year, more than initially projected, but it was largely Italians who swelled the crowds at the great events. Pilgrims from farther away, including the United States, were disappointing in number. Travel was expensive in 1950; much of the world was still on austerity budgets, and the Iron Curtain countries made exit permits for their oppressed believers exceedingly difficult. On the other hand, the modern news media made vicarious participation possible and helped compensate for physical distance. Pictures and articles abounded to make the year a tremendous publicity bonanza for Roman Catholicism. A feature-length documentary on the Holy Year, unabashedly papalist, was shown in movie theaters across America and around the world. All in all, the Holy Year of 1950 was far more important as an event in religious history than any other before or since, and it was a prime channel for the spiritual surges of that apocalyptic-seeming year.

Holy Year in Rome was an appropriate symbol for Roman Catholicism in 1950 as well, for it was indeed in that year the church of Rome, rather than of, say, Galilee or even Jerusalem. The Christian qualities midcentury Catholicism brought to the world were profoundly Roman: order, discipline, dedication, surety, pride, spectacle, administrative sense. The church of 1950 was an empire of the spirit such as the world had never seen, an imperium of mind as well as an institution, supported by worldwide vision and a complex but logical cosmology. It was Christ in the person of his Vicar magnified by the Roman lens into the spiritual Caesar of a new imperial realm, its legions mighty on behalf of the forces of light. This empire was nowhere more truly perceived in its better nature than in the relatively new American provinces, uncontaminated by too much history and eager to believe in all that Rome professed to be in 1950.

Yet even by 1950 there was some slippage behind the scenes in Catholic America and its priesthood. A younger, more affluent and better-educated postwar generation of Catholic youth, often veterans, was entering the priesthood or, if lay, moving with their families away from the old ethnic neighborhoods to the suburbs, leaving behind the old-fashioned powerhouse churches and the clerical prefects they had supported. Furthermore, though it would not become readily apparent until the Vatican II era of the next decade, younger Catholics, even younger priests, were becoming restless, more prepared than their forebears to ask questions and countenance reform.

Sally Whalen Cassidy had written of certain Catholic youth even in 1950: "Every college has a few of these militants. Morose and bitter though they may seem now, they are the seed of any change to come." For now they were held back, not only by the rigidity of the church in an anxious and conservative year, but also by its "commercialization" and the "infantilism" of the laity.[31] But already the perceptive could detect signs of change to come.

In 1950, though, all this was well concealed behind the Roman Church's carefully constructed façade. In the United States, it was growing perceptibly in numbers—of laypeople, priests, monks, and nuns—in financial strength, in buildings and institutions, and in self-confidence. That church may have been exclusivist, ingrown, and rigid, but the virtues corresponding to those qualities—confidence, community, stability in thought and life—were clearly ones for which millions yearned in times troubled and too rapidly changing.

7

The Week the World Might Have Ended

June 25, 1950! Communist armies from the north pour south across the thirty-eighth parallel, an artificial boundary set up by the occupying powers five years before. Banner headlines and tense-voiced newscasts spread the news around the world. The question on everyone's mind: Would this be it—the beginning of World War III, a conflict many then regarded as inevitable, the Armageddon-lik showdown between the mighty communist and capitalist power blocs? If so, that conflict would very likely become nuclear, and though a victor might emerge, little would be left that was neither dead nor radioactive. Life for millions, might now be a matter of days— and death might be far preferable to the lingering effects of radiation, or existence in a world bombed back to savagery.

Nonetheless, no sooner had the blow come than the world reacted. It is possible that the North Koreans and their sponsors in revolutionary Red China and the Soviet Union expected the West to bluster but do nothing, in the end accepting a military fait accompli on the ground. After all, Dean Acheson, the U.S. Secretary of State, had never promised to defend South Korea even when pressed for a definitive statement. His State Department had earlier protested the dictatorial ways of the South Korean president, Syngman Rhee, and in January 1950 he had said that Korea was outside the U.S. defense perimeter. The declared

Two American soldiers surrender to two Chinese People's Volunteers, Korean peninsula.

149

policy crafted by President Truman and Dean Acheson, infuriating to the administration's vociferous right-wing critics, was not the defeat of communism but its "containment."

Dean Acheson was a special bête noire of the Right, which saw sufficient reason to mistrust him because he happened to be in office at the time of the "loss" of China. The Right was further enraged by his well-known refusal to "turn his back" on Alger Hiss. Nor did the dapper moustache and impeccable suit, together with the elegant, sometimes sarcastic, Ivy League manners of this son of an Episcopal bishop of Connecticut, endear the Secretary to grassroots Americans. He was always able to make international matters sound irritatingly complex, as though only highly educated elites like himself could understand them, much in contrast to the straightforward midwestern anticommunism of the likes of Robert Taft and Joseph McCarthy. Acheson responded in kind, referring in his memoirs to his rightist critics as "primitives," and citing none other than Nathan A. Pusey, president of Harvard, to the effect that back in Appleton, Wisconsin, where they had both lived, the young McCarthy used to read Hitler's *Mein Kampf*. Chuckling, the future senator would reportedly say of that authority's rhetorical methods, "Now that's the way to do it!"[1]

Stung by criticism of his January remarks that Korea was outside the defense perimeter, Acheson was now determined to show that he could stand up to the communists as well as anyone. In actuality, though his discourse on the matter might have been more diplomatic than that of the "primitives," the Secretary of State was as anticommunist as any of them, and so were the overall objectives of his policies.

Even more important, the invaders of South Korea failed to reckon with the stubborn determination of President Harry S. Truman. While he might have been willing to "contain" communism at the thirty-eighth parallel, the man from Missouri refused to concede the whole Asian peninsula and vowed to fight. He reflected in his diary, "It looks like World

War III is here—I hope not—but we must meet whatever comes, and we will." To his daughter Margaret he said, "We are going to *fight*. By God I am not going to let them have it,"[2] though later, in words he was to regret, the chief executive referred to the engagement as only a "police action." Personally religious, the President added, "We are on the right track, and we will win—because I think God is with us in that enterprise."[3]

General Douglas MacArthur was commander of U.S. troops in East Asia as well as head of the occupation government in Japan, and also a man who generally believed that God was on his side. Following instructions from Washington, he ordered the bombing of North Korean airfields and rushed to Korea on an inspection tour. There he was appalled to see the South Korean army retreating pell-mell before columns of huge Russian-made T-34 tanks, against which it had no effective weapons. On June 28 the enemy took Seoul. MacArthur immediately requested two combat divisions; U.S. ground forces were put into action by President Truman on June 30. However, even American soldiers, weakened by anemic postwar appropriations and years of cushy peacetime duty at home or in occupied Japan, were at first no match for the invaders. They and the Republic of Korea forces were pressed far to the south into an enclave around the port city of Pusan, until MacArthur's famous Inchon landing of September 15 temporarily reversed Allied fortunes to enable a powerful drive north.

The North had also reckoned without the United Nations. Like the division of Korea, the international body was now only in its fifth year, and its full potential remained to be tried. To its ardent supporters, Korea seemed an excellent opportunity for the concert of nations to make and enforce peace with justice in its name. With the Soviet Union providentially absent in protest of Red China's exclusion from the UN and unable to cast another of its innumerable vetoes, the way was clear for the anticommunist West to act as the conscience of the whole world and to oppose the invasion.

On June 27 a hastily called meeting of the Security Council passed a resolution urging all governments to aid South Korea in resisting the aggressor and to restore peace. But although eventually no less than sixteen nations sent troops to the UN peacekeeping mission, the United States in fact supplied fifty percent of the men, 86 percent of naval power, and 93 percent of air, with South Korea providing most of the rest. For all intents and purposes the Korean War was an American venture, under American command and answering to the American cold war objective of containing Communist power in East Asia, holding that aggressive force to the limits reached by the postwar occupation agreements and the Communist victory in China the previous year.

Religious leaders were also aroused by the ominous developments in East Asia. Some spiritual internationalists saw a gleam of hope in the engagement of the United Nations as well as a single powerful nation, the United States, in the police work. Perhaps, they thought, this act of world cooperation could mark the inauguration of a new era in which the planet as a whole, working in harmony through the UN, would suppress rogue states. So it was that on July 15, 1950, the General Committee of the World Council of Churches, meeting in Toronto, defended the UN presence in Korea as a necessary police action, commending the UN for undertaking that task. Reinhold Niebuhr, the celebrated "Christian realist," and Pastor Martin Niemöller of Germany, famous for his courageous stand against Hitler and subsequent imprisonment, were two of the most prominent supporters of the World Council position. Said Niemöller, "We in Germany do not think of what is happening in Korea as war, but police action against armed violence in defiance of authority."

The Toronto resolution read in part:

> An act of aggression has been committed. . . . Armed attack as an instrument of national policy is wrong. We therefore commend the United Nations, an instrument of world order, for its prompt decision to meet this

aggression, and for authorizing a police measure which every member nation should support.

At the same time, governments must press individually and through the United Nations for a just settlement by conciliation and negotiation. . . . We must not regard the world wide conflict as inevitable. We stand for a just peace under the rule of law, and must seek peace by expanding justice and by attempting to reconcile contending world powers. The Korean situation need not be the beginning of a general war.[4]

At the same time, the threat of war was sufficiently ominous that the committee could summon little enthusiasm for planning the next full meeting of the World Council of Churches, scheduled for Evanston, Illinois, in 1953. Henry Van Dusen, president of Union Theological Seminary, expressed "grave doubts if we will be able to meet in 1953," and suggested that the committee postpone setting a motif for that conclave. The Toronto body concurred. (In the end the World Council did meet at Evanston, though not until August 1954, under the theme "Christ—The Hope of the World." That gathering in relatively more peaceful times attracted immense media attention and was, in a real sense, the high point of the World Council as a highly visible and hopeful presence on the stage of world events.)

The Toronto statement on the Korean War drew two abstentions, both by Christian pacifists. Fred Haslam, a Canadian Quaker, responded, "A world organization speaking for Christ should not make such a statement as this. I doubt whether this action in Korea can rightly be called a police action."

On the other hand, the liberal Protestant *Christian Century* initially vigorously supported the "police action" editorially, emphasizing its character as a work of the UN, and thus as the beginning of the internationalist future of which one-world idealists had long dreamed. A common police action mounted by the family of nations appeared a powerful advance in world affairs, one that liberals could only applaud. Warming to the theme, *The Century* went so far as to propose that American foreign policy in Asia should now be put entirely in the hands of the United Nations.[5]

First opposition to the war in the religious community came from the pacifist left rather than the right. A. J. Muste, Executive Director of the Fellowship of Reconciliation and dean of U.S. pacifism, wrote a letter to the magazine suggesting, first, that the proposal to give over U.S.-Asian affairs to the international body was an exercise in futility; it would entail a "virtual revolution in American foreign policy" to which the Truman administration would certainly never accede. Second, there was the issue of what was meant by the United Nations, given that its role in Korea was owed to the fluke of Soviet absence at the critical vote. If UN conduct of U.S.-Asian policy meant control by the UN with the Soviet Union's participation, then that would require first the resolution of the cold war between the two superpowers, in 1950 a daunting and unlikely prospect. But if it meant the UN minus the Russians, then it would amount to nothing more than U.S. anticommunist policy under another label—which in effect was what, according to Muste, the Korean war was anyway. On July 25 Muste and seventy-four other pacifists issued a statement contending that the Korean conflict was simply "a phase of the global power struggle between Russia and the United States." It was, in their eyes, no more than a continuation of the cold war by other means, and hardly the dawn of a new internationalist era.

The Christian Century, clearly stung but as yet unwilling to give up its utopian dreams even as the bloodletting and the situation on the ground grew more and more desperate, answered with a vehement attack on Muste. The editorial's tone, strained and immoderate for that liberal magazine, immediately brings home the high tension, the nerves on edge even in the most broad-minded of quarters, in 1950.

Mr. Muste is right in his characterization. We are talking about a revolution in our foreign policy. He is wrong in his assessment of what has happened. The revolution has already started! Our contention is that the road to peace is to be found by pressing forward in the direction pointed by the decisions which have been made since the beginning of the Korean crisis. It is to expand a role which the United Nations has already assumed and to which we are already committed.

It is true that the American people and their government have as yet only dimly recognized where this is going to lead. *But we are on our way!* We are moving into new territory which must be explored under conditions of extreme peril. Retreat is precisely what a group of 75 pacifists, of whom Mr. Muste was one, proposed in a statement issued on July 25. They refuse to recognize that the relation of the United Nations to the Korean situation has any significance. . . . They urge that "the United States withdraw from the conflict and itself take the initiative in seeking a peaceful solution and developing a Gandhian nonviolent means for resistance to aggression and tyranny." If there is any better formula than that for wrecking the United Nations, strengthening isolationism, turning the world over to a galloping communist advance and bringing on atomic war, it has not come to our attention.[6]

Much of the national religious press and religious leadership took positions broadly comparable to *The Christian Century,* supporting the war on as highly idealistic grounds as could be mustered and saving questions for later. The liberal Catholic journal *Commonweal,* for example, opined, "At a time when the world wavers on the verge of the most hideous slaughter imaginable, we submit that the Truman-Acheson policy of exhausting every honorable means of defeating the Soviets without provoking a general war is the only position a Christian can take in good conscience."[7]

There were significant variations, however. Harold H.
Osmer, in U.S. *Religious Journalism and the Korean War*, has
sorted out four basic responses to Korea appearing in 1950.[8]
Referring to the Truman-Acheson containment policy, the
administration's bedrock justification for the war, as the
touchstone, Osmer finds religious editorials ranging themselves under four categories: (1) support of containment with
a focus on the present military means; (2) support of containment with a non-military focus, that is, with a moral
rather than bellicose anticommunism that, while sometimes
reluctantly endorsing the war as a distasteful but necessary
"police action," called for increased social programs to
undermine the enemy's appeal in such overseas places as
Korea; (3) opposition to containment with a military focus—
the position of the far Right that wanted to carry the Korean
war on the total victory over communism and considered
that U.S. troops on the peninsula had been hobbled by Acheson's "cowardly" policy; and (4) opposition to containment
with a nonmilitary focus, the stance of the Christian pacifists
and others on the Left who considered that the United States
had not sufficiently explored possible avenues to peace
between the superpowers, or recognized that legitimate
national aspirations might lie behind some of the appeal of
communism overseas.

Under support of containment using military means
Osmer cites two Jewish journals, the Reform journal *Opinion*
and the American Jewish Congress's *Congress Weekly*. Both
emphasized the totalitarian nature of the Communist world
and declared that aggression from that source could not be
tolerated by the "free world," but must be defeated completely in order to maintain the "rule of law."[9] The Roman
Catholic, Jesuit-edited periodical *America* took a comparable
position, constantly praising the U.S. role in backing the
UN's opposition to aggression. It also continually called for
aid to "free peoples" everywhere who were fighting communism, declaring negotiation with an enemy of this nature
hopeless, and concluding that "all we can do to keep them

from taking everything in sight is to meet their armed might with our own."[10] The Protestant, nondenominational, mainstream-to-evangelical *Christian Herald* voiced similar opinions, and moreover looked back before June 1950 to claim, with the hard Right, that all through the Truman era Washington had allowed "atheistic Communism to engulf China, to invade Korea, and to threaten all other Asiatic lands."[11] It may be noted that these several periodicals offering a strong pro-military stance on Korea came out of three powerful but, in 1950, still somewhat marginalized American religions, Judaism, Roman Catholicism, and evangelical Protestantism, although other voices could also be heard in all those camps.

Containment with a nonmilitary focus developed a bit more slowly, but was visible by the end of 1950 in such mainstream Protestant magazines as *The Lutheran, Presbyterian Life*, and Reinhold Niebuhr's voice, *Christianity and Crisis*. All approved of the initial action in June but by year's end were expressing such sentiments as *The Lutheran*'s December 13 comment that "The counter-attack against the red tide will not be won by armies or A-bombs," and Niebuhr's October 11 opinion that "our first business is to stop the advance of Communism by improving the moral and economic health of the free world."[12] *Presbyterian Life* summed it up in December by saying, "If America is to be, under God, the instrument of salvation for the free world, she must also accept responsibility for the moral leadership of the world."[13] Comparable Jewish positions were taken by the Orthodox *Jewish Life* and the liberal *Reconstructionist*.

A further word might be said about Niebuhr's position on Korea. The great moral theologian of the cold war did not contest using force of arms to stop communist aggression there or anywhere else on grounds of principle, though as we have seen he certainly believed that the real war against that foe called for more than military means. But, scanning the conflict from a global perspective, he feared that excessive American involvement in East Asia might tempt the Soviets to move elsewhere, particularly in Europe, which in his eyes was far more valuable. The "free world can live if we lose Asia, but we cannot live in security if Russia should come into possession of the economic and technical resources of Europe." Thus he thought of Korea as a sort of diversion that should not mortgage all of America's resources; for that reason he opposed MacArthur's yearning to carry the war to the Yalu River and beyond.[14] In November of 1950 Niebuhr became an official consultant of the State Department. This honor led to the Union Theological Seminary professor's undergoing a lengthy loyalty investigation by the FBI. That probe raised endless questions and awkward moments as various dubious statements and associations came out, some from back in the 1930s. As these, together with his flimsier enthusiasm for fighting communism in Asia than in Europe, became known, they provided critics on the extreme Right with ammunition. Niebuhr survived, but not without learning something of the cold war's moral cost.

Militant opposition to containment came from others who, far from opposing the war, wanted to expand it into a general anticommunist crusade conducted by all means possible. They reiterated criticism of the alleged softness of the Truman-Acheson policies leading up to Korea, and castigated the limited goals of the U.S. /UN activity. *Columbia*, the journal of the generally rightist Knights of Columbus, called for abandoning the United Nations as a world peacekeeping vehicle. That Catholic periodical, well aligned to the uncompromising anticommunism of Pius XII and Francis Cardinal Spellman, wanted to establish a "new covenant of nations" out of the present United Nations. This rump body would exclude those governments that impeded peace, meaning of course the Communist powers. Discounting the UN stand in Korea, the far Right quickly made opposition to the UN one of its touchstones. Another was opposition to "containment" and to the Truman administration, despite its formulation of the Marshall Plan and NATO, its defense of Berlin, its anticommunist aid to Greece and

Turkey, and now its military action against Communist aggressors in Korea.

This was not enough. The prominent ecumenical lay leader John Foster Dulles, son of a Presbyterian minister and soon to be Secretary of State in the Eisenhower administration, said of Korea in 1950, "We have borne a Christian witness. We need have no remorse. Also we need not despair. We have acted as God gave us to see the right."[15] Then Dulles added that he wanted not only the current policy of "containment" of communism, but a new policy aimed at "liberating" those under its domination.[16]

The case of John Foster Dulles is an interesting and significant bit of religion in 1950. There were really two John Foster Dulleses. Prior to the end of World War II, the future Republican cabinet member was an ecumenical church leader, like many of his ilk an idealistic seeker of peace and advocate of international harmony, as well as a "Christian Realist" of the stamp of Reinhold Niebuhr and John C. Bennett. From 1940 to 1945 he was wartime chair of the Federal Council of Churches's Commission to Study the Basis of a Just and Durable Peace.

Then, after 1945, there emerged the cold warrior, convinced beyond his previous position of the righteousness of America and its need to be God's instrument against the Soviet threat. Dulles himself saw this transformation as a move from "naiveté" to "realism," and posited for it four stages between 1945 and 1950. At first, at the end of the war, he said he favored cooperation between the victorious allies. But he quickly perceived that to be a disastrous miscalculation that only resulted in the "large Soviet postwar expansion in both central Europe and Asia." The second stage, therefore, was one of favoring "noncooperation." It was succeeded in his mind by an American policy of "prevention," apparently about the same as Acheson's containment, that was "marked by the realization that there was an irreconcilable conflict between the ambitions of Soviet Communism and the interests and welfare of the United States." The fourth stage in the evolution of Dulles's cold war thinking was sparked by the July 1950 attack on South Korea; it was "opposition."[17]

Dulles went on to say, "Any soldiers who fight in response to a United Nations appeal can be pretty sure that they are fighting for a just cause and they are not sacrificing their lives merely to satisfy the ambitions of rulers who think it would be exciting to be a conquering hero."[18] A bit of the idealism also returns in Dulles's 1950 book, *War or Peace*, which provides a snapshot of his mind-set in that year, when he asserts that "Western ascendancy was not so much the work of generals as it was of diplomats, merchants, and missionaries," and calls on his readers to return to faith and an American sense of mission equal to that of the Communists.[19] Yet the emphasis is not so much on the missionary spread of Christianity as such, as on the propagation of American ideals with the same fervor as that of the Communist cadres disseminating theirs. The book contains such chapter titles as "Know Your Enemy" and "No Appeasement."

Another celebrated Christian opponent of mere containment was Billy Graham, rising fast as the nation's star evangelist in 1950. All through the 1950s he had no doubt that the United States was the hand of God for defeating communist evil. As he supported the war the evangelist seized on the opportunity to hammer away at communism. After the enemy first invaded South Korea he sent President Truman a telegram saying, MILLIONS OF CHRISTIANS PRAYING GOD GIVE YOU WISDOM IN THIS CRISIS. STRONGLY URGE SHOWDOWN WITH COMMUNISM NOW. MORE CHRISTIANS IN SOUTHERN KOREA PER CAPITA THAN IN ANY PART OF THE WORLD. WE CANNOT LET THEM DOWN. EVANGELIST BILLY GRAHAM.[20]

Before long, though, Graham's confidence in the chief executive waned as he reiterated the conservative Republican theme that the unpopular conflict was "Truman's war." Later, with other conservatives, he contended that General MacArthur's all-out drive for victory should have been supported, not the "cowardly" and "half-hearted" equivocating that dragged out the conflict.[21] In 1952 Graham went to Korea to visit the troops, in the manner of Cardinal Spellman. Evangelicals were also understandably interested in the fate of Korean Christians; there were reports of persecution in Communist-occupied Korea, and of revivals elsewhere in the peninsular nation.[22]

Among nonmilitant opponents of containment Osmer cited *The Christian Century*, the Baptist *Watchman-Examiner*, the Methodist *Christian Advocate*, the Disciples of Christ *World Call*, the Quaker *Friends Intelligencer*, and the liberal Episcopalian *Churchman*. Although, as we have seen, *The Christian Century* supported initial resistance to the North Korean invasion in opposition to the pacifist A. J. Muste, it soon moved to criticize the United States for relying on military means alone, for failure to negotiate a settlement with the Soviet Union and its satellites, and for not adequately recognizing that real "situations of strength" are found not where arms are engaged but where standards of living are being raised and "in which governments are improving in democratic effectiveness," not at all the case in Korea.[23]

Others in this category voiced similar sentiments, contending that the United States was not sincerely pursuing every avenue to reaching a peaceful conclusion to the fighting. Nor was it honestly recognizing the right of peoples everywhere, including East Asia, to choose whatever government or economic system they wished, even communism if that was their desire. Thus, in August, the *Friends Intelligencer* claimed that Marxist ideology had adherents in Asia because "it appeals to the desire for national independence and offers satisfaction to the most elemental drives for security and a minimum standard of living."[24] A contributor added that the rest of the world wants "neither a *pax Americana* nor a *pax Russiana*," but merely to emerge from poverty and to find a place of dignity in the world.[25]

The Korean War dominated the news in the last half of the year, providing a grim backdrop to everything else. The vicissitudes of religion news swung back and forth with stunning blows in those months, as the Holy Year progressed in Rome and the dogma of the Assumption was proclaimed and then, amid some of the gloomiest news out of Korea, the National Council of Churches was inaugurated.

After the last great example of MacArthur's military genius, the Inchon landing, had relieved the Allied entrapment around Pusan, the United Nations advanced up the peninsula, retaking Seoul and then continuing to push north heedlessly across the thirty-eighth parallel toward the Yalu River on the Chinese border. The fateful decision in Washington and the other Allied capitals to cross the former demarcation line between the two Koreas, a move demanded by the Right, which wanted to "liberate" the North, was taken almost casually, so much was momentum on the side of the advancing Republic of Korea and UN armies. It would have required almost superhuman will, not to mention a political risk of historic proportions, to stop there.

Nonetheless the crossing of the line ended in disaster for American troops. Four-fifths of U.S. casualties occurred north of the thirty-eighth. The move brought China into the conflict and nearly provoked an Asian war on a much larger scale. It led to one of the worst defeats in U.S. military history, and not coincidentally ended the career of one of the nation's greatest military figures. And when all was over the border between the two Koreas was set where it was when the war began.

Soldiers from the South reached the vicinity of the Yalu River separating Korea and China by mid-November, and for a moment it seemed the war had been won and was virtually over. But China then sent "volunteers" in vast numbers across the river, and UN reversals commenced. General Douglas MacArthur countered with unauthorized bombings of Yalu River bridges, and with a dangerous and unauthorized offensive on northward toward the river. This venture was terribly mauled by the seasoned and well-armed enemy, and on November 25 the Chinese responded with an offensive of their own. The UN forces were overwhelmed by up to a million enemy troops, and once again backed down the peninsula in full retreat. Seoul fell for a second time on January 4, 1951, and the enemy drive was not halted until January 15. Although Seoul was retaken by the UN on March 14, 1951, no attempt to drive north was now undertaken; the front was eventually stabilized near the original thirty-eighth parallel separating North and South Korea.

In the meantime, in one of the greatest political fracases of the early 1950s, General MacArthur was dismissed for insubordination by President Truman on April 11, 1951. Despite the brilliance of his Inchon landing, the later reverses on the Yalu were certainly the consequence of MacArthur's arrogance and impulsive proclivity for exceeding his orders. His unauthorized actions against the enemy, which in the end were ruinous for the Allied cause and could very easily have led to full-scale war with vast China, left the commander-in-chief no alternative. But the viceroy of Japan and reconqueror of the Philippines was popular back home, particularly with the Right, which yearned for a hero and was, at the same time, all too eager to portray Truman and Acheson as "soft on communism."

The drama of MacArthur versus Truman was virtually of mythic dimension, but it ended in the squelching of myth by messy political reality. The hero of the South Pacific was forced to confront a new world of limits and compromises, and neither he nor the public at large liked that world. A man made for World War II, with its vast stage and immense dramas, and who now personified anticommunism as the apocalyptic cosmic battle of light against darkness, MacArthur was compelled to submit to what Richard Nixon, in the 1952 presidential campaign, was to call "Dean Acheson's College of Cowardly Communist Containment." But though the rhetoric of heroic battles for world liberation sounded grand, neither Nixon nor Dulles nor anyone else was able to do better than containment. The containment world was the world in which humanity lived from Korea until communism collapsed of its own contradictions on a day far beyond the vision of 1950.

So it was that in April 1951 many in the nation were not yet ready to recognize the contradictions in MacArthurism either. Two thirds of the nation, according to one poll, opposed the firing of the five-star general. The Michigan state legislature passed a resolution stating that "World Communism achieved its greatest victory of the decade in the dismissal of General MacArthur." Senator McCarthy, overlooking such matters as the Russian and Chinese revolutions, concurred by saying that the general's removal was "the greatest victory the Communists have ever won." In Los Angeles the flag was flown at half-mast. Senator William E. Jenner, Republican of Indiana, claimed that the deed only proved the McCarthyite allegation that "agents of the Soviet Union" were running the Democratic administration, and called for President Truman's impeachment. Billy Graham, looking at the dismissal from a higher vantage point, said that "Christianity has suffered another major blow." In New York, as the elderly general's limousine rolled through the city in a traditional ticker-tape parade, onlookers were seen crossing themselves, as though in the presence of a sacred icon.[26]

But after his no less triumphant address before a joint session of Congress, MacArthur commenced to fade away, as he said old soldiers were wont to do, and containment, rather than actions in the spirit of his "no substitute for victory" speeches, prevailed. Perhaps even some of those who cheered and wept for the grand old man of American arms would, in soberer moments when the cost was considered, have concurred that more limited policies were wisest. The Republican Eisenhower administration, even with Dulles as Secretary of State, quickly came to the same conclusion when the responsibility was actually theirs in 1953. Here was a true irony of American history. As Stephen J. Whitfield had pointed out, "Dean Acheson had not vowed to defend South Korea, but then his administration did so—at a cost of 54,246 American lives. Dulles promised to emancipate the Captive

Nations, and then did *not* do so—with tragic consequences for the embattled East Germans, Poles, and Hungarians."[27]

For in the end deadlock, marked by lonely bunkers set in muddy fields, was what Korea became. It was an unwelcome stasis for the Communist side as well as the other, teaching Moscow and Beijing that revolutionary momentum alone was not enough to carry the red tide irresistibly forward. In point of fact the Communist side won few major geopolitical victories after 1950, and they were not enough to save its cause. But no one in 1950 was willing to accept that the cosmic spiritual and apocalyptic conflict was over, even though the Korean War would end not as Armageddon nor a new dawn of internationalism nor the site of exemplary Gandhian peacemaking, but as a stalemate, which after 1950 everyone wanted to forget as soon as they could. "The Forgotten War," as it soon became, preached no sermon and conveyed no lesson that anyone wanted to hear. Its homily had to be spoken again in Vietnam and, on the Soviet side, in Afghanistan, and indeed was reiterated until the end of the cold war, an end that has also left the world with a messy and uncertain look.

Perhaps that was the overall message of Korea: the defeat of myth by the confused complexities of ordinary life, whether for individuals, for nations, or for ideologies. But what of religion, which tends to live by myth? What did Korea mean to American religion? It was certainly not *the* "moment of truth" about anything, but it was one of a series of moments that defined the culture of the cold war and the postwar world. This was the 1950s before Elvis and rock 'n' roll, before Ike and hula hoops and everything else that was to soften slightly the decade's culture. This was the cold war 1950s in all their starkness, ameliorated only by nostalgia for pasts that probably never were—the faux World War II of *South Pacific*, the dreamworld pasts of various true faiths before the acids of modernity had gotten to them, and those of Spengler's timeless peasant cultures. This was the 1950 of hopes for a future American "greatness" that had not yet fully come nor been fairly defined.

Apocalypse, if it means anything, means a radical sorting out of what had heretofore been mixed and ambiguous, so that the sides can be seen definitively. So far as the Communist issue was concerned, that had of course been going on before, thanks to cold war headlines, the spy trials and Hiss/Chambers hearings, and then McCarthy. Korea only augmented this "us versus them" mentality, this sense of a battle to the death of the children of light against the hordes of darkness, for it added to all the other spheres in which the struggle was being waged actual military combat. GIs were again freezing, bleeding, and dying, this time at Communist hands.

Korea no less called for clarification of church responses to war. Among Protestants, Korea strengthened the Niebuhrian "Christian realism" approach, entailing support of the military police work by raising hope, like that of *The Christian Century*, for its UN sponsorship to evolve into a full-blown international peacekeeping force. As the Federal Council of Churches's committee statement on Christian conscience and weapons of mass destruction, presented in chapter 5, suggested, the Christian pacifism of Kirby Page, A. J. Muste, and their associates in 1950, now looked too simplistic and did not address the "hard realities" faced by adherents of the Niebuhrian mentality. This issue had been simmering for decades; Korea, and the publication in 1952 of Reinhold Niebuhr's *The Irony of American History*, were to highlight the difficult but exhilarating choices involved. At the same time, Korea also gave rise to religious criticism of cold war attitudes and willingness to rely on military means alone, critiques that in 1950 were like a trial run for the much more vociferous debate on those issues in the Vietnam 1960s.

As was characteristic of 1950, the Roman Catholic Church's position was clear and well distinguished from that of the adversary. Fortuitously, the Holy Year only brought the See of Peter and its modes of waging war more sharply into focus than ever. No music could have sounded more dissimilar than that of ethereal choirs celebrating the mysteries of faith in Rome on the one hand and the sounds of guns in Korea on the other. The dogma of the Assumption of the Mother of God's virgin flesh into heaven contrasted forcefully with both the mutilated flesh desecrating Korean hillsides and the dogma of Communist materialism that church apologists said lay behind the war.

The Roman Catholic Church in those desperate times of 1950 appeared more than ever to be a vast and disciplined army under the authority of a single earthly commander, the Holy Father in Rome. In the same way, the communist apparatus of rule or conspiracy everywhere was as widely perceived to be a mighty engine under the total control of the Kremlin. There were those who regretted that the United States and its allies, not to mention the Protestant world with its hundreds of voices, was not so unified. But by the end of the century both images of superhuman unity, Catholic and Communist, would be shown to have been partly illusions and, insofar as they were true in 1950, ephemeral. But that was not how they appeared then.

In the end Korea became irony, though not exactly as Niebuhr intended. It seemed at first an apocalyptic moment in a climactic struggle. Lt. Gen. Matthew Ridgway, later to succeed MacArthur as commander in Korea, wondered to himself as the first cables about the invasion came in if it was "the beginning of World War III . . . Armageddon, the last great battle between East and West."[28] But the conflict was to play out into compromise, a wide notch down from apocalyptic. Roman Catholicism and communism would change, the latter to collapse as the sovereign ideology of a world power; all this would happen more as the consequence of ordinary human imperfection on all sides than as defeat in spiritual warfare between armies of almost angelic and demonic stature. None of this was clear then.

A treatment of U.S. religion and East Asia in 1950 would not be complete without reference to the continuing occupation of Japan under Douglas MacArthur. Although nominally Supreme Commander of Allied Powers (SCAP), the U.S.

general was for all intents and purposes ruler of the country—American Shogun, the Japanese called him—and the occupation a U.S. affair. That shogunate's career from 1945 to its official end in 1952 is a wonderful mirror of the American mind in those years. For the supremely confident victors wanted nothing so much as to remake Japan as closely as possible on the model of America.

The early years of occupation were full of idealistic change for the defeated nation. The country was demilitarized and the postwar constitution forbade the government to maintain armed forces or engage in war. Land reform broke up large estates, including some belonging to Shinto and Buddhist institutions, in favor of the peasant farmers who actually worked the land. Titles of nobility (except those of the imperial family) were abolished, women were given the right to vote, and the political process became thoroughly democratic. It excluded only those who were "purged" because of their reported close association with the militaristic wartime regime and its ideology.

The U.S.-induced reforms in Japan put special emphasis, as one would expect from Americans, on the separation of religion and the state. The ideology of the extreme nationalism that had led Japan into war had emphasized the sovereign's descent from Shinto divinities and his present role as "manifest deity" whose "imperial will" was unquestioned.

But the emperor was spared the war crimes trial some demanded, and which was inflicted on such others as Hideki Tojo, who had acted in his name and, as they saw it, in accordance with that will. Under the occupation and after, Emperor Hirohito remained the figurehead sovereign, or rather "symbol," of the state. The wise retention of the emperor, which undoubtedly prevented much bitterness and quite likely much bloodshed, was favored by MacArthur.

That policy was in recognition of Japan's religious veneration of the monarch as an earthly manifestation of the divine order, and perhaps also in recognition that Hirohito, unlike many of his subordinates or the rulers of Nazi Germany, was basically a decent person who had been forced into an uncongenial wartime role and who had played a major part in Japan's decision to surrender. Paradoxically, though, the ruler was constrained to issue a declaration on New Year's Day 1946 renouncing his alleged divinity (in which that scientifically minded individual probably never believed anyway) in his celebrated "Declaration of Humanity." The erstwhile high priest of Shinto continued to perform the rituals of his station at the palace shrines, but these were now technically considered personal rather than state acts of worship.

Secularization did not stop there. Separated from state support and landed estates, religious bodies in Japan faced financial problems but for the first time had real freedom to control their own lives and pursue their own ends. Before 1945, they could function legally only if chartered by the state; obtaining that recognition entailed doctrinal conformity to the official mythology and ideology, and much detailed regulation of the religion's internal affairs. Several of the "new religions" and their leaders suffered severe restriction or persecution in those days. The tiny Christian minority in Japan was also hampered on both practical and intellectual levels; during the war, for example, all major Protestant denominations were forced to unite into one church for the convenience of the government, and had to recognize in some way the spiritual authority of the emperor.

All this was very different once SCAP arrived. The links between Shinto and the government were abolished, and ownership of shrine property and appointment of priests reverted to the local community represented by elected shrine trustees, rather as though they were congregational churches. Many shrines, and also Buddhist temples and monasteries, lost considerable revenue from the land reform, which was made up American-style through pledges, fund drives, and money-making enterprises.

Symbolic changes also took place. Shinto holy days were no longer national holidays, being replaced by such innocuous celebrations as Adult's Day, Children's Day, Vernal

Equinox, Autumnal Equinox, Culture Day, and the like. The small Shinto altars that had been omnipresent in schools and government offices were removed. Of course ambiguities occurred. At the end of 1945, as Japanese government workers were busy removing their tiny *kamidana*, shoebox-sized shrines on an office wall, loudspeakers outside the entrance of SCAP headquarters in the heart of Tokyo were blaring out Christmas carols.

That scene suggests a larger ambiguity: the relation of the occupation to Christianity. While sincerely promoting religious freedom, Douglas MacArthur and certain other high SCAP officials strongly believed that Japan needed Christianity to become truly democratic and that the defeat, and therefore the discrediting of the traditional religions that had generally supported the imperial war effort, should open the way for the island empire's evangelization. There were urgent calls for armies of missionaries to come. On February 24, 1950, MacArthur sent a cable to a stateside convention of Youth for Christ stating,

> My often repeated conviction remains unchanged that acceptance of the fundamental principles of Christianity would provide the surest foundation for the firm establishment of democracy in Japan. Therefore, distribution of scriptures and interdenominational evangelistic rallies carried on in cooperation with established religious missions capable of providing continuing follow-up are highly welcome. Entry into Japan of Youth for Christ will be welcome on same basis as other operating missionaries.[29]

An interesting concomitant of this enthusiasm was the way in which, despite denials from the palace, persistent rumors made the rounds that the emperor, the empress, the crown prince, or the whole imperial family were about to be converted. Some missionaries dreamed that, if this happened, the ruling house would bring the entire nation into the faith with it, in the manner of kings of old. Others, including

MacArthur, found their feelings more mixed. While in principle any conversion ought to be welcomed, it was recognized that such a change on the part of the sovereign to a faith not that of the great majority of his subjects would be extremely divisive if not disastrous from the political point of view. It would even be divisive for Christians. Would the ruler become Protestant, Catholic, or perhaps Quaker, like the American tutor to the crown prince? Emissaries of all faiths were reportedly seen entering the palace.

June 1950 and the Korean War just across the narrow Straits of Tsushima from Japan quickly put all such heavenly concerns into abeyance. Even before then, cold war concerns had pushed SCAP away from utopian idealism about democratic reforms toward making sure that Japan stayed on the right side. Now that nation had to become a redoubt and arsenal for one side in a nearby conflict. The Korean War role did much to start the Japanese postwar economy rolling toward its ultimate place as a world economic powerhouse.

The peace treaty leading to the end of the occupation, largely negotiated by John Foster Dulles, was signed in 1951. Though forbidden an army, Japan then raised a "Self-Defense Force," and the emperor remained a Shintoist whose successor would ultimately be enthroned in Shinto rites, just as his nation remained mostly Shinto/Buddhist and unconverted to Christianity. These were matters distant from American shores and alien to American public life. But they were issues the United States inherited through victory and its subsequent world role. For Japan, Shinto, the United States, and their complex interrelationships, as for so much else, the years around 1950 proved to be pivotal for the shape of affairs up to the end of the century.

8

African American Religion before the Beginning

In 1950 seeds were almost invisibly planted that would grow into some of the sturdiest trees of the civil rights movement of the late 1950s and the 1960s. It was in 1950 that Martin Luther King Jr., then a student at Crozer Theological Seminary in Pennsylvania, heard the President of Howard College, Mordecai Wyatt Johnson, lecture in Fellowship Hall, Philadelphia. Johnson who had just returned from a visit to India, spoke on Mahatma Gandhi. The college president, himself a towering figure in African American religion, suggested that Gandhi's philosophy of nonviolent resistance might be applicable to the race situation in America. Deeply stirred, King immediately purchased a half-dozen books on the Indian "great soul."[1]

In the same year Malcolm Little, later known as Malcolm X, was incarcerated at the Norfolk Prison Colony in Massachusetts, to which he had been transferred in 1948. He had been introduced in 1947 to the teachings of Elijah Muhammad, the Black Muslim leader, and in 1950 he was assiduously studying them. As soon as he was released in 1952 he began propagating those doctrines, which were to him profoundly liberating.

Certain signs of hope and change for African Americans, though modest in comparison with what would come later, were evident in 1950. President Truman had already

---

Elijah Muhammad, leader of the Nation of Islam.

173

commenced integration of the military, opening the way for what would become a reliable vehicle for black education and career advancement. When the Korean War began in the middle of the year, thousands of blacks fought alongside whites. On June 5, 1950, the Supreme Court issued several rulings involving race and integration. It declared that segregating blacks and whites in railroad dining cars violated the Interstate Commerce Act. In ruling that the University of Texas Law School must admit a black student who had argued that available black schools were unequal in size and quality, the Court insisted that "separate but equal" involves more than identical physical facilities, thus preparing for *Brown vs. Board of Education* in 1954. In *McLaurin vs. Oklahoma*, the Court determined that once a black student had been admitted to a previously all-white school, as McLaurin had been, no further distinctions could be made on the basis of race.

It was also in 1950 that the African American diplomat, Ralph J. Bunche, was awarded the Nobel Peace Prize for mediating the Palestinian dispute, and Gwendolyn Brooks of Chicago became the first black person to receive the Pulitzer Prize in poetry. All these were very important symbols of black advancement at the higher levels of American educational, political, and cultural life, but admittedly did little for the millions of ordinary blacks trapped in Southern segregation or the hopelessness of the Northern urban ghetto.

Apart from the court decisions, 1950, with its anticommunist anxiety, was not a banner year for progress in race relations. A modest civil rights program advanced by the Truman administration in 1950 was interred after a Southern filibuster. The fall 1950 elections for Congress were also a setback; a number of Northern Democrats, who had favored forward movement in race relations under the leadership of the federal government, were retired.[2] Anticommunism and the Korean War were far more on the minds of most white voters than race, and the Republican argument that Democrats were "soft" on communism clearly swayed many of them away from liberal candidates.

Indeed, despite some largely symbolic progress, American blacks were still quite aware of their distinctive place in American society, and it was not a privileged one. On April 1, 1950, Dr. Charles Richard Drew, the originator of a method of storing large amounts of blood plasma in "blood banks," died as a result of a car accident in North Carolina. In need of blood, he had been denied admission to a whites-only hospital because he was black.

Paul Moore, distinguished priest who was later Episcopal Bishop of New York, tells in his memoirs of traveling in 1950, when he was a young clergyman, to Groveland, Florida. Together with several others later eminent in the civil rights movements, including the future Supreme Court Justice Thurgood Marshall, he was part of an NAACP legal defense team assisting three black men, who had been convicted of the rape of a white woman, in their effort to obtain a new trial with a change of venue because of community prejudice. He was appalled to learn of the physical brutality the small-town police had used to extract confessions from these defendants. The deposition of one of the accused included these lines:

> When they were beating me they said to me, "Nigger, you the man picked up this white girl last night?" I said to them, "What white girl?" They said, "Well you might as well tell us you're the one did it 'cause we gonna beat the hell outta you until you tell us you did it."

Moore adds,

> And so it went until they put him in jail. You can imagine the fear, the terror, of that world. I could not begin to deal with it. This was the country that I fought for [in World War II] because I believe in our democracy,

our freedom. And here we were in a place that
felt like a police state. This was a turning point in my
life.[3]

Moore was hardly less profoundly shocked by the lack of
sympathy—indeed, the lynch mob mentality—of the local
whites. Later the Supreme Court threw out the first verdict
of guilty and ordered a retrial with a change of venue. The
defendants confidently expected an acquittal. But the three
were shot dead on the way to the courthouse with the sher-
iff, allegedly while trying to escape. Moore was with Thurgood Marshall when he received the telephone call
conveying that dreadful news, and the expression on the
face of the gallant African American civil rights warrior
as he heard the word "shot" was seared forever on his
soul.

For Moore as for many others, the years around 1950
were inwardly pivotal, even if—or because—nothing
seemed to be changing outwardly at that hour. Though his
intervention seemed fruitless and the final result of the case
tragic, he confessed that this episode did much to make him,
a son of wealth and privilege, the dynamic clerical social
activist he became in the 1960s and after.

Discrimination extended to religion. As Liston Pope was
to write a few years later, "The church is the most segregated major institution in American society."[4] Thus it was
also in 1950 that the Alabama Supreme Court upheld the
conviction of Glen H. Taylor, the U.S. senator from Idaho
who had been Henry A. Wallace's vice presidential candidate on the 1948 Progressive Party ticket. During that campaign, Taylor had attempted to enter, through the "colored"
door, the Alliance Gospel Tabernacle, a small black Baptist
church in Birmingham where he was to speak at a Southern
Negro Youth Congress. Since both whites and blacks were
expected to attend, the church had been compelled to erect
temporary partitions between pews to segregate them and to

label the front entrance "Colored" and the rear entrance "White." When directed by the police to the "White" entrance, Taylor tried again to force his way in via the entrance his black audience would be required to use, allegedly calling officers of the law "vile names" in the process. The senator was arrested and convicted of disorderly conduct. His detention had been under the supervision of Birmingham Police Commissioner Eugene "Bull" Connor, later notorious for turning fire hoses and police dogs on black demonstrators led by Martin Luther King Jr. The Taylor incident did much to strengthen his reputation as a hard-line segregationist. Taylor appealed, but the state supreme court in 1950 upheld the judgment and in the process affirmed the requirement that churches maintain separate entries, seating sections, and other facilities for the two races. Persons of both races could only coexist at the same event if it were possible for each to avoid recognizing by sight or sound, much less physical contact, the presence of the other class of human beings.[5]

What kind of inner spiritual life could an African American who wanted a religion that was not merely escapist maintain in the face of this kind of segregationist mentality? Howard Thurman's 1949 book, *Jesus and the Disinherited*, was much discussed at the time and was a source of strength to many.[6] The celebrated African American clergyman and mystic had been chaplain of Howard University's Rankin Chapel, then (in 1949) became pastor of the nation's first intentionally interracial congregation, the Church for the Fellowship of All People in San Francisco, and finally dean of Marsh Chapel, Boston University. In *Jesus and the Disinherited* Thurman proclaimed that the Galilean is with those who throughout history have been on the outside, with their backs to the wall. One can be coerced in one's outer self, Thurman declared, but is not destroyed till the inner self submits.

One could well ask, however, how much African

American religion in 1950 had itself submitted. Back in 1945, St. Clair Drake and Horace R. Clayton, in *Black Metropolis*, had written of the increasing irrelevancy of the black church to radicalism.[7] Not a few black churches in effect moved into a conservative political stance, their clerical and lay leaders in northern cities like Chicago or Detroit allowing themselves to become clients of political machines, who delivered the black vote in exchange for token honors and boons that did little to change the basic situation of blacks. Either that, or they responded to the desperate economic state of the 1930s by withdrawing into the revivalist sectarianism of the storefront church.[8]

Gayraud S. Wilmore in *Black Religion and Black Radicalism* follows a chapter on "The Deradicalization of Christianity" with one on "The Dechristianization of Radicalism." Many urban blacks, he claims, in the 1930s and after had come to regard the church as a "racket" in which ministers who failed to practice what they preached played on people's emotions to rake in tithes and offerings; it would be better in the eyes of doubters if blacks were less religious and more realistic. With such skepticism on the rise, the black church was gradually being displaced as the center of black life.[9] In the 1930s and 1940s, Wilmore argued, the thing to watch had been the turning of radical-minded black intellectuals from the church to Marxism, sometimes even to membership in the Communist Party, with its doctrinaire proclivity in those days for seeing religion as a major part of the problem rather than the solution.[10]

However, by 1950 the glow was off that path.[11] Quite apart from the disadvantage of being aligned with a force now perceived as America's mortal enemy, Marxism had come to seem too arid for the black soul, too far removed from its emotional and spiritual roots. The church was not the enemy of black society, some were beginning to realize; it *was* black society. As W. E. B. Du Bois had perceived long before in *The Souls of Black Folk*, in America the black church had been there even before the black home: that is, given the disruption of family life by slavery and its aftermath, "as a social institution it antedated by many decades the monogamous Negro home."[12]

And it was an active institution. As early as 1935, black pastors like Martin Luther King Sr. led the members of the Ebenezer Baptist Church as they attempted to register to vote in Atlanta. The Rev. Adam Clayton Powell Jr. of the Abyssinian Baptist Church in Harlem, later an effective if controversial black congressman, had organized street protests on behalf of black civil rights and economic issues in the 1930s. By the late 1950s and the 1960s, civil rights leaders, beginning with Martin Luther King Jr., would to a remarkable extent have "The Rev." (if not "Imam") in front of their names. But in 1950 a gulf was often fixed between the religious and the activist sides of American black life.

It was the day of the urban black religion described in James Baldwin's quasi-autobiographical writings, such as *The Fire Next Time* (1962), and in his powerful novel *Go Tell It on the Mountain* (1952). This was a world of storefront churches, led by honey-voiced preachers, authoritarian and natural, if sometimes compromised, leaders of their communities; of praying mothers who virtually lived in the church; of pious, spirit-filled young men like Baldwin himself at one point; and of young women who sang in the choir, also pious but a distraction to the pious young men. Of course the black metropolis was not just church. Outside on the street one had to weave one's way through relics of drugs, drink, or abusive and broken homes, conditions themselves engendered by crime and hopelessness. The limits of a black person's world, enforced by Jim Crow on the one hand and police brutality on the other, were discovered all too early in life, as Baldwin made clear. The only ways out of poverty, and the despair of entrapment in a life of demeaning, low-paying, and uncertain jobs, seemed to be crime or religion, or the pseudoreligions of the needle and the bottle.

The church was indeed the most secure haven for blacks in a white man's world, and its ministry the most respectable black profession. But because it meant above all security, and even because in some sense it had an investment in the way things were, the black church was not quite ready yet to leave the sanctuary for the streets. The great civil rights demonstrations and protests of a decade later were not yet on the agenda of 1950.

The church and its pastors could be aroused, however. In 1950, the black Birmingham (Ala.) Baptist Ministers' Conference objected to traveling to the National Baptist Convention on the Pennsylvania-Southern Railroad when it was discovered that a curtain would segregate white and African American passengers.[13]

There were further signs that the wind was rising in 1950. Baldwin pictures not only mainline black churches of Methodist and Baptist type in the "black metropolis," but a colorful variety of Pentecostalists, seance-holding "readers," occultists, the likes of Daddy Grace's United House of Prayer for All People, Father Divine's Peace Mission, and the Nation of Islam, or the "Black Muslims."

The last, under the leadership of Elijah Muhammad (born Elijah Poole), was not yet prominent in 1950 but growing in importance, as it did all through the 1950s. This movement had been founded by W. D. Fard in Detroit in 1930; after Fard mysteriously disappeared in 1934, Elijah Muhammad assumed leadership. He basically taught black nationalism and separatism, saying that blacks as a "lost-found" nation were naturally Muslim and a superior race—the original humans. Whites were the inferior handiwork of Yakub, a "black scientist" who had rebelled against Allah and manufactured this sorry people, whose natural religion was Christianity, to enslave God's best creation. Now

Allah—portrayed as the supreme black man and not a "spook"—is returning to vindicate and liberate his people. The black Muslims fostered a strong sense of identity and confidence through a strict moral code, symbols of separateness in diet and dress, firm discipline, and vigorous recruitment.

The Muslims were a new kind of black spiritual movement, the first, on a large scale, to reject Christianity as a "slave religion" imposed by the white man. It asserted the priority and superiority of Africans in the eyes of God, calling for retributive justice in the form of a proudly black nation and the real separation of the races. But like most non-normative African American religions, except those with Creole connections, black Islam was primarily a product of the diaspora in the large Northern cities where new opportunities and new frustrations alike were shaping a new black culture, one at once intellectual, creative, frustrated, and angry in ways different from in the old South.

Turning now to the rural South of around 1950, a 1947 study by Harry V. Richardson of black churches in four disparate Southern counties found significant patterns and differences.[14] Despite the common assumption that rural blacks were overwhelmingly churchgoing, membership varied widely. In Virginia's Northumberland County black farm ownership, education, and cultural level were high, and so was church membership, at 89.7 percent of the black population. In contrast, in Mississippi County, Arkansas, where these values were very low, church membership stood at only 10 percent.

Moreover, these churches were troubled. The poverty, low educational level, and oppressive social conditions of Jim Crow often meant demoralization and lack of adequate support even for the one institution that was wholly and securely black. Churches were also afflicted by black migration to the North, which often took away the brightest and best of their members. Ministers were not of one mind, Richardson found, in their views of emigration. Nearly half (46.8 percent) favored it, understanding the reasons for leaving the South. Another 41.9 percent professed to be indifferent, and 19.4 percent opposed emigration.

This sociologist also found that dealing with returning black servicemen from World War II was problematic for their pastors. Some of the young veterans were more given to drink and "fast" living than those who had stayed home, and were also conspicuously less ready than the older generation to accept Southern social conventions. In Dallas County, Alabama, a returned black army flyer had recently been beaten by a group of white citizens because he had refused to say "Yes, Ma'am" to a white woman clerk at a gasoline rationing board. The atmosphere was such that blacks could not buy firearms anywhere in the area, even for hunting.

There were signs of new things coming in the North. It was considered national news in 1950 that an interracial fellowship service was held at the Cathedral of St. John the Divine in New York, and that a black clergyman, Roland T. Heacock, was chosen as pastor by the white congregation of the Staffordville (Conn.) Congregational church. But these straws in the wind were not enough to compensate for the fact that in 1950 only a slight glimmering of the dawn to come was lighting the sky.

Nineteen fifty was a pivotal year nationally in many respects. But it was for African American religion pivotal only in a rather negative sense; it was the still point between one era and another, when changes were preparing but were so far barely visible. The age of 1930s' despair, of storefront sects and accommodating pastors, was passing. The returning black veterans and the new generation of black leaders, typified by Martin Luther King Jr., then in seminary, wanted more and would see to it as soon as they could.

Change in American race relations was coming; anyone with any perception could see that. In 1950, though, the process was moving with glacial slowness. But the weight behind change was building, and when critical mass had been reached, it would accelerate like an avalanche.

9

Evangelicals
on the Rise

The years around 1950 were a time of postwar evolution for
evangelicalism, as for so many facets of American life. The
old evangelicalism still lingered, rooted in the losing end of
the traumatic modernist-fundamentalist wars of the 1920s,
and the embittered 1930s, when conservative Protestantism
sometimes bore a sulfurous whiff of nativist anti-Semitism
and anti-Catholicism.[1]

Carl McIntire still used his Bible Presbyterian Church and
his American Council of Christian Churches as platforms for
his harsh, take-no-prisoners crusades against any hint of modernism. Gerald L. K. Smith, the notorious Christian anti-
Semite, was moving to his final retreat in Eureka Springs,
Arkansas, but remained active and seemed genuinely puzzled
that the nation no longer paid much attention to him.[2]

Their time was passing. The founding of the state of Israel
in 1948, universally regarded in prophecy-oriented conservative Christian circles as a supernatural sign of immense
importance, put a new light on Jewish-Christian relations.
While some still urged Jews to repent of their apostasy, it was
also clear that the children of Abraham now had a new and
tremendously significant role, in which they needed to be
supported by Christians, as the doomsday clock ticked toward
the consummation of all things. In 1950 the *Moody Monthly*,
that mainstay of evangelical, prophecy-oriented Christianity,

Evangelist Billy Graham.

ran a series of articles on Israel by Victor Buksbazen, identified as a "Christian Jew." Called "The Miracle of Israel," they
glorified the promise and the spirituality of the new state. Not
only that, but the postwar mood of tolerance and "brotherhood," and of chastened feelings in the face of the immense
suffering experienced by the Jews of Europe, affected even
those on the Christian Right for whom these were not easy
virtues.

But the old evangelicalism put up a fight, and 1950 represents a key year in the battle. The founding of the National
Council of Churches at the end of November was a lightning
rod for fundamentalists. Carl McIntire and those of his style
attacked the Council on several grounds, and they endeavored to relate their charges to American nationalism and
Protestant religious populism. Pictures from the Cleveland
gathering, revealing processional crosses and banners,
together with Eastern Orthodox prelates in their rich vestments, suggested how far the new "superchurch" had moved
from true Protestantism. Always an anticommunist crusader,
McIntire went on to attack such liberal churchmen as the
great missionary E. Stanley Jones and Methodist bishop G.
Bromley Oxnam on the grounds of their alleged leftist sym-
pathies.

McIntire was actually in Cleveland during the NCC's
founding meeting in 1950, hovering around the fringes of the
snowbound conclave and denouncing it to any who would read
or listen; this presence bothered some of the "cooperative"
churchmen. In an address, Charles P. Taft told the story of an
outsider who had visited Texas and, on his return home, was
asked by a friend what was wrong with that state. "Well," the
visitor said, "all Texas needs is more water and a better class of
people." The questioner commented, "That's all hell needs."
This story somehow reminded Taft of McIntire; the eminent
Ohioan then mentioned the latter by name, saying, "When we
really try we can do better than Carl McIntire any day."[3]

Some evangelicals were trying to do better. In 1941 Carl
McIntire had founded his fundamentalist American Council

of Christian Churches as a bulwark against modernism. In 1942 the much larger National Association of Evangelicals was formed under the leadership of Harold John Ockenga, a Boston pastor, in part because many evangelicals thought McIntire too negative in his rhetoric. Ockenga continued to argue that evangelicalism must have a wide vision and offer something more than fundamentalism. In a landmark 1947 speech, "Can Fundamentalism Win America?" Ockenga had said, "Fundamentalism is divisive. Fragmentation, separatism, censoriousness, suspicion, solecism is the order of the day for fundamentalism." It can never win America; it is too negative and full of backbiting, Ockenga thought.[4]

By the middle 1950s a new style of evangelicalism had emerged. It had several characteristics. Intellectually, it was a style that was being pioneered by the brand-new (founded in 1947) Fuller Theological Seminary in Pasadena, California: friendly and well informed toward science and culture in ways the old evangelicalism certainly was not; serious about building a rational philosophical foundation for traditional Christianity; tolerant in nonessentials and able to reexamine itself; and willing to accept social responsibility.[5] Among the funding faculty was Carl Henry, later (in 1956) to become founding editor of *Christianity Today*, ever since a major voice of American evangelicalism.[6]

Particular mention should also be made of Edward John Carnell, professor and sometime dean of Fuller Seminary, who in books like *An Introduction to Christian Apologetics* (1948) and *A Philosophy of the Christian Religion* (1952) strove to show that evangelicalism, not liberalism, was both rational and compatible with the best current science and philosophy. For Carnell, Christianity offers the profoundest interpretation of the human situation of any worldview. It should present itself on the basis of reason, not just existentialist faith, starting, Carnell always insisted, with the law of noncontradiction. Ironically, the new evangelical theology was more rationalistic than the fashionable existentialist neoorthodoxy then regnant in the prestigious seminaries. In its rationalism it was more like the old liberalism, or the then-dominant Roman Catholic Thomism, though drawing different conclusions from reason than they. Nonetheless, Fuller was firmly biblical in a way that could be interpreted as fundamentalist or literalist. On January 31, 1950, Fuller Seminary's faculty and board of trustees adopted a ten-point statement of faith that both faculty and trustees were formally to affirm each year. Its second article declared that "the books which form the canon of the Old and New Testaments as originally given are plenarily inspired and free from all error in the whole and in the part. These books constitute the written Word of God, the only infallible rule of faith and practice."

All in all, though, the new evangelicalism presented an open and loving spirit in contrast to the old-fashioned preacher's prophetic condemnations of the world, including supposedly worldly voices within the church. There were those who thought the new evangelicalism was nothing but liberalism in disguise, but the new model prospered in large part because it fitted well with the new sociological realities of American evangelicalism.

By 1950 evangelicalism was less a matter of particular denominations than a mass cultural movement that touched millions of followers, of varying degrees of commitment, scattered through most denominations. As Jon R. Stone has astutely noted, these masses were often reached less by the standard church than by the numerous parachurch organizations: evangelical educational institutions, publishing houses, radio ministries, and student movements that had, almost unnoticed by the "mainstream," enabled the old faith not only to survive but to thrive after the setbacks of the twenties. Indeed, Harold Ockenga once commented that the denomination is no longer the boundary between the world and the church, but only adds to the confusion.[7] The real "church" was instead an unstructured but potentially powerful evangelical subculture serviced as much by books, radio, summer camps, certain colleges, cross-denominational groups, and freelance evangelists as by denominational churches; this was the constituency so well mobilized beginning in 1949–50 by the evangelical crusades of Billy Graham. Nineteen fifty was then as much a pivotal year between an old style of religion and a new, postwar version of the same in American evangelicalism as in any other faith.

Most of all, the new postwar evangelicalism was a religion of a large but once-looked-down-upon sector of the population now acquiring a new level of prosperity and, many evangelicals hoped, a place in the mainstream. The makers of postwar evangelicalism, from populists like Billy Graham and Oral Roberts to the founders of the faith's new intellectual bastion at Fuller, sought language that symbolized both continuity with evangelicalism's revivalist past and its new place in the prosperous cold war world. The old-time religion would now adroitly emphasize evangelicalism's uncompromising opposition to communism along with all other destructive aspects of modernity. At the same time it tacitly accepted the accoutrements and mores of the postwar suburban lifestyle to which many of its people were heir. Revivals could now be held in air-conditioned auditoria, transmitted over radio and television, or celebrated in tents or under the trees, and preachers could drive late-model cars and wear well-tailored suits. In an almost indefinable way, the songs and rhetoric of the new evangelicalism suggested an upbeat, positive emphasis on the joy and benefit of accepting Christ, more than the have-not's sense of sin and bitterness.

A very important precursor to the new evangelicalism was Charles Fuller's "Old Fashioned Revival Hour," in the 1930s and 1940s the most popular of all radio programs of the era. It offered an upbeat message and music that, even if it was of recent composition, suggested a romanticized traditional revival atmosphere in an earlier America of simple piety and sturdy virtue. During the war it was beamed to soldiers in the nation's far-flung battlefields. Letters from them were often read on the air, symbolically bringing divided families closer together as well as closer to God in a time of great anxiety. In the immediate postwar years, the message incorporated cold war anticommunist rhetoric as well as traditional preaching into its appealing, nostalgic format.

Fuller's program was broadly nonsectarian and nondivisive, at least for those who could accept basic evangelical premises. Paradoxically but significantly, it originated in Hollywood, otherwise often considered a bastion of sin and secularism. But like later evangelical institutions the Old Fashioned Revival Hour effectively adopted the methods of the movie capital—professional quality, expert pacing, popular entertainment value—as vehicles for its piety. The program did much to create the postwar evangelical subculture's vision of America past and present. It was Charles Fuller who sought to perpetuate his style of evangelicalism in the namesake seminary he founded.

After the war, this mood was continued or created anew by the Youth for Christ organization, and above all by Billy Graham, the great evangelist of the postwar era who had earlier worked with Youth for Christ. (That organization's 1950 convention was noted in the previous chapter in connection with the evangelization of Japan.) Nineteen fifty was Graham's first full year of national celebrity status.

One must also mention C. S. Lewis, the unlikely pipe-smoking, sherry-drinking Anglican Oxford don whose elegant apologetics for orthodox Christianity made him a favorite—virtually a cult—among American evangelicals eager to see their faith put in up-to-date language and, perhaps on another level, to perceive it linked to the culture and sophistication that Oxford symbolized everywhere in the English-speaking world. Lewis also penned wonderful children's stories that expressed the Christian message on subtler levels; his famous Narnia series commenced in 1950 with the publication of *The Lion, the Witch, and the Wardrobe*.

Perhaps a definition of evangelicalism is now called for. Here are three characteristics of the religion that may help to describe its nature, especially compared to liberal and so-called mainstream Protestantism. First, evangelicalism insists on the importance of using distinctive and unchanging language on the key points of Christian faith. The keystone of theological liberalism, on the other hand, is conviction that the faith can and should be put in words compatible with the best scientific, philosophical, and cultural language of the day. The essence of Christianity is, like Schleiermacher's "feeling of absolute dependence" or Tillich's "ultimate concern," not itself a word-package but something prior to words that could be expressed through the means of several linguistic or conceptual frameworks and that must be made relevant to all times and places.

But for the evangelical, the use of the exact words of scripture—God, Christ, Atonement, Redemption, Heaven, and Hell—is crucial because they betoken that the gospel message is not cultural but transcendent, standing above all cultures in judgment and with a call to individuals to come out of the world to eternal salvation. To make the gospel truly transcend the seasons of this world it must be put in its own definite and specific language; its preachers must hold fast to the form of sound words (2 Tim. 1:13) while proclaiming the words of eternal life (John 6:68).

Second, evangelicalism gives central, even saving, importance to religious feeling and experience, above all feelings of conversion or "being saved," of receiving the Holy Spirit, and of joyous life with Christ. There are exceptions among some of the more intellectual though conservative Calvinists and Lutherans, but most of American evangelicalism has been deeply affected by the pietistic Wesleyan or Baptist belief that profound religious experience is a hallmark of real faith and salvation. So it is that feeling-laden religious experience is continually felt, testified to, discussed, and sought in evangelical circles, whereas religious liberals tend to be indifferent, or at least very private, about experience in comparison to other ways of knowing and expressing faith. It has been said, perhaps wryly but with some point, that the real difference between religious liberals and evangelicals is that liberals

cannot talk about religious experience without embarrassment, whereas evangelicals make a point of talking about it in
season and out.

Third, establishing well-defined boundaries is important
to evangelicalism. Whereas liberals may pride themselves on
continuity with the best in the culture and their openness to
the world, evangelicals want to know where the limits of the
circle of faith are. They want to bring as many as possible into
it, of course, but it must be on scriptural terms; incomers must
be saved in the right way and share the right beliefs. The
"world" outside is unsparingly castigated. Indeed, the evangelical mentality tends to need an Antichrist, which at various
times has been liquor, modernism, Roman Catholicism, communism, secular humanism, the New Age movement—one
characteristic of evangelicalism around 1950 was its shifting
of the central Antichrist focus from Jews, modernism, or
Catholicism to communism, in the process making alliances
with conservative, McCarthyist Roman Catholics and, in
conjunction with the prophetic importance of the state of
Israel, with Judaism. The antimodernist theological bias
remained, since modernists were liberals and as such too soft
on communism. As we have seen, however, modern culture
was increasingly though tacitly accepted; old blanket stric-
tures against dancing and movies, and even against smoking
and drinking, have tended to fade. But the separatist spirit in
evangelicalism, though muted in some arenas by its postwar
role, retained its potential; witness the "culture wars" of the
late twentieth century.

At this point a further distinction between evangelicalism
and fundamentalism may also be useful. Fundamentalism
may be taken here to denote the mentality of a religion that
senses itself under siege and feels anxiously compelled to safe-
guard its boundaries. Evangelicalism, while still protective
about the language of faith, is more outgoing and relatively
less legalistic, prepared to mount conversion-minded sorties
away from the citadel. This does not mean, however, that fundamentalism is necessarily less populist than evangelicalism,

even though Harold Ockenga was probably right in asserting the former could never "win" America. Although Carl McIntire's strident version of the cause was to pass into history, new forms of fundamentalism as well as the softer "new evangelicalism" continued to flourish for the rest of the century, and midcentury was important for them as it was symbolically pivotal for the "mainstream" churches and the new evangelicalism.

On May 22, 1950, the Baptist Bible Fellowship was created as the result of conflicts in the leadership of a loosely structured Baptist denomination, the World Baptist Fellowship. The highly fundamentalist Baptist Bible Fellowship grew rapidly, in large part by incorporating into its free polity a number of independent Baptist churches. Its main contribution has been to provide a denominational framework for several large autonomous churches under powerful pastors, such as Landmark Baptist Church in Cincinnati and, for a time, Jerry Falwell's Liberty Baptist Church in Lynchburg, Virginia. Even more than most Baptists, Bible Fellowship gave scope to dynamic independent preachers with a conservative message. At least in some symbolic sense, this Fellowship formed in 1950 was a prognosticator of the world of conservative televangelists and megachurch preachers that was to flourish in the second half of the century. Ostensibly, the individualistic Fellowship churches looked to be remnants of the old-time separatist tradition of fundamentalism. But events in 1950 and later would show that separatism—and even fundamentalism—could become culturally voguish. In time it would be mainline denominations that began to appear dated.

So it is that those developments consort with several seemingly contrary indicators of late-century American evangelicalism highlighted by Joel A. Carpenter in *Revive Us Again; The Reawakening of American Fundamentalism*. Carpenter notes that recent evangelicalism has had a symbiotic relationship with modernity, in the sense that evangelicalism is actually able to compete well in the pluralistic world modernity has created. This fact has often been overlooked by social scientists because of their readiness to assume that modernization always produces secularization. The secularization hypothesis, however, has increasingly been questioned, and the reawakening of evangelicalism in the late modern era is a case in point.

As a largely subjective, indeed intensely personal, rather than societal religion, evangelicalism fits well into the compartmentalization of modern life. Its institutions, based on congregationalism and charismatic preachers, flourish in the "free enterprise" spiritual arena left after the withering away of state churches and other forms of cultural faith. Its egalitarianism—the idea that anybody can have a saving experience or have as much insight into the scriptures as anyone else—fits the individualistic, antiauthoritarian consciousness of much contemporary seekers. To be sure, much of life in a complex modern society is governed by "experts" and technocrats, but the very pervasiveness of the "rationalized," bureaucratic system makes for conditions favoring rebellion in subjective areas of life such as religion. One yearns to find some different and more exciting experience in the secret places of the heart.[8]

So it is that evangelical Christianity, perhaps the quintessential American religion, has developed its contemporary role in American life in interaction with the country's modernization. It is instructive to note that in the colonial period, the South, which was to become the "Bible Belt," was spiritually mostly served by a tepid Anglicanism that produced such persons as Thomas Jefferson, icon of the Enlightenment who expected Unitarianism to become the religion of the future. Then it was New England that was the home of serious puritanical Protestantism. The roles more or less reversed as New England's relentless intellectualism chewed its way toward liberalism and as the evangelicalism of the frontier revivals, at first a highly countercultural force, challenged the class and racial hierarchies of the South through a practical application of the Enlightenment, and Christian, premise of American democracy, the equality of all before God. Although Southern evangelicalism certainly compromised with caste and slavery, it was more egalitarian and even interracial than other parts of Southern culture, and ultimately it inspired the civil rights movement of the 1950s and 1960s.[9]

In 1950 evangelicalism and the antisecularization forces that were to give it fresh entry into late twentieth-century America were only starting to gather. Joel Carpenter notes that evangelicalism was beginning to occupy a different place in American life in 1950 than it had only a decade earlier. But that emerging reality was hardly noticed: "Mainline Protestant leaders were not quite aware as yet that there was another Protestant force out there that they had to take seriously; the *Christian Century* published no stories or commentary on Billy Graham's phenomenal urban campaigns in 1949 and 1950."[10] One could certainly perceive religious antimodernism in 1950, but it was not yet clear that evangelicalism would ultimately convey it better than, say, more intellectually respectable rivals such as Protestant neoorthodoxy, the resurgent neomedievalism of Thomistic Roman Catholicism, or Anglo-Catholicism with its Oxford connections.

In retrospect it is clear that evangelicalism, boasting individualism, experience-orientation, quasi-anti-institutionalism, and deep roots in the American past, had assets these alternatives could not match. Overinstitutionalized and continually looking toward Europe, they could hardly have expected to gain evangelicalism's hold on the heartland. All that was needed was for evangelicalism to update itself, which it did with the help of Graham and Fuller Seminary. The updating, the shedding of anti-intellectual negativity and the acquisition of a joyousness to match the new prosperity, was achieved in tandem with the religion's growing popularity. It is a rare movement that, becoming popular and accepted, does not somewhat remodel itself to fit the expectation of its idealizers, and American evangelicalism was no exception.

The great icon of the new evangelicalism was Billy Graham. During the "hidden years" of evangelicalism after the Scopes "Monkey Trial" of 1925—which pitted fundamentalism against Darwinism and which evangelicals felt held them up as objects of mockery out of step with American life—followers of the old-time faith tended to withdraw from public life altogether. It was Billy Graham, and the Youth for Christ crusades of the late 1940s in which he was active, that brought evangelicalism back to the center of American consciousness in a new way.

Graham's evangelistic crusades could not be characterized as compromising or lighthearted spirituality. But they did suggest the urgent drive of postwar religion to return to its sources and find ways to bring them whole into contemporary life. Evangelical Protestantism's past was American rather than Asian or medieval European: the revival tent, the camp meeting, the frontier church, above all the trumpet-voiced preacher full of fiery emotion declaiming the greatest challenge of all, Accept Christ, take him into your heart, now! But the saving words were heard today, not in woodsy camps but in the biggest auditoria and amphitheaters of America's vast cities, in the person of the young man with the compelling blue eyes who was making news from coast to coast.

Graham burst on the scene in the fall of 1949 with a seven-week crusade in Los Angeles. There he preached to more than three hundred thousand and won some six thousand converts for Christ. Among them were Hollywood celebrities, and the news media picked the story up; Graham owes much to a internal directive from William Randolph Hearst to his editors: "Puff Graham." This resulted in sudden front-page coverage of the evangelist in the Hearst papers, including the *Los Angeles Examiner*, by mid-October 1949. The "puff" was quickly matched in other newspapers and newsmagazines nationwide, to make the young evangelist an instant celebrity and his revival of sawdust-trail religion among the supposed sophisticates of the City of Angels a topic of conversation. Graham claims, however, that he never learned why Hearst took an interest in him. In his autobiography, *Just as I Am*, the evangelist wrote, "Hearst and I did not meet, talk by phone, or correspond as long as he lived."[11] However, William Martin, in his Graham biography, *A Prophet with Honor*, notes that earlier, in 1946, the Hearst papers had boosted the Youth for Christ organization in which Graham had been an active leader. Hearst had sent a "puff YFC" telegram in that year; for a while Youth for Christ leader Roy McKeown even had a weekly column in the *Los Angeles Examiner*.[12]

In January 1950 Billy Graham repeated his Los Angeles success in Boston, and then went on to even greater achievement in his home country, the Carolinas. The evangelist returned to Los Angeles in June 1950 for a one-night appearance organized by Fuller Seminary, known as the Mid-Century Rose Bowl Rally, thus sealing the relationship between Charles Fuller, Graham, and the Seminary. Carl Henry, in fact, was the major organizer of this event, reporting in his autobiography that he expended nearly all his time and energy for three months to prepare for it. When the night finally came, he was initially disappointed that fifty thousand persons had turned out, rather than the hundred thousand that would have been the Rose Bowl's capacity, but was consoled to learn that it was nonetheless the largest religious event in the history of the Pacific Southwest and that it had enhanced interest in both Graham and the Seminary.[13]

Graham said in his memoirs that in 1950 he turned down a film offer from the president of Paramount Studios, Y. Frank Freeman. It was during a lunch attended by Cecil B. DeMille, then about ready to remake *The Ten Commandments*, and by actors Anthony Quinn, Barbara Stanwyck, and Betty Hutton. "I'd like you to consider doing a film with us," said Freeman, according to Graham. But Graham wrote, "I looked him straight in the eye, with the others listening, and told him that God had called me to preach the Gospel and that I would never do anything else as long as I lived."[14] (The next year, 1951, though, Graham did open his own studio in

Burbank—World Wide Pictures—to make religious dramas that ended with Graham inviting the audience to commit themselves to Christ.)

Graham was controversial. Commentators noted his hand-painted ties, his stylish suits, and his extravagant rhetoric: "America has only three or four more years at the most and then it will all be over and we will fall as Rome fell and Germany fell."[15] When it came to attacking the evils of communism, he was outdone by no one. There were those who regarded him as naive and given to irresponsible extremism. But some of this was the hyperbole of many Southern preachers, understood and taken with a grain of salt by those who comprehended the religious culture out of which they came. What was more significant was the combination in Graham's campaigns of modern sophistication—the sartorial elegance, the elaborate organization—with the antimodern message. He proclaimed an internal cold war between old-time religion and modern worldliness. Yet that message was appealing to many moderns when presented in venues they could understand and respect, because they felt within themselves not only modernity, but also the sort of emptiness that the modern world could not entirely fill.

The organization of a Billy Graham campaign was a remarkable and telling combination of the technology and "rationalized" bureaucracy that sociologists like Max Weber and Émile Durkheim have seen as the hallmark of modernity, with an antimodern though highly charismatic central figure. Behind the scenes, the labor of launching the performance could scarcely have been bettered by a modern political campaign or Madison Avenue product promotion. A Lutheran pastor in Columbia, South Carolina, reported that before the forty thousand gathered in the University of South Carolina stadium in 1950, a well-organized staff had put out advance publicity. Prayer meetings were held at the neighborhood level, and also in stores and office buildings. This pastor, Wynn Boliek, found the revivalist's preaching to be sincere and straightforward, but with an emphasis on fear, for example, in Graham's predictions that five years from now, none of those present would still be on planet Earth. At the end, Graham called for hands. Respondents went to prayer rooms accompanied by well-trained "personal workers." The new converts filled out decision cards with the name of their church preference. In his own conversations with attenders, Boliek found a mixed situation among those who signed the decision cards. Some did so to get rid of a persistent worker; some young people put up their hands and went to the prayer rooms just out of curiosity about what was going on.

Some churches gained a few members; some lost as converts moved to religious communities presumed to be more attuned to the evangelical spirit. But at least, Boliek concluded, people were talking about religion while Graham was in town.[16] There was something very modern about the way, in the end, the Graham crusades made their real impact less through numbers of "decisions"—although these were carefully counted—than through the spectacular national media attention and the modern state-of-the-art impression evangelistic technology imparted. All this suggested an old American tradition definitely come of age and as much at the heart of American life as ever.

We have noted in chapter 7 that Graham took time out from his 1950 campaigns to endorse the Korean War, to meet President Truman, and increasingly to support the conservative Republican agenda. Later, like Cardinal Spellman, he traveled to Korea to conduct services for the troops. These gestures were significant, at least symbolically, for the new acculturation of evangelicalism. As recently as World War I, liberal Christians had accused evangelicals of dubious patriotism in their lukewarm support of the "war to end war." Evangelical lack of enthusiasm for bringing in the kingdom of God through social progress, even when the means of progress was a just war, was then seen by liberals as a sign of hopelessly reactionary obscurantism. There was a lingering, and probably final, hint of the contrary progressivist liberal frame of mind in *The Christian Century*'s editorial, cited in chapter 7, supporting the Korean War as a United Nations operation that could make the 1950 conflict yet another war to end all war. But evangelicals had little confidence that the millennium would be produced by such human actions as fighting a great war; at most that tragedy would be one of the disastrous signs of Satan's rampage just before the apocalyptic end. Yet, without endorsing utopianism—indeed, out of revulsion at it in the anti-Christian Soviet version—evangelicalism for the most part heartily supported the cold war and the military after 1945.

At the end of Word War II even Southern Baptist periodicals and conventions, still retaining something of their Anabaptist forebears' tendency toward pacifism and their radical sense of separation from the state, were opposed to the draft and highly skeptical of militarism in general. Graham helped redefine the military's cold war role as a vital instrument in a crusade against ultimate evil from which Christians could not withdraw. Indeed, he soon went beyond the policies of the Truman administration to side with those who saw the crusade in absolute, one might say positively apocalyptic, terms.[17] For the new evangelical Christian, militarism was not based on liberal progressive eschatology so much as cold war apocalypticism. It meant taking sides in the ultimate battle.

The positive harmonization of the evangelical gospel with cold war emotional and ideological need was only one aspect of Graham's repackaging of that message for the America of 1949 and 1950. Above all, he was extraordinarily successful in reshaping what had once been an uncompromising antimodern message from the fringes into a reassuring evocation of that history that now seemed familiar, comfortable, and easy. Without diluting its core, at least in his own eyes, like the Old Fashioned Revival Hour before him, Graham tamed and updated the timeless call for decision for Christ into something quite compatible with living in a suburban home and driving a late-model car.

The religious revival of the late 1940s and the 1950s has often been attributed to demand on the part of a populace devastated by the experience of war and riddled with anxiety over the atomic bomb, the international scene, and a very uncertain future. Yet no similar revival occurred on anything like the same scale in any other major country, though all the world shared those anxieties and that experience, some far more devastatingly than the United States. As I have argued elsewhere,[18] the American supply side must be given as much or more credit than the demand side. Not only were some spiritual conditions for a revival present, but America was blessed with a number of charismatic purveyors of revivalism able to create demand as well as satisfy it, with a greater and more varied number of religious institutions able to offer spiritual venues, and with a popular attitude toward religion generally more positive than in most other places in the West. Among the supply-side charismatics none equaled Billy Graham in his capacity to awaken religious longing and then meet it in acceptable ways, as well as in his attractive and simple message well couched in the language of the fears and hopes of the day. It was otherworldly and yet accessible in the everyday world; it was supernatural and yet comprehensible to all: Raise your hand; come forward; accept Christ. And all was in the familiar context of a tradition profoundly intertwined with American history and culture, now enhanced by joyous, well-amplified sacred music and businesslike preparation.

Billy Graham was not alone in promoting the evangelical message in 1950. Youth for Christ had pioneered the use of rallies, much publicized in the 1940s—as we have seen, by Hearst above all—modeled after young people's pop music performances and revues rather than the old-fashioned tent meeting. The former and current Youth for Christ presidents, Torrey Johnson and Bob Cook, among many other "smaller" Billy Grahams, held successful revivals in many heartland cities around 1950. Clearly something was burgeoning. The new movement of the Spirit was reflected also in campus revivals. Beginning on February 5, 1950, a spontaneous confession of sins, by one student after another, struck Wheaton College in Illinois, Billy Graham's alma mater, and continued some forty hours. The story was picked up by *Time, Life*, and other media. Shortly after, a similar marathon of confession and testimony lasted five days at Asbury College in Kentucky, then moved on to campuses in Oregon, Washington, California, and elsewhere. In another stratum of society, prayer breakfasts were becoming popular in Washington; the popular song "It Is No Secret What God Can Do" rose high in the charts and sold over a million records; and Hollywood celebrities, including Roy Rogers and Dale Evans, made publicized decisions for Christ.[19]

The flavor of the old-time tent-meeting revivalism also continued in 1950. In September 1950, the celebrated healing evangelist Oral Roberts was in Amarillo, Texas, preaching in a revival tent holding seven thousand, when a tremendous thunderstorm came up. The huge poles fell and the tent collapsed, but no one was killed or seriously injured, an event that Roberts widely proclaimed as a miracle.[20] Marjoe, the subject of a famous 1972 movie based on his checkered career, was a child evangelist in 1950—a later *Life* article about him contains a picture of his performing a wedding in 1949 at age four, and on August 27, 1950, at age six, he preached his most famous sermon, "Hell with the Lid Off."[21] Marjoe Gortner left home to become part of the "hippie" counterculture in the 1960s, returned sporadically to preaching of both social gospel and "old-time religion," and finally, to considerable applause and scandal, revealed the tricks of the trade: the cues his parents had given him as a child preacher, the simulated emotion, the buckets of money hauled in. But by 1972—or even by 1950—serious evangelicalism had left that exhibitionist kind of religious performance far behind.[22]

Anxiety-based evangelicalism lingered nonetheless, now transferred largely to the tribulations of the cold war so far as world-scale issues were concerned. Often it was expressed through the intense study of biblical prophecy scenarios. This long-standing form of studious yet anguished and exciting evangelicalism experienced something of a revival around

1950. A network of premillennialists developed among Southern Baptists; in 1950 they felt out of harmony with the rest of that denomination, though premillennialism would gain strength in the battles to come within the Southern Baptist Convention. The editor of the *Beacon*, the publication of the Eastern Oklahoma Premillennialist Fellowship, doubted in 1950 that the world has "ever known stark fear as it knows today . . .fright is all about us." The only answer was Jesus, and churches were urged to take up evangelistic crusades, because this "may be our last revival."[23] The somewhat more deep-thinking prophecy writer Wilbur M. Smith said that the bomb forced nonbelievers to consider seriously the claims of biblical prophecy.[24] Numerous prophecy writers spread popular eschatology widely, combining a dispensationalist and premillennialist reading of the Bible with observation of the dramatic world events around them.[25] Israel and Russia (usually identified with the biblical Gog) especially fascinated them, and the two foci of prophetic action could easily be combined. Harry Ironside wrote in 1949, for example, that "in the last days" the Soviet leaders would "look with covetous eyes upon the great developments going on in the land of Palestine and . . . determine that Russia must have her part of the wealth," thus inciting Armageddon.[26]

So it was that in 1950 evangelicalism lived between two worlds (Wilbur Smith, the intellectual apocalypticist, was on the faculty of Fuller Seminary along with the likes of Edward Carnell), trying to keep faith with its revivalistic and prophetic roots while also endeavoring to make itself a presence in current mainstream culture and intellectual life. For this movement from old to new, 1950 was a significant crossroads year, at the very crux of the time of transition.

10

Judaism
in Midpassage

For American Jews the year 1950 was something like an island of calm in the midst of terrible storms. Abundant grief, hope, and trauma were near at hand to the Jewish community of the United States and the world in 1950. There was the recent unspeakable devastation of the Nazi death camps, and American Judaism embraced survivors of that horror. The still more recent founding of the state of Israel in 1948 had brought joy that, if it could not assuage the grief—that nothing earthly could do—brought wonderful new hope as well as new challenges.

On a local level, American Jews were dealing with vast postwar social changes. Like many others, young Jewish families were moving out of inner city enclaves and into the new suburbs, in the process often diminishing or changing their relation to religious Judaism. Orthodoxy typically stayed back home and the new suburban synagogues were either Conservative or temples of the more liberal Reform tradition. Still, some 75 percent of Jews were categorized as urban in 1950. According to the *American Jewish Year Book* of 1951 (covering 1950), only about 10 percent of Jews were synagogue members, and of these only 10 percent attended services apart from the High Holy Days; on the other hand, many who were not members were seatholders for those solemn occasions. Estimates of the number of Jews who were associated in some

The flag of the newly proclaimed state of Israel is raised over the Haifa Airport.

way with religious congregations in 1950 ranged from 850,000 to 1.5 million, out of some 5 million Jews in the United States altogether.

Nonetheless, these were years of what Nathan Glazer has termed a "Jewish revival," especially, as indicated, for the more liberal wings of Judaism. In 1937 Conservative Judaism had 250 synagogues with some 75,000 member families; in 1956 the numbers were 500 synagogues and 200,000 families. Reform Judaism had 290 temples and 50,000 families in 1937; and 520 temples with 255,000 families in 1956. Although hundreds of tiny urban synagogues closed in that period and numbers of congregants were decreasing, the Orthodox tradition showed vigor too; its institutions of learning, like Yeshiva University in New York, were flourishing. Nonetheless, a survey of Americans Jews in 1952 showed that 81 percent said that their grandparents were, or had been, Orthodox, but only 16 percent of their parents were. In 1950 Judaism was in the midst of dramatic religious and demographic changes.[1]

Jews also had to contend with changes in the larger social atmosphere that were hopeful yet also disturbing; as "rules" changed, one was not always sure just what they were at the present moment. After the great war against Nazism and its Final Solution, doctrinaire anti-Semitism was definitely out of favor with the majority of Americans, though as we shall see it lingered with vicious potential. Talk of "Brotherhood" and of the "three faiths"—Protestantism, Catholicism, and Judaism— as coequal partners in the nation's spiritual life was in the air. The *American Jewish Year Book* of 1951 identified a list of active anti-Semitic groups, from Gerald L. K. Smith's Christian Nationalist Party to the Ku Klux Klan. But it also noted that human relations organizations (the favored name at the time for civic leadership committees combating religious or racial intolerance and discrimination in particular locales) were being formed widely, as were interfaith councils bringing together the American religious community's varied leaders.

Nonetheless, true equality was not yet a reality. The most appalling anti-Semitic episode of the time was probably that reported in a February 1950 article in *Jewish Frontier*. It gave an account of two young Jewish war veterans who had pooled their resources to purchase a modest home on Chicago's non-Jewish southeast side. In October 1949 they and their families moved in. Almost immediately "Not for Sale" signs appeared in neighboring homes, and a homeowners association was formed for the purpose of ridding the neighborhood of "undesirable elements" and preventing more from coming in.

Then, on November 8, the two families held a reception in their homes for members of the union of which one was secretary-treasurer; the party included black union members. A mob gathered outside, shouting insults at both Jews and "Negroes." The assemblies continued over following days, quickly becoming strictly anti-Semitic when it was realized that the blacks had no intention of moving to that area. Mobs screaming such cries as "Let's go in and kill the Jews" threw rocks and bricks at the house, cheering when a window was broken. The police, although present in force, did nothing to protect the two families, and in fact seemed largely sympathetic with the attackers. By November 11, Armistice Day, parties from Jewish and civil rights organizations, having obtained no satisfaction from police headquarters or city hall, had gathered to try to protect the home and the families. Riot conditions and violence persisted. According to an editorial in Chicago's *Daily News*, when a policeman was asked by a reporter why he did nothing to stop the beatings, he replied that the home protectors were properly beaten because they were Communists.

"How do you know they were Communists?" the reporter inquired.

"Because they were Jews," the policeman explained.

One neighbor, charged with engaging in Hitlerite behavior, retorted, "The only trouble with Hitler is that he didn't finish the job."

Although the pogrom eventually dissipated, for weeks the families did not dare walk the streets of that neighborhood or leave the threatened home alone. Hardly less shameful than the incident itself was the extraordinary indifference shown by the police, the mayor, and the press in dealing with it, or even recognizing its existence. While it was happening the story was typically played down, labeled as an "incident" based on "false rumors," and put on the back pages of Chicago papers, although eventually the *Daily News* ran the previously cited editorial condemning the outrage, and the *Sun-Times* followed suit the next day. Still, American Jews in this part of Chicago might have been excused for thinking they were living instead in Nazi Germany.[2]

Mob violence on this scale was, of course, not characteristic of the experience of most American Jews in 1950, though no Jew lived without the knowledge at the back of his or her mind that it could, and had, occurred. Quieter forms of discrimination were more common. A 1950 survey by the B'nai B'rith Vocation Service Bureau found that in relation to non-Jews, Jewish lawyers earned less, had a harder time getting employment, and more often had to take jobs unrelated to their training. The survey also found that a lower percentage of Jewish applicants were accepted by medical schools than non-Jews. Jews also came up against barriers in housing, employment, private schools, hotels, and resorts. Sometimes these were discreet, virtually invisible until some opening or facility suddenly became unavailable. Sometimes they were as overt as an advertised notice that a particular resort hotel preferred clients who were "Christians of the white race."

In 1950 Jews fought bigotry as best they could—and increasingly successfully when the issues were openly presented and received a fair hearing. Not seldom Jews contended against racial as well as religious discrimination at the same time, seeing their cause as one with that of African Americans and others who were marginalized in the Land of the Free. In response to complaints by the American

Jewish Congress, the *Journal of the American Medical Association* announced on June 5, 1950, a policy of refusing to accept situations-wanted ads that stated racial or religious preferences.[3] The *Congress Weekly* of the American Jewish Congress, in reviewing five years of civil rights in the United States on November 27, 1950, noted progress but vowed continuing action on behalf of Jews, "Negroes," Puerto Ricans, Japanese, and others in four areas: job equality, housing—the "freedom to dwell together"—"policing the airwaves" (i.e., opposing racist and anti-Semitic messages on the radio), and immigration reform.

What kind of religious worldview did Jews have in 1950? As in any community, perspectives varied widely. In January 1950, Israel Knox presented in *Commentary* "A Humanist Religion for Modern Man." He perceived "a reviving interest" on the part of Jewish intellectuals in religion, and Judaism in particular, but called for its interpretation within a "naturalistic framework." Judaism, he said, stands in sharp contrast to Karl Barth, who said, "We are not the ones to change the evil world into a good world. God has not resigned his lordship into our hands." The ancient religion of the Jews insists instead that humans can and must make the world a better place; only by our taking responsibility for answering to human needs and not waiting for supernatural intervention will this happen.

On the other hand, the distinguished theologian Emil L. Fackenheim, writing in the same periodical in May 1950 on "The Modern Jew's Path to God," gave the perspective of the traditionalist and mystic. Dismissing metaphysics he offered in its place the traditional rabbinical concept of Lord of the Universe, saying that naturalist and idealist approaches to God and religion are alike absurd. Like Martin Buber and the existentialists, Fackenheim insisted that one does not understand those ultimate realities as a spectator seeking to make sense of them in a detached, rational way, but only as a participant in their life.

An interesting and revealing 1950 exchange centered

around an article in *Life* for September 11, 1950, by Philip S. Bernstein titled "What the Jews Believe." This eminent rabbi presented what was probably the standard values of reasonably liberal Jews at the time. He began by saying, "The Jew has no single organized church. He has no priests. The concept of salvation by faith is alien to his mind. . . . Judaism is a way of life, here and now. He does not service his God for the sake of reward, for the fruit of the good life is the good life. Thus his answers about the nature of his religious beliefs are profoundly different from the answers made by Christians."[4] This eminent authority, who was currently serving as president of the Reform tradition, then proceeded to discuss the Law as "not a straight jacket" but always interpreted by oral law, and the basic Jewish "creed," the Shema Israel —- "Hear, O Israel, the Lord thy God is One"—as confirmed by "the writings of Albert Einstein" on the universe as a unified field. The oneness of God, or Ultimate Reality, also means ultimate human oneness. Jewish particularism means respect for human differences, not superiority or inferiority on the part of Jews or anyone else. Finally, Bernstein explained why, though Jews respect Jesus as a teacher and prophet, they do not accept him as the Messiah.

Not all Jews were pleased by Bernstein's amiable modern interpretation of the tradition. The Jewish scholar Will Herberg came back with a trenchant response to Bernstein the next month in *Jewish Frontier*. He pointed out what he regarded as misconceptions in Bernstein's piece, citing the latter's assertion that "the concept of salvation by faith is alien to Jews" and his contention that Jews do not believe in resurrection; Herberg maintained there is significant biblical and rabbinical warrant for both those beliefs. Most centrally, however, he criticized the *Life* piece for the "Confucianist" spirit that pervaded it. For Bernstein, he claimed, Judaism becomes no more than "the religion of the respectable man at ease in respectable society." The religion of Abraham and the prophets is thus sunk to "the dead level of mediocrity."

There is nothing in Bernstein's faith, Herberg claimed, of "the dreadful predicament of the human situation, of the depths of evil and unreason in human existence. . . . Strip it of its ceremonial trimmings and what is the Judaism of Rabbi Bernstein's presentation but the optimistic idealism that was already obsolescent a generation ago." Sounding like Barth and the existentialists, Herberg went on to call for a Judaism of the Living God who reveals himself to humanity, observing that the "god" that a person "finds" by relying solely on one's own efforts is never the true God.

There was more; Herberg's response provoked its own trenchant responses. Harold Weisberg, in "Escape from Reason: A Reply to Will Herberg," in *The Reconstructionist* (Dec. 1, 1950), argued from the perspective of the liberal wing of Judaism that "Mr. Herberg's position does not offer us a viable religion for our time." His theology was, instead, "at base, an exercise in wish fulfillment." Desperately yearning for a God, for a purpose to history and fulfillment in human life, even if reasonable evidence for this is lacking, leads people to an "Other" "which on further analysis turns out to be nothing more than human desires masquerading as ontological aristocracy." Letters to the editor in several periodicals carried on the dispute over the fundamental character of Jewish religion from diverse points of view.

Clearly on one level the debate was a variant of the Christian polemics between rationalistic liberalism and existentialism-tinged neoorthodoxy, though the positions in Judaism were even more extremely stated, insofar as the liberal side did not hesitate to identify itself with sheer nontheistic humanism. Even the most liberal Christian thinkers usually preferred to retain some sliver of a metaphysical deity. Judaism, however, far more than Christianity, could and often did present itself as a culture and a people rather than as a theological religion. Indeed, ultimately the argument was probably between those who thought of Judaism primarily as a culture, to which doctrinal ideas were perhaps interesting but of secondary importance; and those who, like Herberg, now wanted it to be a full-fledged, God-confronting faith with all the feelings of angst and sin and all the "dimensions of depth" those qualities entailed.

There were other dimensions of depth for Will Herberg. In April 1950 that prolific author had published a review of *The God That Failed*, the famous 1949 work edited by Richard Crossman that contained pieces by such celebrated writers, and ex-communists, as Arthur Koestler, Ignazio Silone, André Gide, and others, depicting their lives in the Party and their departure from it, sometimes in favor of an equally fervent commitment to a religious faith. Here Herberg described himself as a one-time Communist who had risen to high position in the American Communist Party in the 1920s, and who had left it in the 1930s. He said that ex-communists become implacable enemies of the cause they had once loved wholeheartedly. That is because it is a totalistic religion that one must either love or hate, since for its sake the lover will do evil in good conscience, indeed with a glow of self-righteousness—deeds done in the name of communism and the coming revolution are "stripped of the odium of selfishness and sanctified by the holiness of the cause." Herberg added that since communism is a total faith, no attack from without can shake it; only an inner spiritual turning can disabuse one of its glamour.[5] Such a deep process, and not mere reason or "Confucian" comforts, must have liberated him from the Party's toils and brought him back to Judaism.

Another important issue for Jews in 1950 was the relation of American Jewry to the new state of Israel. Organizationally, there was the matter of the relation of Zionist groups like the Jewish Agency for Palestine and the World Zionist Organization to the new nation, and the future of *halutziut* or pioneer immigration. More immediately, Jews wondered how to respond to the political needs of Israel, such as security against the Arab states, and the question of the internationalization of Jerusalem. To what extent and in what way should they try to influence U.S. foreign policy?

Controversies swirled around the anti-Zionist American Council for Judaism, whose position was much resented by many Jews as well as other supporters of Israel. One issue had surfaced on August 31, 1949, when Premier David Ben Gurion of Israel, speaking to a delegation from the United States, was reported to have appealed to American Jewish youth to emigrate to Israel, whether their parents wished it or not. This call was used by the American Council for Judaism in a series of ads designed to imply that Zionism and Israel were seeking to undermine the family loyalty and American patriotism of American Jews. Its position was basically that Judaism was a religion and not nationalism, that "American Jews are individual American nationals of Jewish faith."

Needless to say, many Jews deeply resented the ads and their implication of dual loyalty—charges that of course had also been raised against Roman Catholics and their relation to the papacy, and against numerous other Americans in respect to their diverse national backgrounds. In reply to an inquiry by the American Jewish Committee, Ben Gurion stated that the quote had been unauthorized, but he did reiterate a parallel between the colonization of the United States by American pioneers and the need for similar Jewish pioneers in Israel. He also spoke of Israel's need for technical aid, both material and in the form of expert personnel. These thoughts, and the deep emotional issues they engaged, reverberated through the American Jewish community in 1950.[6]

The American Council for Judaism, though widely condemned, did not lie low. There was another matter that must have raised painful, though sometimes submerged, moral conflicts in many Jews, themselves so often a displaced people. Just as the pioneers of the American West did not enter truly empty territory, but largely displaced an indigenous people, so the land of Israel claimed by Jewish pioneers was not unoccupied. The American Council for Judaism seized on this point, and in 1950 its leadership supported HELP—Holy Land Emergency Liaison Program—which was concerned with aiding Christian and Muslim refugees from Palestine. But that group was inevitably characterized as partisan or worse, and friends of Israel, including two future secretaries of state, Christian Herter and John Foster Dulles, resigned from HELP on the grounds that it was too critical of Israel.[7]

These issues typified the deep and confused feelings raised by the matter of Jews and their relation to Israel. How much should Americans help? How should they regard the explicit identification of religion and the state in Israel? What about the matter of "dual allegiance"? How could they handle their mixed feelings about Jews and Arabs: admiration for the heroic "pioneers" versus sympathy for the lot of the displaced? After the horrors of Europe, most Jews were convinced that Jews needed a nation of their own, but was it right for it to be founded at someone else's expense?

These travails notwithstanding, modern Israel's founding greatly invigorated Jewish culture. Israeli folk songs became popular among American young people. Israel attracted Jewish artists, writers, and intellectuals who had a worldwide influence in areas ranging from folk painting to kabbalistic studies. Albert Einstein was elected president of the American Joint Board of Directors of the Hebrew University in Jerusalem at the time of its merger with the Weizmann Institute of Science in January 1950, in the hope, declared Dr. Weizmann, President of Israel, of "drawing the attention of American Jewry to the vital importance of Israeli centers of learning."[8] In the same year Einstein published *The World as I See It*, which included the great physicist's impressions of Jewish life and Zionism.

There was considerable coming and going between the New World and Israel, much of it rejoicing in the intoxicating pioneer spirit of the new Jewish land and the wonderful prospects it offered for untrammeled Jewish political and cultural expression. American students, especially rabbinical candidates, began spending time in Jewish institutions of learning in Israel. Whether Israel could or should be the world center of Jewish culture and values was a question that stirred intellectuals, but in practice the Jewish state's vitality was beginning to answer that question in its own terms.

Even so, American Jewish visitors sometimes found they had to explain themselves to Israelis. Arthur Hertzberg, writing on "American Jews Through Israeli Eyes," reported numerous conversations that began and ended with such questions as,ß Why didn't you stay in Israel? Why didn't more Americans come to fight? What are you American Jews like anyway? It was a new country versus the one with half the world's wealth; it was people with grim experience of the diaspora in their background and doubts about the future of Judaism outside Israel versus those who many thought had it too easy as Jews. The oft-unspoken background of these conversations was a recognition by Israelis they needed U.S. international support and material assistance, despite a healthy sense of independence and pride in their own accomplishments, and they thus could not help both appreciating and resenting the American role at the same time. Hertzberg did not always find their discussions comfortable, but they were enlightening.[9]

As always, though, Jewish culture was very much alive in the United States as well. The monumental two-volume *The Jews: Their History, Culture, and Religion*, edited by Louis Finkelstein, was published. The distinguished rabbi Abraham Heschel presented *The Earth Is the Lord's*, a history of the Jewish devotional movement called Hasidism. Several books on the Nazi persecution of Jews in Europe appeared. Two were collections of first-person accounts: *The Root and the Bough*, edited by Leo Schwartz; and *We Survived*, edited by Eric Boehm. Then there was John Hersey's best-selling novel on the Warsaw ghetto, *The Wall*.

In this connection, it may be noted that the Nazi persecution of Jews was not called the Jewish Holocaust in 1950, as it would be subsequently, and not all American Jews in the immediate postwar years looked on the Nazi terror exactly as would Jews of later decades. A controversial book by Peter Novick, *The Holocaust in American Life*, argues that emphasis on the uniqueness and transcendent meaning of the Jewish holocaust was really a product of the 1960s, especially the 1961 trial in Jerusalem of Adolf Eichmann, manager of transportation to the liquidation camps.[10] More tendentiously, Novick argues that the later interpretation of the Holocaust was not so much a consequence of a buried trauma then surfacing, but rather a political movement related to the needs of American Jews: their need for a symbol of Jewish identity at a time of declining religious participation, and the need to support the state of Israel. While the ghastly inhumanity of the Nazi extermination process was certainly known and not minimized in the late 1940s and the 1950s, according to Novick, Jews then did not so carefully distinguish between their experience and that of other victims of German barbarism, and did not want it to be especially emphasized as distinctive to Jewish experience. Instead, it was almost as though that part of Jewish history was seen as something shameful.

When a monument commemorating Jewish victims of the Holocaust was proposed in New York in the late 1940s by several prominent Jews, it was opposed by the American Jewish Committee, the Anti-Defamation League of B'nai B'rith, and the American Jewish Congress: Novick argues that was because, in the eyes of these authorities, it would be "a perpetual memorial to the weakness and defenselessness of the Jewish people," and thus "not in the best interests of Jewry."[11] From this perspective, there was no particular advantage to be gained now by conspicuously recalling days of dread and sorrow. They were over; those who knew what they were like firsthand did not need to be reminded; and for others they had not yet become a timeless symbol always to be kept before the eyes of the world. "The Holocaust had not, in the postwar years," writes Novick, "attained transcendent status as the bearer of eternal truths or lessons that could be derived from contemplating it."[12]

It was better then to emphasize new hope in Israel and to dwell positively on the relative freedom of Jews in a changing and powerful America; it was better to work for Jewish equality and participation in American life, and to stress the "brotherhood" ethic, rather than to emphasize Jewish uniqueness. Above all Jewish uniqueness in suffering need not be stressed, nor should the still-fresh memories of terror and degradation associated with such reflections be unnecessarily evoked. Perhaps that is why fundamentally optimistic novels of Jewish immigration to America, such as Frederic Morton's *The Darkness Below*, Ruth Chatterton's *Homeward Borne*, and Sam Ross's *The Sidewalks Are Free*, were also popular in 1950. Yet the dark nightmares were there and would not forever lie still. If there were those in 1950 who hoped they could be forgotten or even reversed, they hoped in vain. One can understand why many Jews in 1950 chose to recall what was to be termed the Holocaust only reluctantly, and why for the next generation it was important that it never be forgotten. Another reason had to do with U.S. foreign policy: that war was over and in the current pressing conflict, the cold war, Germany was an ally. It was now better to de-emphasize the uniqueness of German sins and stress the universality of inhumanity in a way that enabled a keen focus on the evils of Stalinism.

At the same time, I am not sure the recent terror in Europe was as downplayed in 1950 as Novick implies. My own reading of Jewish periodicals for that year has presented a good number of relevant memoirs and articles, as well as reviews of books of Holocaust memoirs like those mentioned above. It is also not clear that Novick has presented the evidence of alleged de-emphasis in proper context. For example, Nathan

Glazer's study of 1950s' American Jews observes that the Holocaust then "had remarkably slight effect on the inner life of American Jewry."[13]

Actually the statement by Glazer links both the Holocaust and Israel by saying that the murder of six million Jews by Hitler, and the founding of the state of Israel, had slight effect on the "inner life" of American Jewry. But this author goes on to point out that hundreds of thousands of Jews who had little or nothing to do with Jewish life were drawn into Jewish activities by those momentous events, supporting the United Jewish Appeal and Zionist groups by raising vast sums of money. But of those who were not already members, Glazer states, not many then responded to Hitler or Israel by joining a synagogue or temple.[14] "Inner life" is apparently to be construed narrowly to indicate strictly religious sentiments. Perhaps neither the Holocaust nor Israel directly and centrally impacted what was going on in the very different world of American Jewish religious life around 1950: the building of new suburban synagogues and temples, the drift away from Orthodoxy and toward the more liberal traditions with their very different aura from that of Jewish religious life in old Europe or in new Israel. Yet while the hellish Nazi regime and the new nation may have not yet have possessed conscious significance for Jewish religion, it would certainly be incorrect to say they had no hold on Jewish passions and commitments in the midcentury years.

Nonetheless Glazer indicates that the "Jewish revival" of those years, meaning expansion in the strictly religious sphere, the growth of synagogues and temples, had causes nearer to home than Hitler or Israel: the move to the suburbs where community centers were needed; the way suburban middle-class respectability required a Jewish religious membership to match the Gentile suburbanite's church membership; the call for religious education so that Jewish children, now playing and going to school with non-Jewish classmates, could answer the question, "Why am I a Jew?" To all this, European terrors and Israel with its hidebound Orthodoxy so far as Judaism was concerned seemed remote and irrelevant, if Glazer and Novick are correct. Yet one doubts they were entirely absent from the back of the mind of even the most suburbanized Jew; regardless of circumstance, one always knows one is a Jew, and this awareness brings with it the consciousness of a history and a world community.

Jewish life had rarely been easy. In 1950 it seemed to many Jews easier, at least in America, than ever before, but knotty issues persisted and could not be ignored.

11

Getting Ready for the 1950s and 1960s

A *Time* magazine article on "The Younger Generation," though published in November 1951, clearly reflects the year 1950 and gives a valuable concluding insight into that era. It tells us that the youth of what came to be known as "The Silent Generation" were grave and fatalistic, the men especially sobered by the draft and the "Korean business."

These young people are conventional and gregarious, men and women alike wanting careers and marriage and a "traditional" family. Their morals are confused; they can "raise hell, but with an alarm clock in the back of their heads, recalling them to school, work, or war." They are not rebellious, and they expect disappointment. So far as religion is concerned, "they want a faith," but it appears they haven't found one and don't even know where to look. There is no religious revival among the young, yet they are not iconoclasts either, in the manner of the campus atheists of earlier generations, and church attendance among them has increased.

Not being rebellious, they will serve, in Korea, for example, and have no real doubts about the righteousness of the United States. They would not expect to enjoy military service or other calls of duty, and indeed they expect many disappointments in life, including perhaps the imminent end of the world in nuclear holocaust. But they are willing to make the best of a hard and difficult job, whether in life or war.

This was a generation coming of age just after the

John F. Kennedy's inauguration, January 20, 1961.

optimistic returning veterans graduating under the GI Bill in 1950, and just before the neo-rebels of the 1960s. *Time* summarized the Silent Generation in these words: "Youth today is waiting for the hand of fate to fall on its shoulders, meanwhile working fairly hard and saying almost nothing."[1]

This pretty well sums up 1950: a time of waiting for the next move of fate. Its tremendous conflicts, over McCarthy and McArthur, Korea and the cold war, were like birth pangs of a new postwar era, not that era itself. The dead-center, eye-of-the-storm calm of other areas of American spiritual life in 1950, whether African American or evangelical, were likewise moments of rest in that parturition process.

The remainder of the 1950s saw the gradual decline of the grim polarization, both national and international, of the midcentury year. In 1953 and after, President Dwight D. Eisenhower brought a certain welcome sense of stability in national life, even though important issues involving race and foreign policy were postponed. The Korean case was closed, and that war quickly forgotten like a bad dream by most people. After the army hearings of 1954, Senator McCarthy's reputation plummeted, and "McCarthyism" became a nasty word. The civil rights movement accelerated with *Brown v. Board of Education*, the Supreme Court decision outlawing school segregation in 1954, and with the Montgomery bus boycotts of 1955 and 1956, which first brought the name of Martin Luther King Jr. to wide public attention. That movement culminated with the Little Rock, Arkansas, crisis of 1957.

That same fall of 1957 also brought Sputnik, the satellite that suggested to an astonished and alarmed American public that now the Soviet Union might be ahead of us in science and technology. The upshot of that cold war crisis, however, was not more McCarthyist witch-hunting, but a new emphasis on education and space projects that were to lead, in the end, to the U.S. triumph on the moon in 1969. On happier notes, the later 1950s produced its own distinctive popular culture, featuring such varied symbols as Elvis, Disneyland, hula hoops, now-classic television, and the Beats, as well as a continuing religion boom.

Most of this was only latent in 1950. What one can see in that year is a deep-seated conflict between optimism and pessimism, the Class of 1950 versus the decline-of-the-west people and the McCarthyite alarmists about Communist victory. It was the optimists who won, though that was not a sure thing at midcentury. What we can see in 1950 was a year that looked, Janus-like, both forward and backward, trying to adjust the relative focus.

The celebrated activists and counterculturalists of the 1960s were supposedly the children of the postwar baby boom that crested around 1950, who were raised in a bland, conformist fifties culture against which they ultimately rebelled. None of this is entirely true—some were older than that, and the 1950s were by no means as dull as the image seems to assume. Indeed, as we have seen, certain roots of the 1960s can be perceived in 1950: in civil rights, with Martin Luther King Jr., who was reading Gandhi that year; in the antiwar movement; and in the reaction against McCarthyism and the skepticism about doctrinaire anticommunism that it provoked.

But so far as religion in a more institutional sense is concerned, it must be admitted that not many of the massive changes the 1960s brought were visibly on the horizon of 1950. Who then could have prognosticated what John XXIII and Vatican II were to mean to Roman Catholicism, or how large-scale social activism—clerics in peace and civil rights marches—and "Death of God" theology would affect the temper of liberal Protestantism? In Judaism, the religion's strong postwar position in American culture and close relation to the new state of Israel were apparent by 1950, though other aspects of Jewish life later in the century, such as a 1960s' upsurge of interest in mysticism, were not.

On the other hand, the revival of evangelicalism could already be seen in 1950. Possibly a few traces of the counterculture's interest in eastern religion and occultism were also evident—relevant books by Carl Jung, Aldous Huxley, and

Alan Watts were already attracting interest, and Jack Kerouac was living *On the Road*—but for the most part even the precursors of the counterculture had to wait for the public formation of the Beat culture in the middle 1950s.

On the other hand 1950 is also significant as a reverse mirror of the rest of the century. It shows what spiritual America could have become, but did not. There was in 1950 at least the potential for a quasi-fascist national superreligion based on mythological, apocalyptic anticommunism and an idealization of the premodern past, emphasizing conformity for the sake of "freedom" and the cohesion of the nation in spiritual as well as political unity. That this did not happen, or when it did, did not last long, is I believe chiefly due to the real nature of American religion. Unlike those European countries that truly became fascist, the United States does not have the model of a single state church thoroughly intertwined with the history and culture of the land, but rather has long been, to a degree virtually unequaled anywhere else, religiously pluralistic. Moreover, religion is in principle radically separated from the state, and so is voluntaristic. Beyond that, the United States is the only major country in the world largely peopled by religious dissenters from some state church or another.

Even in the crisis atmosphere of 1950, centrifugal forces drawing energy from America's cantankerous religious traditions pulled heavily against conformist ideology or a single anticommunist mythology of light and dark. The varied religious responses to the Korean War indicate as much, as do religious voices raised against McCarthyism to counterbalance those resonating with that master mythologist and witch-hunter of the cold war. Certainly the United States' persistent religious character had much to do with its vehement rejection of communism, but neither could religious America with all its divisive voices abide totalitarian anticommunism. And it was religion, not any secular ideology, that most profoundly shaped the later midcentury movement for social change, the civil rights movement.

Finally, then, 1950 shows American religion for what it has

been since colonial times and probably will be for a good while to come: diverse, pluralistic, frustrating in its inability to find a common voice or any significant unity—yet for that very reason an indispensable protector of individual freedom and nurturer of civil rights. For unless American religion were itself quieted and forced into conformity, all freedoms could not be lost. The seeds of fresh dissent, capable of taking root and crumbling the foundation of any state church or totalitarian superimposition will always be present, awaiting water and sun.

NOTES

Preface
1. Lisle A. Rose, *The Cold War Comes to Main Street: America in 1950* (Lawrence, Kans.: University of Kansas Press, 1999).
2. Tom Brokaw, *The Greatest Generation* (New York: Random House, 1998).

Chapter 1: Journey to the Heart of a Century
1. Mark Sherwin, *The Extremists*. (New York: St. Martin's Press, 1963), 110.
2. From Billy Graham's Los Angeles crusade of 1949. Cited in Stephen J. Whitfield, *The Culture of the Cold War* (Baltimore: Johns Hopkins University Press, 1991), 77.
3. "Five Fecund Years," *Life*, 31 July 1950, 31.
4. John Norberg, *A Force for Change: The Class of 1950.* (West Lafayette, Ind.: Purdue University, 1995), 211–12.
5. Ibid., 29–30.
6. Robert Thomas Allen, "I'm Sick of Sex," *Reader's Digest*, April 1950, 15–17. Condensed from *National Home Monthly*, January 1950.
7. Clyde Brion Davis, *The Age of Indiscretion*, condensation in *Reader's Digest*, August 1950, 145–68. Quote p. 168. From Davis, *The Age of Indiscretion* (Philadelphia: J.B. Lippincott Co., 1950).

Chapter 2: Heir of the 1930s and 1940s
1. Editorial, "Wages and Human Desperation," *The Christian Century*, 4 January 1933, 3.
2. Edwin Lewis, "What Is Barth Trying to Say?" *The Christian Century*, 18 January 1933, 82f.; and "The Theology of Karl Barth, *The Christian Century*, 25 January 1933, 120–21.
3. C. F. Andrews, "Lifting the Deadweight from Missions," *The Christian Century*, 25 January 1933, 115–17.
4. "Ministers on the March," *The Christian Century*, 9 May 1934, 624–25. Based on Kirby Page, "20,870 Clergymen on War and Economic Injustice," pamphlet.

5. Justin Wroe Nixon, "Protestantism for Such a Time as This," *The Christian Century*, 13 June 1934, 194–96.
6. Hubert Herring, "Union Seminary Routs its Red," *The Christian Century*, 13 June 1934, 799–801.
7. "Churches' Growth: Surveys Show Mounting Membership," *Newsweek*, 3 July 1939, 29.
8. Charles Eugene Conover, "Students and Religion: A Reply," *The Christian Century*, 19 July 1939, 901–02.
9. "Karl Barth Receives Double Honor," *The Christian Century*, 5 July 1939, 844–45.
10. "To 50,000," *Time*, 3 July 1939, 45.
11. "For Pacifists," *Time*, 10 July 1939, 36–37. "Niemöller or I," *Time*, 10 July 1939, 37.
12. "MRA in Hollywood," *Time*, 31 July 1939, 33–34.
13. See, for example, the reference in Halford E. Luccock, "With No Apologies to Barth," *The Christian Century*, 9 August 1939, 971–74.
14. Allan A. Hunter, *White Corpuscles in Europe*. (Chicago: Willett, Clark & Co., 1939).
15. Ray H. Abrams, "Preachers Present Arms," *The Christianity Century*, 22 November 1939; 6, 13, 20, 27 December 1939; 3 January 1940. Ray H. Abrams, "Preachers Present Arms," (Ph.D. thesis, University of Pennsylvania, 1933) (New York: Round Table Press, 1933).
16. Charles J. Tull, *Father Coughlin and the New Deal* (Syracuse, N.Y.: Syracuse University Press, 1965), 212. Cited from *Social Justice*, 31 July 1939.
17. Sheldon Marcus, *Father Coughlin*. (Boston: Little, Brown, & Co., 1973), 188.
18. "No Picketing," *Time*, 30 October 1939, 50–51. On the German American Bund, see Susan Canedy, *America's Nazis* (Menlo Park, Calif.: Markgraf, 1990). On other rightist, anti-Semitic voices of the time, particularly William Dudley Pelley, Gerald B. Winrod, and Gerald L. K. Smith, see Leo P. Ribuffo, *The Old Christian Right* (Philadelphia: Temple University Press, 1983).
19. "Christian Affronters," *Time*, 27 November 1939, 52; Tull, *Father Coughlin*, 218–19.
20. "Did Catholics Bet on the Wrong Matador?" *The Christian Century*, 12 July 1939, 868.
21. "'*Gott Sei Mit Uns*,'" *Time*, 18 September 1939, 62.

22. "Rev. Reds," *Time*, 11 December 1939, 44–45. Hewlett Johnson, Dean of Caterbury Cathedral, should not be confused with the primate of England and head of the Anglican communion, the Archbishop of Canterbury.
23. "Christian Program," *Time*, 25 September 1939, 54.
24. Norman Thomas, "War, Peace, and the Churches," *The Christian Century*, 11 April 1945, 458–60.
25. "Now He Belongs to History!" *The Christian Century*, 25 April 1945, 510–11.
26. "Gazing into the Pit," *The Christian Century*, 9 May 1945, 575–76.
27. "Horror and Shame," *Commonweal*, 24 August 1945, 443–44.
28. "Atrocities and War," *The Christian Century*, 29 August 1945, 974–75.
29. For a review of these positions sec "Godless Götterdämmerung," *Time*, 15 October 1945, 62–64.
30. Francis X. Murphy, C. SS.R., "God, Man, and the Atom Bomb," *Catholic World*, May 1946, 144–51.
31. Robert L. Calhoun, ed., *Atomic Warfare and the Christian Faith* (New York: Federal Council of Churches, 1946).
32. "Survivor," *Commonweal*, 6 January 1950, 356.

Chapter 3: Things Old and New

1. Norman Mailer, "Our Country and Our Culture: A Symposium" in *Advertisements for Myself* (New York: Putnam, 1959), 189–92.
2. "Religion and the Intellectuals: A Symposium," *Partisan Review*, February, March, April, May 1950.
3. "Editorial Statement," *Partisan Review*, February 1950, 103.
4. Philip Rahv, in "Religion and the Intellectuals: A Symposium," *Partisan Review*, March 1950, 237.
5. Editorial, "If People Ever Required Religious Faith, It's Now," *Saturday Evening Post*, 11 November 1950, 10–12.
6. Oswald Spengler, *Der Untergang des Abendlandes* (München: Beck, 1922–23). English translation, *The Decline of the West* (New York: Alfred A. Knopf, 1926).
7. See Paul Freedman and Gabrielle M. Spiegel, "Medievalisms Old and New," *American Historical Review* 103, no. 3, June 1998, 681.
8. Jack Kerouac, "'On the Road Again,' excerpts from Journals 1948–1950." *The New Yorker*, 22, 29 June 1998, 59.

9. William F. Buckley, Jr., *God and Man at Yale* (Chicago: Henry Regnery, 1951; 1971, lx–lxi.

10. "Protestant Architect," *Time*, 19 April 1954, 62–66.

11. Karl Barth, "We Are Not Against the East," translation from *Die Wahreit* [Graz], 17 April 1949), *Christianity and Crisis*, 14 November 1949, 152.

12. "Stalin Has a Birthday," *The Christian Century*, 4 January 1950, 3.

13. See "The Trouble with Keeping Calm," *The Christian Century*, 16 January 1950, 60–62, and Hendrik Hauge, "Barth as Church Politician," *The Christian Century*, 11 January 1950, 47–49.

14. Cited in William Lee Miller, *Piety along the Potomac* (Boston: Houghton Mifflin Co., 1964), 151.

15. Richard Fox, *Reinhold Niebuhr: A Biography* (San Francisco: Harper & Row, 1987), 228–29.

16. "Faith for a Lenten Age," *Time*, 8 March 1948, 70–76.

17. Fulton J. Sheen, *Peace of Soul* (New York: Whittlesey House, 1949).

18. David Riesman, Nathan Glazer, and Deuel Denney, *The Lonely Crowd: A Study of the Changing American Character* (New Haven, Conn.: Yale University Press, 1950).

19. William H. Whyte Jr., *The Organization Man* (New York: Simon and Schuster, 1956), 404.

20. R. S. Lee, *Freud and Christianity* (New York: Wyn, 1949), Benjamin Gilbert Sanders, *Christianity after Freud* (London: Bles Geoffrey, 1949).

21. Editorial, "The Novel Goes to Church," *The Saturday Review of Literature*, 24 June 1950, 22.

22. For the fascinating story of *Worlds in Collision* and the controversy, see James Gilbert, "Two Men of Science," in *Redeeming Culture: American Religion in an Age of Science* (Chicago: University of Chicago Press, 1997).

Chapter 4: Lies, Spies, and the Junior Senator from Wisconsin

1. Matt Cvetic as told to Peter Martin, "I Posed as a Communist for the FBI," *Saturday Evening Post*, 15 July 1950, 17ff.; 22 July 1950, 34ff.; 29 July 1950, 30ff. The movie, *I Was a Communist for the FBI* was released by Warner Brothers in 1951.

2. Cited in Rebecca West, *The New Meaning of Treason* (New York: Viking, 1967), 187.

3. See Ellen W. Schrecker, *No Ivory Tower: McCarthyism and the Universities* (New York: Oxford University Press, 1986).

4. See Greg Mitchell, *Tricky Dick and the Pink Lady: Richard Nixon vs. Helen Gahagan Douglas, Sexual Politics and the Red Scare 1950* (New York: Random House, 1998).

5. Whittaker Chambers, *Witness* (Chicago: Regnary, 1952), 9.

6. Ibid., 482.

7. Alistair Cooke, *A Generation on Trial* (New York: Alfred A. Knopf, 1950). See also Sam Tanenhaus, *Whittaker Chambers: A Biography* (New York: Random House, 1997).

8. Joseph McCarthy, *Major Speeches and Debates of Senator Joseph McCarthy Delivered in the United States Senate, 1950–1951* (Washington, D.C.: U.S. Government Printing Office, 1951), 8–9.

9. Editorial, "Call for Mobilization," *Moody Monthly*, 7 September 1950, 7.

10. Editorial, "Call for Jeremiah," *Moody Monthly*, May 1950, 599.

11. See Robert Newman, *Owen Lattimore and the "Loss" of China*. (Berkeley, Calif.: University of California Press, 1992).

12. Cited from John Cooney, *The American Pope: The Life and Times of Francis Cardinal Spellman* (New York: Times Books, 1984), 148. See also "Francis, Cardinal Spellman," in Benjamin Frankel, ed., *The Cold War 1945–1991*, vol. 1, (Detroit: Gale Research, 1992), 460–62.

13. Cooney, *The American Pope*, 221. See also Donald F. Crosby, *God, Church, and Flag: Senator Joseph R. McCarthy and the Catholic Church, 1950–1957* (Chapel Hill, N.C.: University of North Carolina Press, 1978), 167–69.

14. Crosby, *God, Church, and Flag*, 47–52.

15. Warren L. Vinz, *Pulpit Politics* (Albany, N.Y.: SUNY Press, 1997), 116.

16. L.P. [Liston Pope], "The Great Lie," *Christianity and Crisis*, 17 April 1950, 41–42.

17. J.C.B. [John C. Bennett], "The Self–Defeating Attitudes of America's 'Reactionaries,'" *Christianity and Crisis*, 15 May 1950, 57–58.

18. Editorial, "Why Not Guilt by Association?" *The Sign*, May 1950, 8.

19. Editorial, "Thoughts about Witchcraft," *Christian Advocate*. September 1950, 11.

20. Editorial, "The Strain of the Cold War," *The Living Church*, 16 April 1950, 11.
21. Milton Mayer, "Both Your Houses," *Motive*, January 1951, 10ff.
22. Paul Nelson Poling, "Alger Hiss Is Not Alone," *Presbyterian Life*, 4 March 1950, 3.
23. "The Sounding Board," *Presbyterian Life*, 15 April 1950, 3.
24. "The Fourth of July and McCarthy," editorial, *The Sign*, July 1950, 5.
25. Editorial, "The Secret," *The Living Church*, 4 April 1954, 15.

Chapter 5: The Protestant Establishment
1. "Donegan Inducted as Head of Diocese," *The New York Times*, 19 November 1950, 1ff.
2. "Diluted Pacifism," *Time*, 3 July 1950, 56.
3. "The Christian Conscience and Weapons of Mass Destruction," *The Christian Century*, 13 December 1950, 1489–91.
4. "Emphasis on Religion," *Newsweek*, 13 November 1950, 82. See also Karl Quinby, "Religion in American Life," *The Christian Century*, 13 November 1950, 1356–58.
5. "Protestant Advance Reaches Mid-Point," *The Christian Century*, 7 June 1950, 694; "Evangelistic Advance Is Led by Laymen," *The Christian Century*, 5 April 1950, 421.
6. "Evangelism," *Time*, 13 November 1950, 61.
7. "The Sales Approach," *Time*, 11 December 1950, 80–84. William A. Pleuthner, *Building Up Your Congregation* (Chicago: Wilcox & Follett, 1950).
8. "Trend," *Time*, 27 November 1950, 54.
9. Reinhold Niebuhr, "Is There a Revival of Religion?" *New York Times Magazine*, 19 November 1950, 13ff.
10. "Mount Olivet Lutheran Church," *The Christian Century*, 25 January 1950, 105–111.
11. "Evangelical and Reformed, New Knoxville, Ohio," *The Christian Century*, 22 February 1950, 233–38.
12. Randall Balmer, *Grant Us Courage: Travels Along the Mainline of American Protestantism* (New York: Oxford University Press, 1996), 99–107.
13. Balmer, *Grant Us Courage*, 53–54.
14. "The First Church of Christ (Congregational), West Hartford, Connecticut," *The Christian Century*, 22 March 1950, 362–68.

15. "Theological Emphasis Is Shifting," *The Christian Century*, 11 January 1950, 37.
16. Norman Vincent Peale, *A Guide to Confident Living* (New York: Prentice-Hall, 1948). Norman Vincent Peale and Smiley Blanton, M.D., *The Art of Real Happiness* (New York: Prentice-Hall, 1950).
17. Norman Vincent Peale, *The True Joy of Positive Living* (New York: William Morrow & Co., 1984), 181–84. For a scholarly, critical biography, see also Carol V. R. George, *God's Salesman: Norman Vincent Peale and the Power of Positive Thinking* (New York: Oxford University Press, 1993).
18. See George, *God's Salesman*.
19. David R. Bains, "Tradition, Church, and Changes in Protestant Appreciation of Liturgy: The Order of St. Luke in the 1950s." Paper presented at the American Academy of Religion, San Francisco, 1997.
20. "Getting Together," *Time*, 8 May 1950, 47.
21. Eugene Carson Blake, "The American Churches and the Ecumenical Mission," in *The Ecumenical Era in Church and Society*, ed. E. J. Jurji (New York: Macmillan Co., 1959), 77–78.
22. "For Christ: 31,000,000," *Newsweek*, 11 December 1950, 78–79.

Chapter 6: The Church of the Triple Crown
 1. Jay P. Dolan, "Patterns of Leadership in the Congregation," in *American Congregations*, vol. 2, *New Perspectives in the Study of Congregations*, ed. James P. Wind and James W. Lewis (Chicago: University of Chicago Press, 1994), 248.
 2. Evelyn Waugh, "The American Epoch in the Catholic Church," *Life*, 19 September 1949, 146.
 3. Ibid., 137.
 4. James Kavenaugh, *A Modern Priest Looks at His Outdated Church* (New York: Trident, 1967); see, for example, J. F. Powers, *Prince of Darkness and Other Stories* (Garden City, N.Y.: Doubleday, 1947).
 5. Whitley Strieber, *Communion* (New York: William Morrow & Co., 1987), 115.
 6. Editorial, "Waugh Appraises American Catholics," *The Catholic World*, November 1949, 81–85. Quote p. 83.
 7. Emanuel Romero, "The Negro in the New York Archdiocese," *The Catholic World*, October 1950, 6–12. Quote p. 6.

8. See Peter McDonough, *Men Astutely Trained: A History of the Jesuits in the American Century* (New York: The Free Press, 1992), especially ch. 7, "Political Change."

9. Sally Whalen Cassidy, "The Catholic Revival," *The Catholic World*, February 1950, 375–76.

10. John Cooney, *The American Pope: The Life and Times of Francis Cardinal Spellman*. (New York: Times Books, 1984), 90.

11. Francis Cardinal Spellman, *The Foundling* (New York: Charles Scribner's Sons, 1951).

12. Ibid., 176–79.

13. Paul Blanshard, *American Freedom and Catholic Power* (Boston: Beacon, 1949). Editorial, "Lopsided Liberalism," *America*, 1 July 1950, 349. For a substantial Catholic rebuttal of Blanshard's *American Freedom and Catholic Power*, presenting alleged examples of his misuse of sources, see the review by Francis J. Connell in *Cornell Law Quarterly*, 35, no. 3 (Spring 1950): 678–84. See also Blanshard's reply, "Father Connell and Mr. Blanshard," *Cornell Law Quarterly* 36, no. 2 (Winter 1951): 406–15.

14. Waugh, "American Epoch," 149.

15. See Paul Hendrickson, *Seminary* (New York: Simon & Schuster Summit Books, 1983), especially p. 41, for certain of these figures and insights, and especially for a fascinating account of Roman Catholic seminary life in the 1950s.

16. "Carthusian Solitude," *Time*, 11 December 1950, 84–85.

17. See Patrick Allitt, *Catholic Converts: British and American Intellectuals Turn to Rome* (Ithaca, N.Y.: Cornell University Press, 1997). See also his *Catholic Intellectuals and Conservative Politics in America 1950–1985* (Ithaca, N.Y.: Cornell University Press, 1993).

18. Allitt, *Catholic Converts*, 206.

19. See Peter A. Huff, *Allen Tate and the Catholic Revival* (Mahwah, N.J.: Paulist Press, 1996).

20. Fredric Wertham, "The Air-Conditioned Conscience," *Saturday Review of Literature*, 1 October 1949, 8 ff.

21. See "Religion Marries Psychiatry," *The Catholic World*, December 1949, 161–65.

22. Cooney, *American Pope*, 250–56.

23. John F. Cronin, S.S., "Communism," *The National Catholic Almanac, 1951* (Paterson, N.J.: St. Anthony's Guild, 1951), 116.

24. "Humani Generis," text in *National Catholic Almanac, 1951*, 62–68.
25. Text in ibid., 69–76. "Dogma of the Assumption," *Newsweek*, 13 November 1950, 82.
26. Editorial, "Assumption Dogma to Be Announced," *The Christian Century*, 30 August 1950, 1012.
27. "A Dogma Is Proclaimed," *Life*, 13 November 1950, 128–29.
28. Graham Greene, "The Assumption of Mary," *Life*, 30 October 1950, 50–58. Quotes pp. 56, 58.
29. "Year of Pardon," *Newsweek*, 2 January 1950, 32–33.
30. Paul Blanshard, "The Holy Year: Fact and Fiction," *The Nation*, 23 September 1950, 260.
31. Cassidy, "Catholic Revival," 376.

Chapter 7: The Week the World Might Have Ended
1. Dean Acheson, *Present at the Creation* (New York: W. W. Norton & Co., 1969), 334, 370.
2. Cited in David Haberstam, *The Fifties*. New York: Villard Books, 1993), 69.
3. Cited in Martin E. Marty, *Modern American Religion: Under God, Indivisible, 1941–1960*. vol. 3 (Chicago: University of Chicago Press, 1996), 120.
4. "Next Meeting: 1953?" *Time*, 24 July 1950, 52.
5. Editorial, "Out of Darkness, Hope," *The Christian Century*, 12 July 1950, 837.
6. Letter by A. J. Muste, *The Christian Century*, 9 August 1950, 941. 952; Editorial, "Revolution in Foreign Policy," *The Christian Century*, 9 August 1950, 941.
7. Editorial, *Commonweal*, 9 February 1951, 438.
8. Harold H. Osmer, *U. S. Religious Journalism and the Korean War* (Washington, D.C.: University Press of America, 1980), 27–59.
9. Ibid., 28.
10. Editorial, *America*, 30 December 30, 1950, 370.
11. Editorial, *Christian Herald*, September 1950, 16.
12. Cited in Osmer, *U. S. Religious Journalism*, 31.
13. Editorial, *Presbyterian Life*, 9 December 1950, 7.
14. Richard Wightman Fox, *Reinhold Niebuhr: A Biography* (New York: Pantheon, 1985), 241.
15. Cited in Marty, *Modern American Religion*, 120, 129.
16. Ibid., 128.
17. John Foster Dulles, "U.S. Military Action in Korea,"

Department of State Bulletin 23 (17 July 1950): 88–91. Cited in Mark G. Toulouse, *The Transformation of John Foster Dulles: From Prophet of Realism to Priest of Nationalism* (Macon, Ga.: Mercer University Press, 1985), 161.

18. John Foster Dulles, "Universal Bible Sunday Broadcast," 20 November 1950. Cited in Toulouse, *Transformation of John Foster Dulles*, 232.

19. John Foster Dulles, *War or Peace* (New York: Macmillan Publishing Co., 1950), 75.

20. William Martin, *A Prophet with Honor: The Billy Graham Story* (New York: William Morrow & Co., 1991), 131.

21. Ibid., 147–48.

22. See "Korean Aftermath," *Christian Life*, December 1950, 24.

23. Osmer, *U.S. Religious Journalism*, 37; Editorial, *The Christian Century*, 26 July 1950, 886.

24. Editorial, *Friends Intelligencer*, 5 August 1950, 459.

25. Cornelius Kruse, "Friendly Proposals for Better Relations with Russia," *Friends Intelligencer*, 22 July 1950, 427.

26. Stephen J. Whitfield, *The Culture of the Cold War* (Baltimore: Johns Hopkins University Press, 1991), 59–60.

27. Ibid., 9.

28. Matthew Ridgway, *The Korean War* (New York: Doubleday, 1969), 192.

29. Cited in William P. Woodard, *The Allied Occupation of Japan 1945–1952 and Japanese Religions* (Leiden: E.J. Brill, 1972), 358. This entire book is highly recommended for the topic. For a 1950 evangelical, missions-oriented look at Japan, see Donald E. Hoke, "Crisis Hour in the Orient" and other related articles in *Christian Life*, December 1950, 33–52.

Chapter 8: African American Religion Before the Beginning

1. Henry J. Young, *Major Black Religious Leaders Since 1940* (Nashville: Abingdon Press, 1979), 33. See also William Robert Miller, *Martin Luther King, Jr.* (New York: Weybright & Talley, 1968), 30, and the civil rights leader's own testimony in Martin Luther King Jr., *Stride Toward Freedom* (New York: Harper & Brothers, 1968), 96. However, King's major biographer, Taylor Branch, in *Parting the Waters: America in the King Years 1954–63* (New York: Simon & Schuster, 1988), 69–81, curiously does not mention the influence of Mordecai Johnson's lecture, preferring to emphasize the longer-term

impact on King of Crozer Professor George W. Davis, a pacifist and admirer of Gandhi.

2. See William C. Berman, *The Politics of Civil Rights in the Truman Administration* (Columbus: Ohio State University Press, 1970), 178–81.

3. Paul Moore, *Presences: A Bishop's Life in the City* (New York: Farrar, Straus and Giroux, 1997), 122.

4. Liston Pope, *The Kingdom Beyond Caste* (New York: Friendship Press, 1957), 105.

5. William A. Nunnelley, *Bull Connor* (Tuscaloosa, Ala.: The University of Alabama Press, 1991), 33.

6. Howard Thurman, *Jesus and the Disinherited* (New York: Abingdon-Cokesbury Press, 1949).

7. St. Clair Drake and Horace R. Clayton, *Black Metropolis* (New York: Harcourt, Brace & Co., 1945).

8. See C. Eric Lincoln and Lawrence H. Mamiya, *The Black Church in the African American Experience* (Durham, N.C.: Duke University Press, 1990), 209.

9. Gayraud S. Wilmore, *Black Religion and Black Radicalism* (Garden City, N.Y.: Doubleday, 1972).

10. Ibid., 223.

11. For tensions between Communist and noncommunist black intellectuals around 1950, including the role of Paul Robeson's Communist-oriented 1949–1950 magazine *Freedom*, see Harold Cruse, *The Crisis of the Negro Intellectual* (New York: William Morrow & Co., 1967.

12. W. E. B. Du Bois, *The Souls of Black Folks* (New York: Penguin Books USA, 1969), 217. First pub. 1903.

13. Wilson Fallin Jr., *The African American Church in Birmingham* (New York: Garland, 1997), 134.

14. Harry V. Richardson, *Dark Glory* (New York: Friendship Press, 1947).

Chapter 9: Evangelicals on the Rise

1. See Leo P. Rubiffo, *The Old Christian Right: The Protestant Far Right from the Great Depression to the Cold War* (Philadelphia: Temple University Press, 1983).

2. See Gerald L. K. Smith, *Besieged Patriot: Autobiographical Episodes Exposing Communism, Traitorism, and Zionism from the Life of Gerald L. K. Smith*, ed. Elna M. Smith and Charles R. Robertson (Eureka Springs, Ark.: Elna M. Smith Foundation, 1978).

3. Louis Gasper, *The Fundamentalist Movement* (The Hague: Mouton Publ., 1963), 57.
4. Jon R. Stone, *On the Boundaries of American Evangelicalism: The Postwar Evangelical Coalition* (New York: St. Martin's Press, 1997), 91–92.
5. See George Marsden, *Reforming Fundamentalism: Fuller Seminary and the New Evangelicalism* (Grand Rapids: Wm. B. Eerdmans, 1987).
6. For a vivid personal portrayal of these years of American evangelicalism, including the founding of Fuller Seminary, see Henry's autobiography: Carl Henry, *Confessions of a Theologian* (Waco, Tex.: Word, 1986).
7. Stone, *On the Boundaries of American Evangelicalism*, 92.
8. Joel A. Carpenter, *Revive Us Again: The Reawakening of American Fundamentalism* (New York: Oxford University Press, 1997), 234–35.
9. See Christine Leigh Heyman, *Southern Cross: The Beginnings of the Bible Belt* (New York: Alfred A. Knopf, 1997).
10. Carpenter, *Revive Us Again*, 233.
11. Billy Graham, *Just as I Am* (New York: HarperCollins, 1997), 150.
12. William Martin, *A Prophet with Honor* (New York: William Morrow & Co., 1991), 117.
13. Henry, *Confessions*, 125.
14. Graham, *Just as I Am*, 175.
15. "Billy and His Beacon," *Newsweek*, 1 May 1950, 66–67.
16. Wynn Boliek, "Estimate of an Evangelist," *The Lutheran*, 5 July 1950, 13–18.
17. Anne C. Loveland, *American Evangelicals and the U.S. Military, 1942–1993* (Baton Rouge, La.: Louisiana State University Press, 1997).
18. Robert S. Ellwood, *The Fifties Spiritual Marketplace* (New Brunswick, N.J.: Rutgers University Press, 1997).
19. Carpenter, *Revive Us Again*, 230–31.
20. Oral Roberts, *The Call: Oral Roberts' Autobiography* (New York: Avon Books, 1971), 173–74.
21. Hal Wingo, "The Confessions of Marjoe," *Life*, 8 September 1972, 60. See also Steven S. Gaines, *Marjoe* (New York: Harper & Row, 1973). This book contains the six-year-old preacher's sermon of Aug. 27, 1950, " Hell with the Lid Off."
22. C. Dwight Dorough, *The Bible Belt Mystique* (Philadelphia: Westminster Press, 1974), 166–69.

23. "Simultaneous Revivals," *Baptist Beacon*, April 1950, 1. Cited in Helen Lee Turner, "Myths: Stories of This World and the World to Come," in *Southern Baptists Observed*, ed. Nancy Tatom Ammerman (Knoxville: University of Tennessee Press, 1993), 103.

24. Cited in Paul Boyer, *When Time Shall Be No More: Prophecy Belief in Modern American Culture* (Cambridge, Mass.: Harvard University Press, 1992), 119.

25. For a bibliography of primary sources see Jon R. Stone "The Cold War Period (Part 1), 1949–1957," in *A Guide to the End of the World* (New York: Garland, 1993).

26. Cited in Boyer, *When Time Shall Be No More*, 163.

Chapter 10: Judaism in Midpassage

1. Nathan Glazer, *American Judaism* (Chicago: University of Chicago Press, 1957), 108–10.

2. Mike Hecht, "Civil Rights on Peoria Street," *Jewish Frontier*, February 1950, 15–17.

3. The information in the preceding paragraphs is largely from Morris Fine, ed., *American Jewish Year Book* (New York: American Jewish Committee, 1951).

4. Philip S. Bernstein, "What the Jews Believe," *Life*, 11 September 1950, 161.

5. Will Herberg, "After Communism—What?" *The Reconstructionist*, 7 April 1950, 28–32.

6. Fine, *American Jewish Year Book*, 123–24.

7. Ibid, 119.

8. Ibid, 124.

9. Arthur Hertzberg, "American Jews Through Israeli Eyes," *Commentary*, January 1950, 1–7.

10. Peter Novick, *The Holocaust in American Life* (Boston: Houghton Mifflin, 1999), 133–34.

11. Ibid., 123, quoting Jules Cohen in minutes summarizing a meeting of an ad hoc committee to consider the monument proposal.

12. Ibid., 110.

13. Ibid., 105.

14. Glazer, *American Judaism*, 114–15.

Chapter 11: Getting Ready for the 1950s and 1960s

1. "The Younger Generation," *Time*, 5 November 1952, 46–52.

INDEX